COACHING IN THE CLASSROOM

COACHING IN THE CLASSROOM

Bringing out the best in learners

Mark Jamieson and Rachel Wood

LONDON AND NEW YORK

First published in 2024 by Critical Publishing Ltd

Published 2025 by Routledge
4 Park Square, Milton Park, Abingdon, Oxon OX14 4RN
605 Third Avenue, New York, NY 10017

Routledge is an imprint of the Taylor & Francis Group, an informa business

Copyright © 2024 Mark Jamieson and Rachel Wood

All rights reserved. No part of this book may be reprinted or reproduced or utilised in any form or by any electronic, mechanical, or other means, now known or hereafter invented, including photocopying and recording, or in any information storage or retrieval system, without permission in writing from the publishers.

Trademark notice: Product or corporate names may be trademarks or registered trademarks, and are used only for identification and explanation without intent to infringe.

British Library Cataloguing in Publication Data
A CIP record for this book is available from the British Library

ISBN: 9781041054559 (hbk)
ISBN: 9781915713698 (pbk)
ISBN: 9781041054566 (ebk)

The rights of Mark Jamieson and Rachel Wood to be identified as the Authors of this work have been asserted by them in accordance with the Copyright, Design and Patents Act 1988.

Cover design by Out of House Limited
Text design by Greensplash

DOI: 10.4324/9781041054566

CONTENTS

About the authors		vii
Acknowledgements		viii
Introduction		1
PART 1	**COACHING IN AN EDUCATIONAL SETTING**	**3**
Chapter 1	The relationship between coaching and education	5
Chapter 2	Coaching as an accompaniment to learning	26
Chapter 3	The six new dimensions of learning	55
PART 2	**HOW TO COACH YOUNG PEOPLE IN SCHOOLS**	**79**
Chapter 4	Coaching for the new dimensions of learning	81
Chapter 5	Who gets coached and distinct learning pathways	116
Chapter 6	Team-based coaching	141
Chapter 7	Coaching leadership for learning	163
Chapter 8	Evaluating the impact of coaching	192

PART 3	**HOW TO EMBED A COACHING CULTURE IN SCHOOLS**	**221**
Chapter 9	Making space for leadership coaching in schools	223
Chapter 10	Psychological dimensions	245
Chapter 11	What the future holds: six critical questions	271
Index		297

About the authors

Mark Jamieson is an award-winning coach specialising in leadership. His consultancy work with national youth and homeless charity Centrepoint inspired him to practically connect coaching and leadership to wider youth development ideas. He founded the GreenWing Project in 2020 to concentrate on bringing high-level leadership coaching to schools and underserved youth communities. His experiences and research are recorded in his recent book, *Coaching Young People for Leadership*. Mark is an expert in evaluation and has published works about the impact of leadership coaching.

Rachel Wood is a coach and expert educational practitioner specialising in Team-Based Learning, unconditionality and creativity. She has 20 years' experience working in education and development across all sectors and age groups. Rachel is a PhD researcher at the University of Bradford, an advisory teacher and a director of her own consultancy company. She has had a number of her educational resources published digitally and has worked with numerous schools, universities, charities and companies.

Acknowledgements

I would like to thank all those like-minded souls who have enthusiastically engaged and supported our work. Specifically, I would like to acknowledge the intellectual contribution of Eve Mpanda and the specialist advice from Marc Pescod. I am indebted to the editorial expertise and patience of Janine Watson, the creative space-making of LB Watson-Jamieson and the critical analysis of James Jamieson. Finally, I wish to congratulate all the extraordinary young people we have worked with and thank them for taking the leap of faith, without which this book could not have been written.

Mark Jamieson

I would like to thank the schools, partners and sponsors that we have worked with for their open-mindedness and willingness to help open closed doors. Without your support and trust in us to deliver outcomes there wouldn't be the evidence for book. Similarly, the hundreds of young people that we have worked with in the classroom have given us the backdrop for this book and the drive to write it. Your engagement and progress have said everything that needs saying. Additionally, I would like to thank Professor Simon Tweddell, Michael Glenn and Dr Mark Jamieson who have all opened up a pedagogy of Team-Based Learning and leadership coaching; they have inspired me to stay in the world of education. Finally, thank you to my family, colleagues and friends who have supported me throughout this process.

Rachel Wood

INTRODUCTION

The relationship between coaching and education has conventionally been primarily focused on the interaction between coaches and teachers. Focusing on the professional development of educators has been proved to enhance the academic achievements of pupils and improve the overall learning experience for young people. This book accepts the work of coaches in this field and in this particular context; however, it also presents an alternative perspective for the relationship between coaching and education, which is currently overlooked; that of coaching learners directly.

Its aim is to contribute to the wider debate around education by entrusting young people with dedicated space to develop their unique intrinsic skills, values and aspirations in an academic context. In this way, it presents coaching as an active learning methodology. Simultaneously, it successfully taps into the longer-term ambitions of young people and, using leadership as a focus, prepares them to thrive in the future.

It is careful to acknowledge the restrictions of a curriculum that emphasises replication of knowledge over independent thought, creativity and curiosity. In doing so, it presents coaching as complimentary to traditional teaching (and coaching), accepting that change is part of an evolutionary process.

This book is a faithful reflection of our experiences working in secondary schools nationwide. It is representative of the myriad opinions of teachers, learners and educationalists with whom we have been privileged to come into contact, and these voices set the tone for the book. Inevitably, amongst many of the uplifting, life-affirming and forward-thinking narratives, there is also criticism of the current system and some of the personalities within it.

In part, this book was written in response to the ongoing movement to address the fault lines in the education system. In its own modest way, it sets out to make a contribution to this movement but, at the same time, it is unapologetically ambitious and reflects some of the frustrations from those working on the ground with the incremental pace of change.

We hope that you find the content of this book thought-provoking, challenging in places, but ultimately optimistic in its vision for coaching learners.

Part 1
COACHING IN AN EDUCATIONAL SETTING

Chapter 1

THE RELATIONSHIP BETWEEN COACHING AND EDUCATION

> **CHAPTER OVERVIEW**
>
> **A hypothesis**
>
> The premise for this book is based on the following enquiry: *What happens to conventional academic targets and emerging educational goals when we coach students directly?* This book sets out to prove the hypothesis that coaching – unfamiliar cognitive and non-cognitive development interventions characterised as a matter of personal choice – when directly applied to young people in a school setting can simultaneously enhance academic achievement, help modernise the scope of learning and enrich the student experience.

This opening chapter investigates the relationship between coaching and education. It asserts that coaching currently takes place in the margins of education, misdirected by being predominately associated with the professional development of teachers. It argues that the claimed positive knock-on effect to students underserves them and, as a strategy, is emblematic of the wider problems faced by a UK education system stuck in a steady state of underachievement. Accepting that the current relationship with education is marginal, it sets out the case for coaching as a response to the state of education today, generally described as failing, disconnected and complex. Using coaching methodologies to negate these criticisms, it goes on to imagine a new relationship between coaching and education.

Introduction

Failing, disconnected and complex sums up the conclusions of the recent report *Bringing Out the Best* (Times Education Commission, 2022) on the state of education in the UK today. Specifically, in terms of emerging goals for education, it is claimed to be failing young people on all counts, while findings and recommendations from new research provide evidence of the disconnect between the policies of government and the needs of the education system (National Education Union, 2023). Finally, the constituent parts are deemed to be overly complex and too often self-serving. The first three chapters of this book provide a reasoned discussion around the concept of coaching in schools, examining criticisms to understand the current context for education and where coaching might fit. In this opening chapter we begin by recognising the need for coaching to form a meaningful relationship with education in order to be accepted and, subsequently, influence the agenda for modernising learning and learning outcomes.

The current state of education in the UK

If, as it is variously claimed, schools reflect society and education, and are the seedbed for future prosperity, then the outlook is not promising. Headline statistics taken from the recent seminal report from the Times Education Commission (2022) provide grim reading about the current state of education and the future prospects for young people inside and outside of the classroom.

The prognosis from inside the classroom is an unhealthy one, revealing a third of pupils in state secondary schools are defined as failing under the current system for assessing progress. One in six children show signs of poor mental health, while 65 per cent of parents are worried that the present system of exams places too much pressure on young people. Furthermore, one-third of teachers are classified as being disillusioned and considering quitting their vocation. Outside of the classroom, the implications of a failing education system are equally gloomy. Here, employers are reportedly frustrated by the lack of qualifications and preparedness of young people to enter the workforce, with around two-thirds struggling to recruit young people with the basic skills they need and three-quarters having to provide supplementary learning in literacy and numeracy for those they do employ.

The implications for the big picture suggest that the current state of education undermines government planning at national and global levels: 40 per cent of employers predicted a shortage of skills needed to deliver net zero strategies; around the same percentage anticipated a dearth in technological and digital skills and 85 per cent were pessimistic about an imminent shortage of requisite skills in key economic sectors. Or, put another way, three-quarters of businesses estimated an increase in productivity of around 25 per cent if young people were equipped with up-to-date commercial behaviours (boosting the economy by as much as £125 billion a year – alternatively, failure to close the skills gap is predicted to cost the economy £140 billion in lost GDP by 2028).

These numbers reveal alarming patterns and themes about our direction of travel across national economic, social and demographic terrains. In terms of global status, the UK is now perceived as an education outlier, moving counter-clockwise to capture traditional, some may argue archaic, systems while the rest of the world has gone in a modernising direction. A preoccupation, to the point of obduracy, with institutional structure and governance, given precedence over an agenda to modernise the scope of learning to keep pace with change, sits at the heart of an education stasis. The resultant frustration was encapsulated by one of the teachers we spoke to:

> *I think Covid should be a watershed moment. We should stop talking about returning to pre-Covid as a 'normal' and focus on moving on – looking at learning in a completely different way. It's frustrating as a teacher not to be able to spend time exploring facets of a subject that would throw open the windows of knowledge. They're not going to be tested on it so I don't bother exploring it – it's the antithesis of a learning culture that I would choose. Basically, we're teaching kids to be incurious.*
>
> S, London

Later in this book, we propound the theory of education as part of a dysfunctional environment characterised by a lack of trust in professionals from overbearing ideologues obsessed with irrelevant key performance indicators (KPIs), targets and managerialism, bereft of creativity, artistry and invention. The Times Education Commission findings allow us a foreglimpse of this dysfunctional environment and raise flags about emerging problematics and barriers that coaching must overcome if it is to establish a meaningful relationship with education and enter the learning mainstream.

The relationship between coaching and education reality

On the one (practical) hand, there is no relationship between coaching and education. Active or self-regulatory learning approaches share similar methodologies but coaching, per se, is disregarded, seen solely as an adult development strategy, generally within the domain of the private sector and, for non-profit organisations, where finances are severely squeezed, a budget anomaly. On the other (conceptual) hand, coaching is a natural partner for education, where handing young people responsibility for the way they learn, and supporting them by developing unique cognitive and non-cognitive skills, spike engagement with the curriculum and enhance academic performance. At the same time, the confidence and sense of self-worth that coaching unlocks create a basis for wider school strategies such as inclusion, well-being and mental health.

The issue we have is that, so far, the practical version is dominant and has created a seemingly immutable relationship stasis. In our experience, the reasons for this are threefold: affordability, inundation (of coaching) and misconception.

Affordability: if it is free then it has no value

It is a simple fact that schools do not have the budget for coaching and therefore building any kind of relationship will be problematic. Coaching, necessarily subsidised or fully funded by external sponsors, is perceived by schools as a gift. However, an absence of internal funding also creates a psychological inhibitor to relationship building as a verisimilar irony is generated – if it is not in the budget, it has no value. In an environment of intense financial scrutiny, perversely, *free stuff* can be treated with suspicion, even disdain, and is greatly underestimated by schools. In our experience, a lack of financial investment from schools represents a lack of overall commitment and is a major barrier to a working relationship. Ironically, coaching is simultaneously assumed by schools to be an unaffordable transaction that is out of reach until it is made available for nothing, when it then becomes a faddish initiative of little consequence. In other words, when it is free, the perceived (non-financial) value of coaching plummets.

Inundation: the rise of the self-help-book coach

Any potential coaching relationship with a school begins by being mired in a fog of confusion through misrepresentation. Because coaching is unregulated, there is a proliferation of underqualified, unsupervised and ineffective education professionals side-lining as coaches. Despite good intentions and an intellectual and/or instinctive interest in coaching, the casual nomenclature *coach* dilutes the offering and corrupts the relationship. An inundation of coaches means that the school is entitled to ask itself why, with a number of in-house coaches, does it need to have a relationship with an external provider?

Misconception: the system is out of sync

Despite a so-called inundation of coaches, the school environment is not designed to accommodate coaching. Entrenched structural rigidity does not sit comfortably beside free-style interventions. The contradictory nature of any relationship between coaching and education means that, as a serious accompaniment to learning, schools view coaching as an arcane dark art. We have observed that anything sitting outside the conventional wisdom of education, whether intellectually or financially, inhibits the working relationship. Here, it is the dysfunctional environment (see Chapter 9) that is out of sync where, regardless of the enthusiasm to form partnerships, teachers are confined by the institutional straitjacket of the education system.

The relationship between coaching and education imagined

Clearly, the systemic failings in education cannot be rectified by coaching alone, but building a meaningful relationship between the two can be part of the solution. In continuing to make the case for entente between coaching and schools, we have examined the key words – *failing, disconnected* and *complex* – that negatively characterise the current state of education and drawn connections to the positive corresponding interpretation brought about by coaching (Figure 1.1 and Table 1.1). As an exercise, it was not difficult to see how coaching could benefit the education system by shifting focus to, and interacting with, pupils. In this way, negative characteristics are now reframed as positive outcomes: *potential, connection* and *creative*.

Figure 1.1 An imagined relationship focused on learners, placing negative characteristics in a positive light

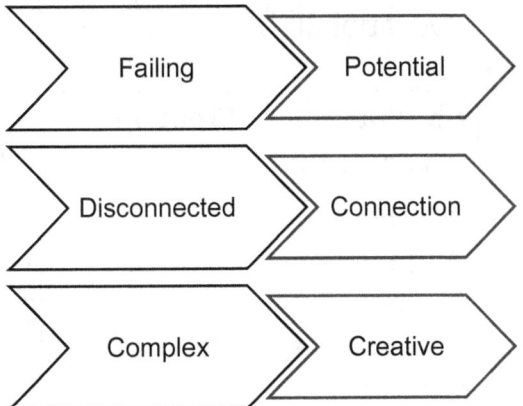

In Table 1.1, the negative dimensions of education, categorised and described in the first two columns, are positively reframed by their coaching counterparts in the third and fourth columns. The process is described in terms of individual relationships below.

Table 1.1 Building relationships using the transformative characteristics of coaching

The state of education today	Characteristics of the education system	Imagined relationship between coaching and education	Characteristics of coaching (pupils)
Failing	• Academic metrics for success • Aiming for average • Exclusion	Potential	• Identifying and developing potential • Stretching • Inclusion • Prevention
Disconnected	• Irrelevant • Systems • Non-vocational	Connection	• Relevant • Ambition and aspiration • Soft skills
Complex	• Multiple stakeholders • Competing priorities	Creative	• Connection to the outside world • Originality • Single focus on pupils

Education is failing: coaching's relationship with potential

Success in education is measured in academic terms and exams are an unassailable way of fairly and accurately assessing learners. These two facts (or fictions) are representative of the one-dimensional approach to learning that means schools are currently failing young people. In simple terms, coaching is the antithesis of this: working with young people to help them identify, develop and fulfil their potential. Focusing on potential rather than the ability to absorb and replicate a set of prescriptive facts, coaching works with the unique intelligences, competencies and instincts of the learner, accentuating originality as opposed to aiming for the anonymity of being average.

Aiming for average

Accepting the need to expand the scope of the curriculum, recent recommendations to introduce a Baccalaureate (Times Education Commission, 2022) are welcomed but arguably unambitious in terms of a radical overhaul of the education system. In search of practical solutions, there is a danger we become transfixed by what is already known, refining the tried and tested, and not addressing fundamental ideological fault lines (assessing pupils by their ability to pass exams). In a system driven by averages, *average* (rather than excellence) becomes a self-fulfilling prophecy. Such a system fails all, effectively incentivising schools to exclude pupils who are likely to score poorly in exams, while star learners are not sufficiently stretched to reach their potential (Figure 1.2).

14 COACHING IN THE CLASSROOM

Figure 1.2 The lose–lose outcomes of aiming for average

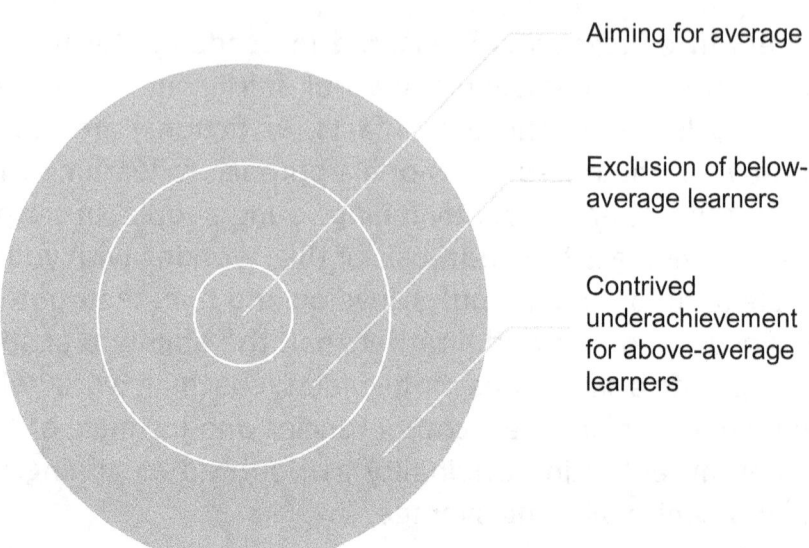

- Aiming for average
- Exclusion of below-average learners
- Contrived underachievement for above-average learners

One of the key challenges for the coach is to convert the ecosystem in Figure 1.2 to the Venn diagram representation in Figure 1.3 by highlighting how different types of learners can share the same coaching outcomes. To do this, we introduce leadership, as a positive focus for the coach, to access the unique potential of individual learners.

Figure 1.3 Using leadership coaching to access different types of learners

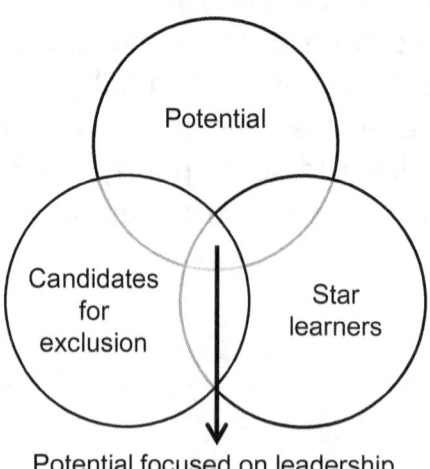

Potential focused on leadership

Introducing youth leadership: a strategy for inclusion and prevention

A swathe of pupils is lost to the proscriptive morality of the current education system. Some muddle through, but others are excluded, temporarily or permanently. Muddling through or being excluded is one of the most severe consequences of the narrow-minded one-dimensional assessment of young people in schools today. Talking to schools about this, there is a strong sense that the system has painted a number of pupils, often the most vulnerable or those with special educational needs, into a corner. Furthermore, because of the interpretation of success to which schools are currently held, these young people are not only problematic but an inconvenience. Prohibitive time constraints and a lack of capacity mean that this group is lost in the system, dumped out of sight into specious pupil referral units, where they are infrequently accommodated.

In this way, schools are complicit in contributing to wider social problems – excluded pupils are 20 times more likely to live in poverty, 10 times more likely to have mental health issues and only 4 per cent go on to achieve basic English and maths qualifications needed for employment (The Difference, 2022). Most worryingly, the policy of hiding young people out of sight through exclusions or simply letting them slip through the education net means that there is now a significant number of *ghost children* who cannot be accounted for in the education system. However, the connection between a failing education system and more general social issues, along with the subsequent need for an alternative approach, is beginning to be recognised. For instance, the national youth homelessness charity Centrepoint puts exclusion from school as one of the major causes for homelessness and now advocates coaching interventions as part of a wider prevention strategy to end youth homelessness (Jamieson, 2023).

To work together with schools as part of an inclusion or prevention strategy, coaching must recognise different groups of pupils and somehow include those from outside of the academic mainstream. To achieve this, we use leadership as a positive focus for coaching. Throughout this book, we refer to leadership as a mechanism that allows us to work with young people from diverse backgrounds with varying levels of recognised or unrecognised potential. We are able to do this because we have revisualised leadership in three ways: as part of a unique personality rather than a template into which young people are required to fit; an action as opposed to a status; and as defined by a set of new, often counter-intuitive, energies including challenging and disruptive behaviours.

Developmental and reorientation coaching

Disavowing entrenched assumptions about a leadership *type* and promoting a new set of counter-intuitive leadership qualities give us access across the classroom, ranging from high-flyers to those in danger of being excluded. In this way coaching is able to negate the characteristics of *failing* by: a) encompassing all pupils and b) shifting from *average* to excellence. For us to achieve this, we must distinguish between two different types of leadership candidate: developmental and reorientation (Table 1.2). Therefore, despite its exclusive connotations, *leadership reimagined* is a vehicle for inclusion, a natural fit for coaches and schools and a firm basis upon which to build a strong and mutually beneficial relationship.

Table 1.2 The distinct characteristics of developmental and reorientation leadership coachees

Leadership components	Developmental leadership	Reorientation leadership
Status	Recognised by others as having leadership potential	Unrecognised and overlooked by others as having leadership potential
	Recognised by self as having leadership credentials	Assumed lack of leadership credentials
	Currently in a leadership role	Currently outside the academic/ organisational mainstream
	Exemplary track record of achievements outside domain of leadership	Marked out as an underachiever
Communication	Assured	Tentative
	Willing	Reluctant
	Serious	Humorous
	Informative	Passionate
	Conformational	Angry
Action	Willing	Reluctant
	Follow conventional guidelines	Push conventional boundaries
	Competent	Creative
EQ	Well-mannered	Combative
	Restrained	Unrestrained
Purpose	Short term	Long term

(Jamieson, 2023)

Coaching developmental and reorientation candidates is discussed in detail later in the book; in the context of this chapter, we are simply setting out to illustrate how focusing on potential, specifically in terms of leadership, is a mechanism for inclusion in schools, counteracting the one-dimensional approach that currently fails learners.

Education is disconnected: coaching's relationship with connection

We cannot expect coaching to single-handedly change the system, but we do believe it can effectively narrow the gap between government targets and education needs. The repercussions of this gap – or the disconnect – to learners is that they leave school unprepared and underqualified to thrive in the future. Relating coaching directly to learners, we focus on two areas of connection: to self and to work.

Connection to self

The idea that schools build happy, confident twenty-first century global citizens with an acute awareness of self and of others is wishful thinking. In this space, coaching can build relationships with learners that schools are not designed for, focusing on authentic and authoritative voices to support young people to make positive decisions about their future. By reinforcing the learner's connection to self, the coach is also introducing the coachee to self-evaluation – the contribution I make; the impact I have; my worth. This sense of self-worth connects the coachee directly to aspiration and ambition, bringing to life academic achievement as relevant to future goals of their own making, thereby unlocking a discretionary learning energy.

In schools, we use two coaching models working in tandem (Figure 1.4) for connection. The Leadership Coaching Hierarchy (the Maslowian-type figure on the left of the graphic) is a sequential series of coaching foci designed to enable the young coachee to discover and develop their voice, authentic (self-awareness) and authoritative (awareness of others), in the context of a task or goal, using appropriate (to the individual's personality) tools to reach a state of unconscious competence. The three stages of the Youth Leadership Coaching model: authentication (self-awareness, awareness of others), development (context, tools) and ambition (unconscious competence) are designed to work in concert to provide a clear development pathway for the coach and coachee.

Figure 1.4 The Leadership Coaching Hierarchy (left) and Youth Leadership Coaching models (right) connecting young people to self

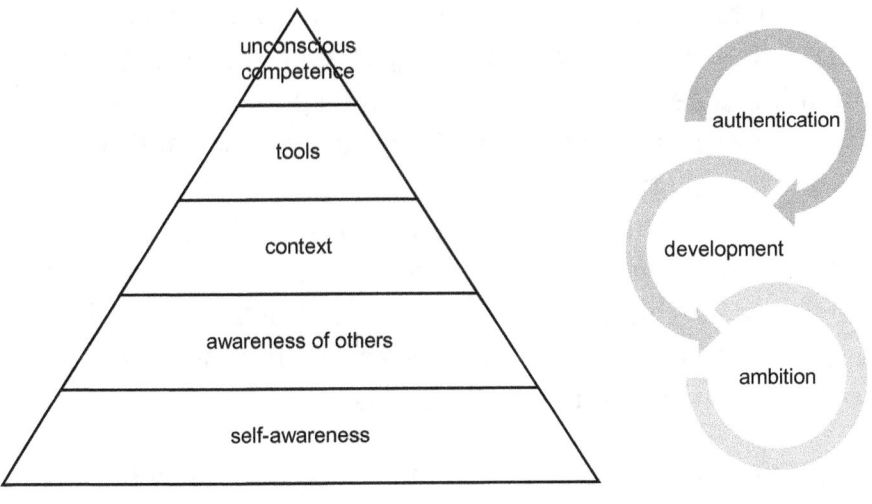

(Jamieson, 2023)

Connection to work

Research (PwC, 2022) shows that employers today set little store by academic qualifications. In Chapter 3 we discuss in detail the disconnect between school and the future workplace, not just in terms of skills and capabilities, but also preparedness. Focusing on non-cognitive and soft skills, coaching connects the young person to a future work mindset with the capacity for independent thinking and the emotional intelligence to provide resilience and professional judgement beyond their years.

Education is complex: coaching's relationship with creativity

Unlike education, coaching serves one master. Multiple stakeholders and accompanying competing priorities provide a complex environment for education, undermining its functionality and deflecting attention away from learners. Coaching has the ability to cut through the complicated network of stakeholders by solely serving the young person, providing a dedicated safe space and a personalised agenda. The uncomplicated relationship between coach and coachee fosters creativity as a kind of controlled agent of distraction, allowing the young person to explore multiple new ideas, but on their own terms, filtering out the noise from external agendas. This singlemindedness enables the coachee to uncover and develop areas of personal interest to crystallise future ambitions outside of the classroom.

In this way, the coach uses creativity and curiosity to inform an intellectual hinterland, which, when applied in school, allows the young person to form meaningful relationships with wider issues such as well-being and mental health and practise nascent leadership behaviours to impact wider goals. In other words, focusing on creativity encourages the young person to prioritise and think originally about those issues that they care about, shutting out the clamour for attention of competing stakeholders that currently confuse the end goals for education.

A word on the relationship between coaching and teachers

When we scoped out this book, we began with the premise that coaching in education was one-dimensionally focused on teaching practice. We then decided we would set out to prove the theory that, redirected towards learners, coaching could provide a significantly higher return on investment and potentially contribute to an education reset. Finally, we reached the conclusion that coaching teachers and learners was not mutually exclusive and, despite being predominately focused on young people, we should not eschew coaching support for professionals. As we progressed our work in schools, it became increasingly clear that coaching interventions with teachers would actually be part of a wider collaborative process.

The relationship between coaching and teachers

In our work, we prioritise the coaching of young people (over professional development) as a direct way of impacting learning. However, in doing so, there is a danger that we underestimate the potential contribution of teachers to a strong conceptual relationship between coaching and education. In Chapter 2, we describe how teachers can help design and manage that relationship, but here we examine the teacher's natural allegiance to coaching and how the outcomes from a functioning professional relationship are mutually beneficial to both.

Teachers face a very steep learning curve post qualification. Training is almost entirely front loaded, which means instruction in different teaching techniques ranges from basics like classroom management through to advanced skills such as assessment design. But by the time teachers are ready to start integrating more advanced techniques into their repertoire, their formal training is a distant memory and they will likely have forgotten the content or relevance. Indeed, with the passage of time and wearied by experience, they may have written these techniques off altogether, as they adopt new improvisational skills to navigate the arduous day-to-day challenges of teaching. The implications of under-developing teachers as they progress through their careers or, worse still, leaving them to their own devices part explains the worrying outlook for recruitment and retention.

Figure 1.5 Teacher development curves with and without coaching

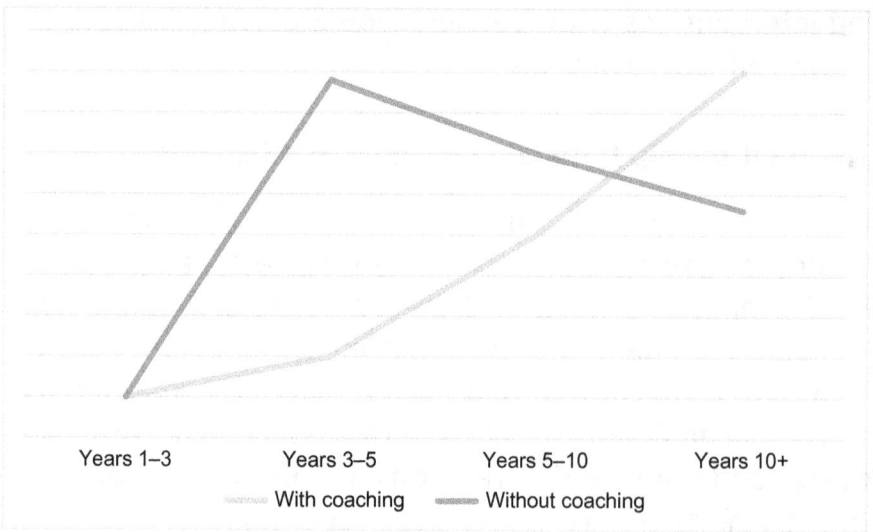

In Figure 1.5, the darker line plots the teacher's career in terms of professional development. It illustrates the steep learning curve over the first two years post qualification reflecting formal training. The flatlining and subsequent drop in the development curve after year three reflect the onerous workload that teachers carry and the inadequate strategies for continuing professional development (CPD). This also explains the high rate of attrition: 44,000 teachers left the state-funded sector in 2021/22, up by 7,800 from the previous year, representing 1 in 10 (9.7 per cent) of all qualified teachers; the highest rate since 2017/18. It is true that some schools provide sustained opportunities for training, practice and feedback so that teachers can continue their learning curve, but this is rare.

If a meaningful relationship between coaching and education is to exist, coaching needs to form a subordinate relationship with teachers. It can be argued that the school environment is seemingly designed to be unhelpful to the basic psychological needs (competence, relatedness and autonomy), whereas coaching nurtures these nutrients to enable teachers to develop and grow by demonstrating and improving ability (competence), feeling valued and needed (relatedness) and being trusted to set personal and professional performance priorities (autonomy).

The lighter line in Figure 1.5 interprets data from recent research and predicts the continuing development of the teacher through access to coaching (Growth Coaching International, 2019). Beyond the obvious benefits to professional practice, coaching acts as an intellectual stimulant, keeping the recipient connected to their original purpose or vocation and often acting as a coping mechanism for the mundane challenges of the daily grind. In turn, this improves retention levels and teacher engagement, providing the stability to build meaningful partnerships with new ideas.

Negating the negative characteristics of education to forge some kind of working relationship between learning and coaching suggests that the coach is doing most of the heavy lifting. We anticipate that as coaching becomes more familiar to schools, the relationship will come to be seen as mutually beneficial and efforts will be equally shared. For now, coaching must accept the role of junior partner, helping it to achieve targets outside of its cultural remit in order to prove useful, growing in influence with teachers in the classroom but not yet sitting at the top table with the decision makers.

Further reading

Jamieson, M (2023) *Coaching Young People for Leadership*. St Albans: Critical Publishing.

Times Education Commission (2022) *How to Transform Education and Unleash the Potential of Every Child*. [online] Available at: https://nuk-tnl-editorial-prod-staticassets.s3.amazonaws.com/2022/education-commission/Times%20Education%20Commission%20final%20report.pdf (accessed 26 January 2024).

van Nieuwerburgh, C (2012) *Coaching in Education: Getting Better Results for Students, Educators and Parents*. Abingdon: Routledge.

References

Growth Coaching International (2019) *Coaching in Education Annual Survey Report 2019*. [online] Available at: www.growthcoaching.com.au/resource/coaching-in-education-annual-survey-report-2019 (accessed 26 January 2024).

Jamieson, M (2023) *Coaching Young People for Leadership*. St Albans: Critical Publishing.

National Education Union (2023) *Educators Deserve Better: The Crisis in Teacher Pay and Supply*. [online] Available at: https://neu.org.uk/sites/default/files/2023-06/NEU%20evidence%20to%20the%20STRB%20March%202023.pdf (accessed 26 January 2024).

PwC (2022) *Global Workforce Hopes and Fears Survey 2022*. [online] Available at: www.pwc.com/gx/en/issues/workforce/hopes-and-fears-2022.html (accessed 26 January 2024).

The Difference (2022) *Impact Report 2021–22*. [online] Available at: www.the-difference.com/our-impact-report-2021-22 (accessed 26 January 2024).

Times Education Commission (2022) *How to Transform Education and Unleash the Potential of Every Child*. [online] Available at: https://nuk-tnl-editorial-prod-staticassets.s3.amazonaws.com/2022/education-commission/Times%20Education%20Commission%20final%20report.pdf (accessed 26 January 2024).

Chapter 2
COACHING AS AN ACCOMPANIMENT TO LEARNING

CHAPTER OVERVIEW

This chapter builds on a basic understanding of the dynamics of any relationship between coaching and education to provide a professional guide for integration. It acknowledges that coaching, as a junior partner, needs to find ways to fit in with the system as an accompaniment to learning rather than a competitor. Using a three-stage model (advocacy, environment and activism), it presents a strategy for the coach to build a working relationship with schools through a series of negotiations and collaborations. Most importantly, it introduces leadership as a mechanism that allows the coach to interact with the function of education and posits that teachers – the middle managers of schools – have a significant role to play.

Introduction

This chapter begins by accepting that relationships need time to form and develop; therefore, the coach is best advised to adopt a strategy of incremental change focused on existing school targets – working with the system not against it. This means managing entrenched expectations by fitting in with the curriculum and aligning with overarching goals. It follows that if we are to manage expectations, we must first of all know what those expectations are: specifically, the vision and function of education.

The vision for education

What is the vision for education? Ideologically speaking, there are four cornerstones for education: democracy, society, prosperity and innovation (Figure 2.1). Education, by fostering an awareness of self and others, allows individuals to make the moral judgements that defend freedom of choice; the emotional intelligence to interact with societies and communities for cohesion and inclusion; the skills for economic success and the creative inventiveness for future relevance. And yet there is a general feeling that education serves none of these: confidence in democracy is at an all-time low, nations are characterised by division, the economic outlook is parlous and we are underprepared for the fourth industrial – technological – revolution.

Figure 2.1 The cornerstones of the vision for education

Democracy	Society
	The vision for education
Prosperity	Innovation

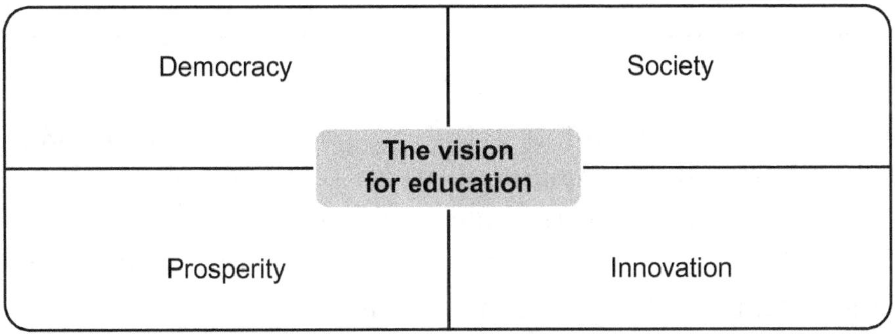

The function of education

On the other hand, a more practical view of education sees it as a function, comprising four variables: potential, inclusion, preparedness and relevance (Figure 2.2). In its functional capacity, every child should be helped to reach their potential, introduced to ambition and aspiration regardless of background, connected to relevant outcomes and prepared for a future in which they should expect to thrive. As with the vision for education, it too is reported to be failing on all counts. Many children leave school with low expectations of future prospects, excluded from certain sections of society, having collected average academic qualifications of little interest to employers and lacking the social skills and professional instincts to be considered good hires.

Figure 2.2 The four functions of education

Potential	Inclusion
Preparedness	Relevance

(The functions of education)

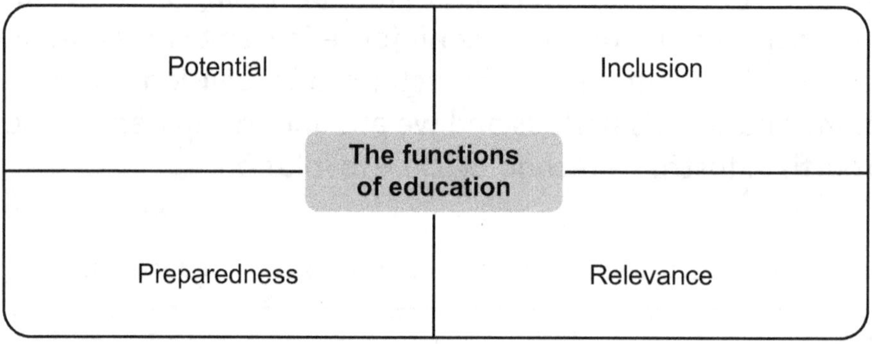

To create a compelling proposition, coaching must manage expectations by aligning itself to both the vision and function of education. Accordingly, it must find its own version for the role of education, one that allows it to access both ideological and practical dimensions.

A coach's definition of the role of education

From the perspective of the coach working in schools, the role of education is to prepare young people, intellectually, emotionally and practically, to prosper in the future. In order to do so, educators must accept the unique personalities of learners and support varying levels of ability and different types of intelligence – emotional, academic and practical (Gardner, 2000) – to bring out the best in every child. If we accept this premise, it follows that education must be adaptable to the needs of individuals and comprise numerous diverse approaches. It is this definition that the coach is tasked with integrating into mainstream learning.

How to integrate coaching

As part of the soul searching that inevitably accompanies the philosophical analysis of society's major problems, education is seen as an avoidable failure (something that can be fixed); hence there is a continuous call for a reset to change what and how young people learn. To contribute to an education reset, coaching needs to find a way of stepping out from the margins of youth development and into mainstream learning. In so doing, it must design and deliver a new pedagogy that is complementary to the curriculum and central to teaching and learning, linking together cognition, metacognition and motivation to create self-regulated learners.

But how to integrate coaching into mainstream learning? Now that we are beginning to understand the dynamics of a working relationship, we are able to put in place strategies upon which to build partnerships with schools (most significantly with teachers) to introduce coaching as an accompaniment to learning. The model in Figure 2.3 shows the constituent parts of a workable relationship: advocacy, environment and activism.

Figure 2.3 The constituent parts of a workable relationship between coaching and learning

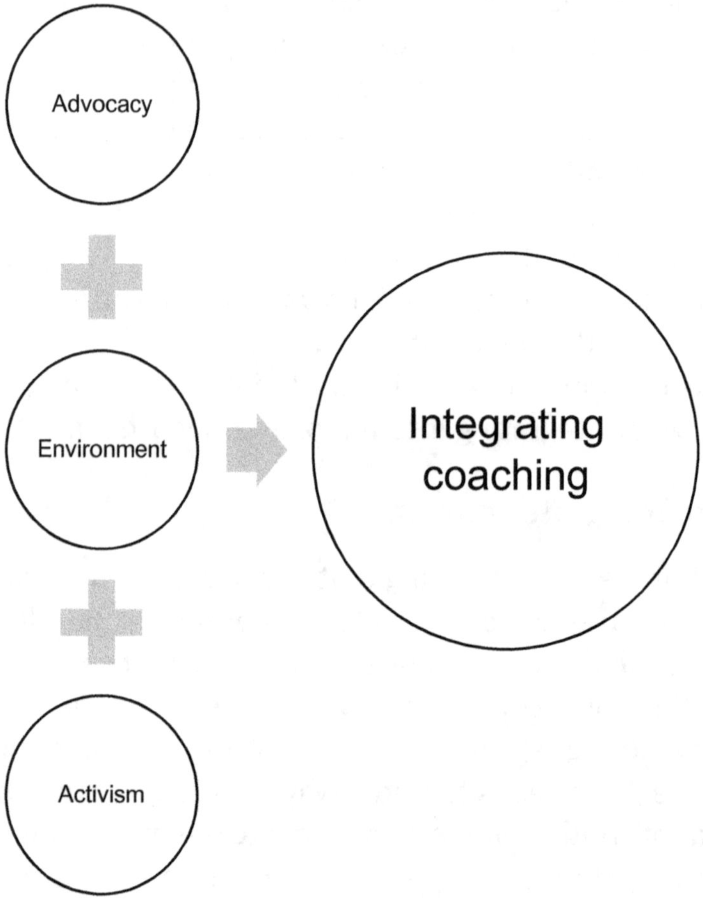

Advocacy
+
Environment
+
Activism
→ Integrating coaching

Advocacy

To integrate coaching into the classroom, the coach needs advocacy – the support of an influential group to help carry the argument for coaching as a credible accompaniment to learning and recommend its formal implementation. The primary target for both advocacy and future advocates is teachers.

Advocacy is achieved by creating awareness to garner support. To create awareness, the coach needs to work within the system, communicating through recurring narratives and storytelling to make sense of coaching in the context of learning. As a framework for advocacy awareness, we work with two complementary narratives: *strategic* and *illustrative*. The *strategic* narrative is used to make sense of the coach's role by aligning with the curriculum and wider school goals, while the *illustrative* narrative effectively demonstrates the coach's activities and their impact on the functions of education and academic targets.

Once the coach's campaign for awareness is underway, they must work to gather support. We recommend using a check-list model such as the one in Figure 2.4. This version uses a keystone framework (Figure 2.5) comprising communication, connection and negotiation prompts to facilitate seven defining principles: clarity, originality, alignment, perspective, navigation, alliances and evaluation.

Figure 2.4 How to achieve advocacy

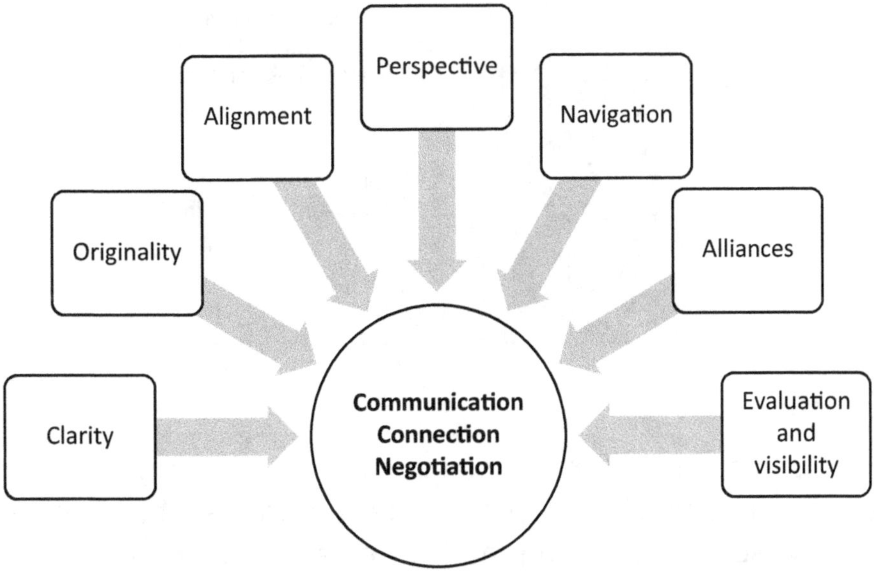

- Perspective
- Alignment
- Navigation
- Originality
- Alliances
- Clarity
- Communication / Connection / Negotiation
- Evaluation and visibility

COACHING TOOL

Advocacy prompts

The keystone in Figure 2.5 provides a series of prompts for the coach to follow. These are designed to help the coach explore and stay aligned to the unique personality of the individual school, ensuring that all coaching interventions are custom-made.

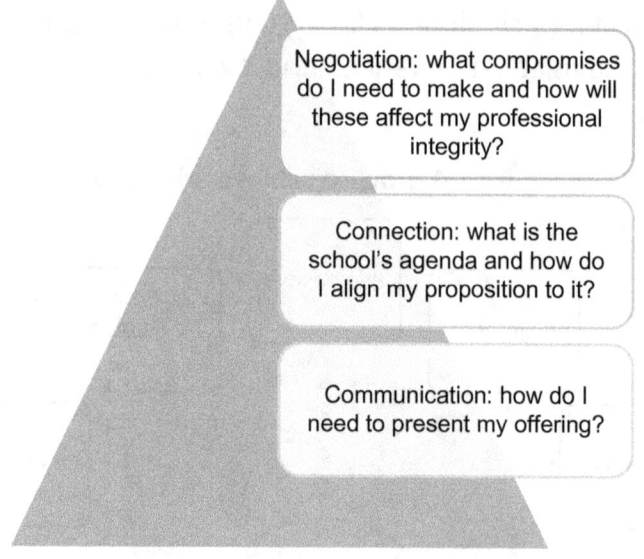

Figure 2.5 Communication, connection and negotiation, the coach's keystone for advocacy to be used in conjunction with Figure 2.4

Clarity

The primary task for any coach seeking advocacy is to be clear about what is on offer. The fog created by inundation, misconception and faddism means that the coaching partnership needs an effective elevator pitch to gain attention. Using relatable strategic and illustrative narratives underpins the pitch; however, the coach, having made sense of the proposal in the eyes of the school, should now focus on delivering the message. This means avoiding jargon at all costs. A profusion of psychobabble or idioms both underserves the coach offering and has the potential to irritate the listener.

Originality

Advocacy is much more readily given if the idea is original. New thinking enables the advocate to have a sense of ownership over the concept and an original idea is a much easier sell than a reheated version of something that has been tried, tested and failed. This also means that the advocate is invested intellectually in the project, free to make their own interpretation of a concept that is continuously evolving.

Alignment

It is not enough to have a clear offering: that offering should satisfy a need. Readily transferable outcomes allow the advocate to align coaching with the whole range of education targets, from tangibles such as enhanced academic achievement to wider issues such as inclusion, social mobility, well-being and mental health, through to more abstract destinations including aspiration and legacy.

Perspective

For effective advocacy, it is critical to understand and take stock of the opposing perspectives for both directive and reciprocal communication as well as positive behaviour management. Such an understanding aids alignment and communication, and it also informs negotiation strategies.

Navigation

Understanding different perspectives enables the advocate to anticipate barriers and navigate a safe passage. Navigation is seen as a broad term for negotiation, encompassing language, diplomacy, deft alignment of outcomes and intellectual agility. Whereas we see negotiation as a series of episodes, navigation is a constant state of awareness that informs behaviours.

Alliances

Effective advocacy requires networks of alliances. Under the harsh light of intense scrutiny that new unfamiliar projects attract, alliances not only support and defend the project when it hits a bump in the road but keep up the momentum going forward once the coach has left the building.

Evaluation

The advocate must be able to visibly prove impact of worth. For intangible goals, impact is difficult to quantify, but the advocate must be alert for snippets of evidence, often reflective or anecdotal, that convince stakeholders of progress. Reporting small wins often gives a sense of success and keeps the project in the spotlight. At the same time, advocacy should also be open to including failures as well as successes when disseminating feedback. This provides credibility and reinforces confidence in the project which, being judged at an experimental stage, is accepting of negative feedback as a positive source of future design.

Environment

Integrating coaching into mainstream learning depends on an understanding of the interaction between the four functions of education and the environment within which they operate. Once a working knowledge of the environment is in place, the coach is looking for an entry point for coaching to be ushered in rather than rudely announced. Using the four functions (potential, inclusion, relevance and preparedness) as a context and applying leadership as a coaching focus (Figure 2.6), the coach is challenging the environment and negating its fault lines while at the same time creating an access point.

> **CRITICAL DISCUSSION POINT**
>
> ### The disempowering and empowering influences of a leadership focus
>
> Leadership, as a concept in schools, is complicated, having the capacity for both empowerment and disempowerment. In a recent coaching workshop with teachers, autonomy – the ability to act independently and make judgements while maintaining collective responsibility for the overarching goals of the school – was reported as the most valued condition for doing the job. At the same time, a total lack of autonomy was reported by all teachers as the single most demoralising characteristic of their working environment, reflecting an absence of trust and respect for their status. Alternatively, from a young person's point of view, the focus on leadership, once accepted, was found to be empowering, instilling a sense of responsibility and choice that, when applied to the functions of education, unlocked a high level of discretionary energy.

How leadership interacts with education

Figure 2.6 Introducing leadership as an access point for coaching to the functions of education

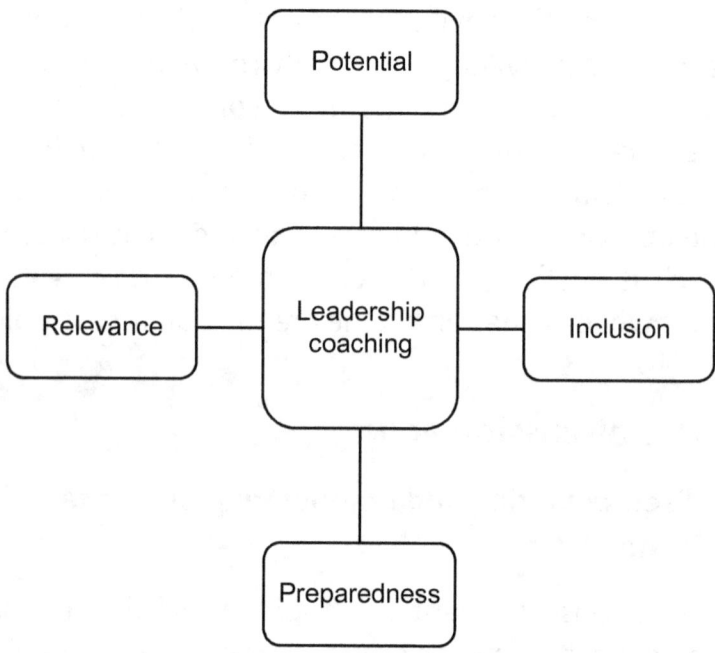

Potential

The findings and recommendations of the recent Times Education Commission survey (2022) identified *helping each child reach their potential* as a primary role for education. If schools are serious about this ambition, specifically to include *every child*, they must look outside the curriculum and conventional school targets and broaden the scope of potential. Restrictive structures and assessment criteria make this difficult, whereas the coach sees potential as a mercurial latent energy that reflects the unique personality, skills and ambitions of the individual towards an, as yet unidentified, end goal.

When leadership is applied as a coaching focus, the direction for *potential* is crystalised. A new vision of leadership (Jamieson, 2023) reimagines qualification to include counter-intuitive behavioural traits and disruptive thought patterns. Therefore, leadership reimagined acts as a filter for potential, using the new vision to give licence to purpose and aspiration, from which ambitions emerge (Figure 2.7).

Figure 2.7 Leadership as a filter for potential

Potential → Leadership → (Purpose / New vision of leadership / Aspiration) → Ambition

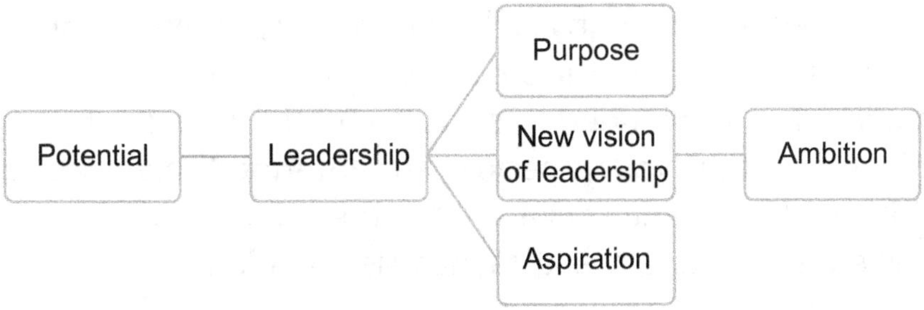

Inclusion

The new vision of leadership treats a hitherto exclusive role as a mechanism for inclusion. By visualising leadership as a unique (to each child) energy rather than a collection of past, outdated hierarchical notions, coaches are able to work with every individual young person regardless of their perceived standing in an educational setting. This means that those deemed troublesome, outside the academic mainstream or on the verge of exclusion are appreciated for their disruptive and challenging personalities, reinterpreted as potential positive leadership qualities. In this way, leadership becomes a shared destination for every child and breaks the shackles of standardised assessment criteria used by schools.

Preparedness

Schools may be able to adapt to the needs of the future workplace, ramping up opportunities for vocational education, but in isolation this is a very one-dimensional approach to preparing young people for life after school. In the context of preparedness, leadership coaching offers two new dimensions to learning. Firstly, it has the capacity to enhance vocational education by equipping young people with a leadership mindset. This includes critical analysis for decision making, independent thought for original ideas, and curiosity for exploration and experimentation, reported to be the distinct characteristics that employers require but are currently lacking in young people. Secondly, coaching can support the soft skills, underserved by schools, that young people need to survive and thrive in the future. This means that young people are entering the workplace with the developing social skills and emotional intelligence needed to navigate the idiosyncrasies of adult life.

Relevance

The current school environment dictates that relevance is defined within the context of standardised education outcomes. Coaching works outside these parameters and is primarily focused on the learner's agenda for relevance, not by disrupting the curriculum but by connecting it to the individual's long-term ambitions and drivers.

Developing a leadership mindset assists the young person to make positive choices about learning, putting sufficient effort into subjects that count and unlocking discretionary energy for subjects that matter to them. This means curriculum subjects can be easily related to current issues and causes relevant to the young learner. For instance, in Chapter 6 we present a case study to illustrate how coaching can work in concert with other pedagogies. The subject for the study was a school history project based on the letters of Richard Cobden, the nineteenth-century activist and campaigner. We found that learners were quick to connect the campaigns of Cobden to a current context and, given the space, enthusiastically related these to areas or causes of personal interest, including the #MeToo movement, modern slavery and the moral dilemmas around refugees.

In addition, employing leadership projects to pursue academic subjects provides relevant real-life experience of using critical thinking and independent thought, as well as a chance to practise the non-cognitive skills they have developed through leadership coaching.

Activism and the role of teachers

Activism refers to the action taken by advocates, specifically teachers, to implement coaching as a legitimate accompaniment to learning.

> **CRITICAL DISCUSSION POINT**
>
> **Teachers as middle managers**
>
> Despite our focus on coaching young people, the subordinate relationship between coaches and teachers should not be underestimated. In the previous chapter, we discussed the impact of continuing professional development strategies on teacher retention and engagement. We have also evidenced that coaching and teaching is a natural relationship, where coaching methodologies provide an intellectual and creative outlet for the teacher and reaffirm original vocational goals (the reasons they joined the profession), making them effective advocates. Now, we posit the idea that, in facilitating a working
>
> →

relationship between education and coaching, teachers should be reimagined as middle managers.

In the margins of our work, conversations with teachers reveal they are actually the middle managers of the school, squeezed between the institution of education and the culture of coaching: beholden to the former but aligned with the latter. The very term *middle manager* in the private sector is a pejorative description of status, representative of limitation and mediocrity. However, in the last 20 years there has been appreciation for the role, both for the contribution they make and the unique balancing act they are required to perform. Organisational academics such as DeLong (2003) and Huy (2001) have challenged us to re-evaluate a role where there is no ownership over decisions that the manager is employed to enforce. Appreciation for middle managers has now moved the discussion on to how they are supported to perform a vital organisational role – moving away from a *kissing up kicking down* caricature to a key function, connecting detached C-suite executives to the frontline workforce or, in schools, closing the gap between what the system provides and what learners need.

CRITICAL QUESTION

- In occupying the space of middle management, why is the unique position held by the teacher (between pupils and decision makers) unrecognised as a source to inform future learning strategies?

COACHING AS AN ACCOMPANIMENT TO LEARNING 41

The four roles of the activist teacher

For coaching to become a legitimate learning accompaniment, the contribution of teachers is indispensable and they must be supported to take action. Continuing with the analogy of middle managers, we assigned four roles to the teacher reflecting their unique position: entrepreneur, communicator, counsellor and arbiter (Figure 2.8).

Figure 2.8 Teachers – activists or middle managers?
The role teachers play in implementing coaching as a legitimate accompaniment to learning

In our capacity as coaches to teachers, the overarching focus is on developing the authoritative voice. From this point, four satellite dimensions of coaching are in play (Figure 2.9):

1. creativity;
2. ambidexterity;
3. emotional intelligence;
4. judgement.

Figure 2.9 The authoritative voice and satellite coaching outcomes for advocacy

The authoritative voice is referred to in Chapter 1 and examined in detail in the first book of this series, *Coaching Young People for Leadership*. In simple terms, it refers to having the professional presence to communicate and be listened to in terms of ideas and opinions in the context of shared goals. For the purposes of introducing coaching to learning, the authoritative voice (usually the teacher's) interacts with the environment like a legitimate disruptor for advocacy.

The teacher as entrepreneur

Most teachers see coaching as a natural fit for learning. However, the notion that they should act as entrepreneurs to crystallise their instincts, taking risks for long-term gain, is challenging, not personally, but in the environment within which they have to operate. When we talk to teachers, the enthusiasm for new ideas and experimentation around learning is palpable. And when it comes to envisioning learning stimulants that sit outside the curriculum, teachers are ideally positioned to gather insights into the creative sparks that stimulate learners to enhance academic performance. At the same time, the sense of not being listened to and passed over for preferred alternative (mostly ineffective) initiatives adds to the sense of hopelessness.

Teachers must be encouraged to think creatively about learning. Here, the coach is working on two levels: firstly, to help the teacher to find the safe space to explore new ideas and, secondly, to formulate creative initiatives that they can sell to the school's senior leadership team (SLT). Where the SLT is sceptical about the entrepreneurial role of teachers, they might need to look to themselves to reassess and ask questions about the overall creative environment and ambition of the school.

The teacher as a communicator

Teachers are actively involved in the coaching relationship at conception and implementation stages. As advocates, they are charged with creating awareness through clarity of message and effective communication. There are four communication targets: learners, SLT, colleagues (cynics) and others (outsiders).

Learners
One of the starting points for coaching young people is to build credibility at the beginning to allow the process to achieve meaningful long-term outcomes. This is particularly relevant when working in schools where the coach should always be mindful of the surreal dimensions of the learner's experience: unfamiliar individual dedicated attention enacted in a familiar lowest-common-denominator classroom setting. For coaching to be accepted into the mainstream, the teacher needs to communicate consistently to keep up momentum, especially once the coaching programme has completed, helping the learner adjust to choice over compliance. The learner will be subjected to plenty of mixed messages in a school environment and the teacher must step in to ensure clarity and maintain enthusiasm for a new and durable way of thinking about learning. If coaching is to succeed, it must not be perceived to take place in a bubble and consistent communication is a way of normalising the process, allowing it to enter the mainstream.

Senior leadership team
The primary goal when communicating to the SLT is return on investment. This does not necessarily refer to financial return but, more generally: what impact has the coaching programme had on specific school targets? As with all coaching interventions, evaluation of impact can be complicated with resultant data often irrelevant or tendentious. Unlike the coach, the teacher has first-hand knowledge of school touchpoints and can communicate precisely,

imparting assessment data and feedback intelligently and in alignment with overarching goals. Certainly, schools will want data for the purposes of financial accountability; however, impact on academic targets and wider social goals is likely to be more eye-catching and a cause for celebration.

Colleagues
The source of most frustration and disappointment is the cynical attitude of colleagues towards coaching, potentially undermining the process by confusing learners and demoralising those teachers involved. The disconnect between coaching and conventional teaching methodologies is a real problem for acceptance into the mainstream, but it is understandable and mixed messages are inevitable because coaching currently only takes place in the margins of day-to-day school life. Where being disconnected is unacceptable and most damaging is in the cynical or dismissive attitudes of some colleagues that belittle the efforts and enthusiasm of those involved. Colleagues outside of the coaching programme need to be brought in and enlightened so that ideas become part of a positive cognitive contagion – the spontaneous proliferation of a way of thinking and related behaviours (Jamieson, 2023) – spreading throughout the school and becoming part of the culture.

Others
We have found that the sense of ownership of new ideas and ways of thinking acts as an intellectual stimulant to teachers – a sabbatical from the curriculum – and can provide a coping mechanism for the daily grind. The attraction of intellectual exploration is that it is expansive and there is a requirement to take it outside the institution, opening up new networks of like-minded people. Communication at this level is not just about the wider advocacy but the new

conversations, surprising partnerships and pioneering ideas that loop back to the entrepreneurial responsibilities of the teacher.

The teacher as counsellor

Promoting an unorthodox counter-intuitive learning methodology inevitably creates uncertainty among both pupils and peers. In their capacity as middle managers, teachers have a vital role to play in creating the safe psychological and practical space for coaching (see Critical discussion point: What is a psychological safe space?). This means simultaneously supporting learners (and, let us not forget, parents) to step into the unknown while coaxing peers to be open-minded towards the unconventional. In our experience, coaching young people can open up personal insecurities or psychological flaws, ranging from a lack of self-worth to an overabundance of self-belief and expectation. Adopting coaching behaviours heightens the teacher's awareness of psychological blind spots, allowing them to either predict potential problems, specifically those emerging from mixed messages, or re-energise flagging interest once any programme has concluded.

The teacher as arbiter

The teacher's role as an arbiter, using an authoritative voice to convey balanced judgements between continuity and change, is critical. Logically, these judgements will be made towards the end of the coaching programme and form part of the wider evaluation process.

Once accepted into the learning system, coaching needs to prove its worth by performing exceptionally, delivering high-level results against specified school outcomes for an enduring relationship. Underperformance means that any coaching programme, as an accompaniment to learning, will wither on the vine. As arbiters, teachers are tasked with connecting unorthodox learning (change) to recognisable school outcomes (continuity). Here, the teacher collaborates with the coach to plan and design creative learning activities that simultaneously exceed the expectations of curriculum targets but, at the same time, can still be measured against them.

CRITICAL QUESTIONS

- How important is the role of the activist teacher in building a working relationship between coaching and learning?
- What is your strategy with parents for dealing with activist pressure points (communication, counselling and arbitration)?
- What is your strategy for dealing with scepticism or criticism from parents as highly personalised stakeholders in learning?

CRITICAL DISCUSSION POINT

The pace of change

The coaching partnership should be acutely aware of the pace of change. Coaches and teachers should not get carried away and try to force the issue, but remember they are helping the institution to learn to change. This means removing coaching from its bubble and

→

> placing it in the mainstream by shaping programmes to fit in with the structure of the school and not the other way around, making coaching a companion to learning rather than a competitor.

Bursting the bubble

If coaching is to become a companion to learning it cannot operate in a bubble. The challenge for the coach is to normalise coaching so that it can enter the learning mainstream, as welcomed rather than treated with suspicion.

Later in this book, we discuss in detail the *dysfunctional environment* that we argue characterises education, but for now we allude to the lack of trust and natural propensity for scepticism and suspicion as part of the school's operating DNA. In such a system, the coach and the partnering teacher(s) (the coaching partnership) need to work hard on a professional charm offensive to usher coaching into an intrinsically negative environment. We found that this is achieved through a combination of perseverance and inspiration.

Negotiating your way to normal

Getting to normal (entering the mainstream) is a straightforward negotiation between the coaching partnership and the school's SLT. As with all negotiations, nuance combines with argument to reach agreement. When coaching negotiation skills, we work on using the authentic voice in a tone that is relatable to the other party to find a middle ground. In this specific context, and in a difficult environment, that simple formula is deconstructed into six coaching focal points: drive, connection, incrementalism, evaluation, experimentation and professionalisation (Figure 2.10).

Figure 2.10 How to burst the coaching bubble – negotiating to *normal*

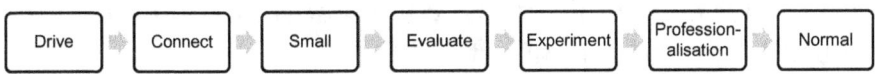

Drive

What is your purpose? Clarity of purpose underpins the drive needed to persevere, construct and articulate a compelling case. Purpose can be both selfish and altruistic, in the sense that using coaching as an intellectual stimulant re-engages the teacher with their original vocation and produces the discretionary energy needed to persevere and inspire. At the same time, by selflessly connecting coaching directly to outcomes for young people, the coaching partnership is aligned to purpose and this drives a compelling narrative that is difficult for sceptics to argue against.

Connection

The requirement to connect is thematic throughout this book; however, in this context it has two dimensions: alignment with existing targets and emotional connection for negotiation. In the first instance, an understanding of the values and goals of the individual school is a prerequisite of any coaching contract. Therefore, alignment with existing targets should require no more than precise targeting and the dexterity to reorient readily transferable coaching outcomes. In the second instance, the coaching partnership should adopt a flexible strategy to shape the narrative to appeal to different groups of decision makers and stakeholders. Shaping the narrative does not solely refer to delivering the message but emphasising specific areas of interest or concern relevant to the individual. For instance, one member of the SLT might need reassurance about financial implications, while another could be more focused on pastoral impact.

Incrementalism

As we have already stated, integrating coaching into mainstream learning is a gradual process of incremental steps. Any new initiative in a dysfunctional environment is subject to either the intense glare of scrutiny and micro-management or indifference and lack of engagement. Either way, it is an easy target for criticism if it is perceived to underperform. Accordingly, the coaching partnership is advised to rein in ambition and strategise managing expectations to avoid failing to deliver. As part of this strategy, cautious enthusiasm and easy relevant wins should appear high on the negotiating agenda. The coaching partnership should treat integration like a campaign rather than a singular event in the knowledge that small steps lead to incremental change.

Evaluation

In the work we do, evaluation of impact is a priority. However, as with any pioneering project at a nascent stage, quantitative evaluation data is difficult to generate due to the lack of benchmarking and the degree of experimentation necessary to deliver the programme (it is constantly evolving). Nevertheless, the coaching partnership should energetically elicit feedback – positive or critical – to inform the future design of the project. Feedback, however it is couched, should be treated as valuable insights towards assessment of impact and qualitative evaluation data should be liberally shared with decision makers, stakeholders and sponsors as part of a lively debate about the direction of travel.

Experimentation

Having elicited feedback, the coaching partnership needs to act on it inside the classroom and be prepared to fail intelligently to enable the evolutionary process. By *failing intelligently* (Edmondson, 2023) we refer to the notion that innovation needs constant experimentation to succeed and, with that, failing is a necessary part of the process. Handling or disseminating failure is a challenge for the coaching partnership where forays into new territories are constantly under the spotlight of a psychologically unsafe environment (see Critical discussion below). Outside of the classroom, the coaching partnership should seek out opportunities to network and engage in dialogues with interesting people outside the domain of education. Youth development and leadership are not confined to education, and connecting with like-minded individuals or groups can widen the purview for coaching and introduce surprising new ideas that are readily transferable to learning.

Professionalisation

Despite genuine enthusiasm at the conceptual stage of a proposed coaching programme, a difficult operating environment means that roadblocks are inevitable. Accordingly, the coaching partnership must work hard not to get discouraged and give up. Barriers to progress are ever-present in any organisation, but in schools frustration from objections is exacerbated because of the vocational nature of teaching and the potential missed opportunities to directly benefit learners. Therefore, it is important that those involved do not get distracted by interpreting these as personal slights but are able to persevere by envisioning an end goal. Professionalising objections from operational non-strategic departments and inflexible systematic barriers means that the coaching partnership engages, as opposed to confronts, to connect with naysayers and argue a case. Professionalisation is not making it about the individual but about the project, and requires a degree of humility, plenty of patience and an unshakable conviction about purpose and goals.

> **CRITICAL DISCUSSION POINT**
>
> **What is a psychological safe space?**
>
> Throughout this book, we refer to creating safe spaces and, sometimes, psychological safe spaces. Psychological safe spaces, more often than not, are profoundly misunderstood. When we talk to partner teachers, there is always agreement about the need to create safe spaces for young people to express themselves freely as part of the coaching process. However, the phrase psychological safe space is often misconstrued as places to practise *niceness*, accept poor performance or engender a moan culture. This interpretation is more easily adopted by schools because it is generally within the sphere of an individual teacher's limited autonomy. The real definition of psychological

safety is a climate that gives permission to challenge and be heard without recrimination or retribution. In such a climate, interpersonal fear (how what you say will be received) negates interpersonal risk-taking (willingness to reframe failure as a learning experience). This interpretation is more difficult for schools to adopt due to the dysfunctional environment (see Chapter 9) and the visceral belief, nurtured from a very young age, that failure is bad and to be avoided and success is good and to be applauded.

CRITICAL QUESTION

- Can a school ever be a psychologically safe space? Explain your answer.

Coach humility

For coaching to accompany mainstream learning, the coaching partnership must work hard to understand the environment and then design a strategy to fit in. The ideas presented in this chapter have worked for us. They assume a developing relationship with the school at a nascent stage and buy-in to the degree that the school is prepared to at least enter a conversation about collaboration.

From the coach's point of view, we would urge professional modesty – it is, after all, about the success of coaching as an alternative learning methodology, not the brilliance of the facilitator. In a number of schools where we have been successful, formal recognition from Ofsted or the Department for Education often overlooks the efforts of the coach as the initiator and facilitator of a highly acclaimed project, and the school is similarly ungenerous in putting our contribution on record. As coaches, this is frustrating from a marketing perspective; however, we also accept that this reflects the fact that schools are operating under intense scrutiny and to exacting assessment criteria. Without wishing to sound pious, it is sufficient to know that we are contributing to an education renaissance and the new dimensions of learning.

Further reading

Curran, T (2023) *The Perfection Trap*. London: Cornerstone Press.

Edmondson, A (2023) *Right Kind of Wrong: Why Learning to Fail Can Teach Us to Thrive*. London: Cornerstone Press.

References

DeLong, T and Vijayaraghavan, V (2003) Let's Hear It for the B-Players. *Harvard Business Review*, June 2003.

Edmondson, A (2023) *Right Kind of Wrong: Why Learning to Fail Can Teach Us to Thrive*. London: Cornerstone Press.

Gardner, H E (2000) *Intelligence Reframed: Multiple Intelligences for the 21st Century*. London: Hachette UK.

Huy, Q (2001) In Praise of Middle Managers. *Harvard Business Review*, September 2001.

Jamieson, M (2023) *Coaching Young People for Leadership*. St Albans: Critical Publishing.

Times Education Commission (2022) *How to Transform Education and Unleash the Potential of Every Child*. [online] Available at: https://nuk-tnl-editorial-prod-staticassets.s3.amazonaws.com/2022/education-commission/Times%20Education%20Commission%20final%20report.pdf (accessed 26 January 2024).

Chapter 3

THE SIX NEW DIMENSIONS OF LEARNING

CHAPTER OVERVIEW

Drawing on published research and real-life experience, this chapter explores the new dimensions of learning as a logical entry point for coaching in schools. Identifying three key stakeholders for educational goals – employers, schools and young people – it discusses in detail emerging targets outside the current curriculum. Aligning stakeholder outcomes produces six new dimensions of learning – creativity, society, leadership, industry, technology and well-being – as a pathway for young people to thrive in the future. From an analysis of new dimensions, it explains how coaching is the natural accompaniment to conventional teaching, as an uninhibited development methodology capable of delivering unfamiliar skills, simultaneously enriching the student experience and enhancing academic achievements.

Preparing young people to thrive in the future workplace

Aiming for known targets

First and foremost, we would like to emphasise that this book is not an ideological tract but founded on evidence, mostly from real-life experience, and focused on relevant and realistic outcomes from schools for young people. Accordingly, much of this chapter is centred on a single transactional goal: preparing young people to thrive in the future workplace. For the school and the (coach's) sponsor, focusing on a relevant known target and a practical outcome provides legitimacy for engaging with a coach due to the prospect of a quantifiable return on investment. At the same time, for the coach we recognise that preparing young people to thrive is a more complex multi-faceted proposition where there is a balance to be struck between tangible and intangible outcomes. A coaching programme heavily weighted towards a short-term known target restricts the coachee's capacity for ambition and aspiration, while overly focusing on ideals sometime in the future ends up as wishful thinking. To achieve a balance the coach has to flex between the two, applying soft skills to hard targets. In practical terms, aiming for a known target is a great place to start but to achieve success in the current reality, both the school and the coach are faced with the same conundrum: how to bridge the gap between curriculum knowledge and life skills.

Originality over replication

The gap between curriculum knowledge and life skills is facilitated by a learning culture that emphasises replication over originality. For young people to thrive in the future we must equip them at an early age with the skills of enquiry, to analyse and interrogate information rather than just accumulate facts – to learn different things differently. However, as schools continue to prepare young people for a world that no longer exists, fake news and social media echo chambers mean that we have taken a backward step and self-preservation is now a more immediate imperative. Furthermore, in a future workplace characterised by technological advancement, knowledge replication simply does not cut it and young people will be required to differentiate themselves by developing human skills such as curiosity, empathy, communication and collaboration that their AI counterparts lack. The spotlight is now on schools to adapt to a new way of learning, encouraging young people to think independently and originally to meet the emerging expectations of the workplace, by developing transferable skills to create well-rounded citizens fit for a twenty-first-century global economy.

Reality check: compensating for the skills gap

An obdurate system and a curriculum that acts as a straitjacket for teachers and pupils alike mean that education is essentially turning a deaf ear to the needs of employers. With the world of work now at odds with the educational landscape, the gap between the curriculum and the workplace is evidenced by the compensatory strategies adopted by employers and the post-school preferences of pupils. For instance, deeming A levels and GCSEs to be meaningless, employers are now favouring CV-blind interviews and their own assessment systems weighted towards creativity and originality. Furthermore, organisations are promoting apprenticeship schemes over graduate recruitment. Although many of these schemes eventually lead to a professional qualification, three years spent gaining experience of the industry are often considered more valuable than a degree.

This is borne out by our own experience, coaching both graduates and apprentices into the workplace, where, despite similar ages, there is a marked difference between the two, with the latter group generally more mature and streetwise. Of course, some professions (eg law and medicine) require conventional academic qualifications; but even in these instances, a balanced approach between IQ and EQ (emotional intelligence) is preferable. Indeed, one of the significant coaching challenges we face is supporting the graduate to make space for the acquisition of behaviours and unrelated knowledge in their pursuit of a highly demanding academic qualification – it does not matter how technically brilliant a doctor is, they will still be judged by their bedside manner.

Many organisations now strive for a diverse recruitment policy, with varying motives: accessing the current workplace zeitgeist, fulfilling quotas or genuinely in search of young people with an intellectual hinterland who break the mould of a brand-traditional recruit type. While recruitment diversity for competitive differentiation and new thinking is a legitimate strategy, those that are motivated by ticking a diversity box often do not know how to support and develop the potential of their young people and forget that they are barely out of school and likely to be from a different cultural background. Here, the gap between the young person's preparedness for work and the expectations of the organisation is most starkly highlighted. It is not only schools that are failing to prepare young people for work; charities and youth organisations supporting young people who have been excluded or who lie outside the academic mainstream work hard to deliver academic qualifications, but fail to support their young people who, vulnerable to low self-esteem, struggle to make a job stick. According to data from the Department for Education, one in three young people from disadvantaged backgrounds are not in any form of education, apprenticeship or employment five years after leaving school with GCSEs (DfE, 2023).

At the same time, more young people are opting for apprentice schemes over university. For the first time in a decade, the number of school leavers applying for university has decreased and half of those registered with UCAS are simultaneously enquiring about apprenticeships (UCAS, 2023). A combination of employers' demands, young people's changing preferences and the soaring costs of higher education tuition fees means that the number of apprenticeships for 16–18 year olds is up 20 per cent on the previous year (Institute of Student Employers, 2022). However, one critical question remains: how much of this shift can be attributed to negative experiences of learning at school?

Emergent outcomes for education

What young people want

When we begin any new coaching project in a school, our first task is to engage with the young people designated to the leadership cohort through a dedicated one-to-one coaching session. This time is spent getting to know them, introducing the concepts of leadership and coaching, and building our credibility to facilitate a future working relationship. As part of the coaching process, this session is discussed in detail in Chapter 5 of *Coaching Young People for Leadership* (Jamieson, 2023, p 120) and is practically covered in the case studies in Chapter 4. However, this session also provides us with valuable insights into what young people want to get from their experience in school – their expectations and their sense of entitlement. Exploratory questions about ambitions and aspirations usually take some time to land, simply because young people are unfamiliar with being asked about what they want. Setting aside the necessary time to build confidence in the coaching relationship is essential, allowing the young person the space to imagine what the future looks like and how they see themselves in it.

Defaulting to classroom expectations, coachees scramble to find the right answers to open questions about intangible ideas that they have probably never thought about before. To move this session on, we ask more general questions about being at school. This depersonalises the conversation and removes them from the spotlight, allowing them to talk comfortably about their environment. From here, the coach achieves two things. Firstly, they introduce the coachee to perspective – the responsibility and influence of authority – what would I do if I was in a position of power? Secondly, having established perspective, they are able to elicit an intelligent balanced critique of the school environment as a reliable source of knowledge about the real needs of young people and how they are (or not) being addressed. In other words, the coach is providing the young person with a voice and a platform to be heard.

Perhaps surprisingly, when invited to speak their mind, most young leaders spend time talking positively about role model teachers. These teachers are distinguished by a set of shared leadership attributes, including: kindness, compassion, humour, consistency, approachability and fairness. At the same time, placing young people in a leadership context also invites them to be critical of perceived negative behaviours of authority figures. For instance, when G was asked how she would lead her group as part of a school project, she was unhesitating:

> *With respect. Not like some teachers – shouting and criticising – I will get the best out of them by showing them all respect.*
>
> G, Bradford

Another negative theme was the blind obedience to the many seemingly meaningless rules and regulations that schools are run by:

> *I get that the discipline of learning in a structured way is a future life skill in itself. It's more about the relevance of the rules in school. There's no flexibility or reason for many of them. Teachers' attitudes when we challenge them is – they are the rules! Even if they are completely irrelevant, they must be followed – that's not a life skill. If anything, it's setting you up to be a robot!*
>
> A, 16, York

Systematic inflexibility was also criticised by some young learners in the context of teaching methodologies:

> *Because I am dyslexic, I don't have the same opportunities as others in my class. What I mean is, there's only one way of learning – reading and writing. And that means, there's only one way to be successful at school. There needs to be other ways of learning that include people like me. It's frustrating because I know I can do so much more.*
>
> Y, 15, London

There was also sympathy from some for the burden placed upon teachers, but, in the same breath, disappointment at missed opportunities:

> *Teachers can be leaders. They have the potential to change lives, when they make the time for you and show they're interested. I know they're all busy, but when you think they can have that positive effect. What's more important than that?*
>
> K, 16, Manchester

By far and beyond the most consistent criticism of school was the irrelevance of the current curriculum as a basis for preparing for the future and a thematic argument that it was actually a counter-productive force:

> *What about the stuff that's not known? I am working hard to be the same as everyone else – what's the point of that? Who cares? How does this make me different? Who's going to notice me? I don't blame my teachers because I think they find it frustrating too – imagine being a teacher, at least we only have to go through this once! I just don't see how what's on offer [learning] is relevant to my future. If anything, it's holding me back – I don't want to be average.*
>
> J, 16, London

Using a version of Maslow's hierarchical framework, we compiled the combined responses collected from young people and parents as part of our own research to create a hierarchy of needs for learners to be met by schools (Figure 3.1). Maslow's original model (the Hierarchy of Needs, 1943) was developed as a motivational theory in psychology, where needs were either deficiency (arising from unmet deprivation) or growth (arising from a positive desire for development). In our version, deficiency needs are confined to the *basic* level and all other levels are seen as growth needs. In reality, schools are designed, through outcomes, assessment and evaluation, to only focus on the basic needs of pupils. In this way, teaching is reduced to a means to an end and there is no motivation for the school to go beyond this basic function. Higher levels become discretionary and random, inconsistent not just across schools but sometimes within the same school, across teachers. *Growth* needs get overlooked because they are intangible and difficult to evaluate, focusing on the unique emotional development of a young person as an ongoing process. They cannot be conveniently categorised, quantified or confined by a timeline.

Figure 3.1 Hierarchy of needs for learners to thrive in school

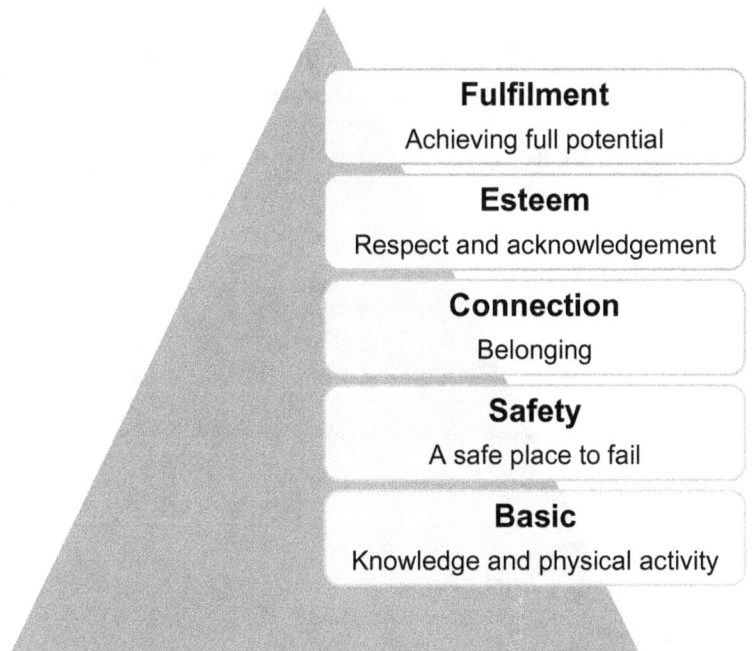

CRITICAL QUESTIONS

- How does your school attend to the growth needs of pupils?
- How can these be promoted?

Balancing needs

For all that has been written and spoken about the problems in education today, the imbalance between growth outcomes (those for the development of the young person) and deficiency outcomes (those for the achievement of school targets) encapsulates the current situation. Despite a clear statement from intellectually and emotionally invested stakeholders (learners and their parents) about the best interests of pupils, the balance of power remains firmly with the sole deficiency outcome to satisfy basic educational needs (Figure 3.2).

Figure 3.2 Counter-balance – how deficiency needs outweigh growth outcomes

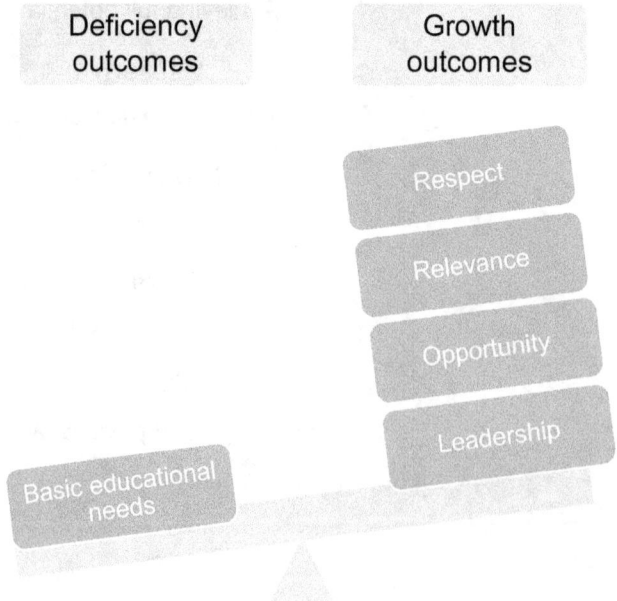

In essence, the role of the coach in an educational setting is to balance the scales, to consolidate the outcomes of schools and young people, so that they are able to exist harmoniously and support each other towards a common goal.

Summary of emergent outcomes

Our research for this book combines real-life experience and interviews with a diverse range of people with an interest in education: teachers, parents, educationalists, employers, third sector leaders, sponsors, psychologists and, most vitally, young people. We have consciously set out to engage with the broadest research sample, talking to specialists across the wider purview of youth development, including experts in the fields of gender dysphoria and social mobility, to provide a comprehensive understanding of needs.

Professionally, we have directly or indirectly worked with over 300 schools across the country, covering a range of sectors including state and independent, free schools and academies. We have also worked with local authorities and children's services as part of an SEMH (social, emotional and mental health) specialist teaching team. We have delivered training and coaching to teachers in schools and universities, and acted as advisers to Education and Training boards. Through our work, we have engaged with thousands of learners and hundreds of educators.

From an analysis of the wide-ranging data gathered, we arrived at a number of new goals for education. We used three stakeholder groups to categorise these goals: schools, employers and young people. We considered extending the stakeholder group to include teachers and parents, but decided they were essentially sub-sections for the Schools and Young People groups, although their responses influenced our understanding of new dimensions of learning and it is worth recording some of the salient points.

Responses from our interviews with teachers invariably turned to pay and conditions; however, one unexpected theme emerged: the public lack of awareness over the values and ideals that drive teachers. Here, one teacher talks about her motivation to take recent industrial action:

> *What disappoints me is how strike action by teachers has become a one-dimensional argument about money. That is an unfair representation of the teacher's mindset. Yes, we deserve more money, but that single focus undermines the reason we've been forced to take action – the general state of education and the effect on the children we teach. Teachers genuinely believe that the system is failing young people – this is not what we signed up for.*
>
> A, Leeds

CRITICAL DISCUSSION POINT

The litmus test for the potential impact of one of our projects in a new school is the quality of the partnerships we forge with the teachers. There are occasions when teachers are unresponsive or disengaged from the programme, claiming limited capacity or lack of financial support (to work outside the curriculum in the school's time). Mostly, we find teachers are keen to be involved in the coaching process and learn more about adopting coaching behaviours to enrich their professional practice. These teachers told us they were attracted to coaching because it provided them with the vocational opportunities they imagined when they joined the profession: one-to-one engagement, professional autonomy, creative interventions and relatable learning. Throughout our work, we are constantly amazed by these highly motivated, caring practitioners; however, if headline research is to be believed, nearly half plan to leave the profession within five years (National Education Union, 2023).

CRITICAL QUESTION

- As a teacher, how can you navigate the rigid inflexible structures in school to use coaching behaviours to enrich your professional practice?

In our informal conversations with parents, we found that, although academic achievement was a primary requirement from their child's school, the way in which it was attained was critical. Parents were looking for an educational hybrid model that meant that their children would pass exams in good mental health and with a strong sense of well-being. As part of a wider well-being agenda, a significant number wanted their children to be given the space to enjoy creative, sporting and social activities outside of the academic curriculum. There was also an emphasis on equipping young people with life skills and the emotional and social intelligence to survive and thrive in the future.

Most of all, I want my children to be happy, welcomed and included. I want to feel that their personalities are recognised in the way they're taught and that the school is able to adapt to their individual needs. Of course, I want them to be successful in their school work but I also want them to gain a wider global knowledge that will make them both interesting and interested.

S, London

Insights from teachers and parents were incorporated into our findings from the three stakeholder groups to produce our interpretation of a wish-list for emergent outcomes for education (Table 3.1).

Table 3.1 The emergent outcomes that inform the new dimensions of learning

Stakeholders	Emergent outcomes
Schools	To create brilliant human beings who want to change the world
	To prepare young people for life not just exams
	To create active learners
	To support and educate for twenty-first-century competencies
	To be inclusive
	To create the next generation of leaders
Employers	Judgement and decision making
	Project management
	Negotiation skills
	Critical thinking
	Creativity
	Emotionally intelligent communication
Young people	Respect
	Relevance
	Opportunity
	Role models/leadership

Aligning emergent outcomes across stakeholders

Aligning the outcomes of stakeholders (Table 3.2) will go on to produce the new dimensions of learning. This process also provides a framework for advocacy for the coach, making sense of intangible soft skills by connecting them to hard targets. As the outcomes of schools and young people are, to a certain extent, already aligned, this exercise introduces a transactional dimension which ensures relevance.

Table 3.2 Framework for aligning the interests of stakeholders

Schools	Employers	Young people
To create brilliant human beings who want to change the world	Creativity	Opportunity
To prepare young people for life not just exams	Judgement and decision making	Relevance
To create active learners	Critical thinking	Relevance
To support and educate for twenty-first-century competencies	Project management Negotiation skills	Relevance
To be inclusive: identifying and drawing out the talent in every young person	Emotionally intelligent communication	Respect
To create the next generation of leaders – young people leading young people	Creativity	Role model/ leadership

From a deep-dive analysis of stakeholder responses, data was distilled and six new dimensions for learning emerged: creativity, society, leadership, industry, technology and wellbeing. These are summarised below.

The six new dimensions of learning

Dimensions are multi-faceted, having a practical definition, leading to qualification or transactional target, as well as a more subtle subtext focused on self-development. Simply put, they are designed to deliver the ideal – *well-rounded citizens fit for a twenty-first-century global economy* – described earlier in this chapter. We expect that the responsibility for transactional learning focus will naturally sit mainly with the school, in terms of providing opportunities, initiatives, capacity and resources. The self-development learning dimensions are envisaged to be the responsibility of the coach. It is the combination of the two facets, working in concert, that is expected to bring out the best in learners.

Creativity (transactional)

At one level, emphasising creativity requires the school to simultaneously make space for, and realise the importance of, co-curricular activities such as art, sport, drama and debate. At another level, creativity, as a learning mindset, when applied to everyday school tasks will enhance academic achievement. Our experiences provide evidence that encouraging learners to think independently, challenge conventional wisdom and learn from things that do not work means that they become inspired – learning is now perceived as a choice over which they have control (the case studies in Chapter 4 illustrate the impact of creativity on day-to-day academic projects).

Creativity (self-development)

Focusing on a young person's creativity develops a number of transferable skills and positively reframes conventionally perceived negative behaviour, such as disruption and challenge. Learning to be creative is not simply confined to enhancing academic achievement, but is essential to developing a mindset that thrives on curiosity, intuition and imagination. Creativity flips the conventional teaching dynamic as the learner loses the inhibition to strive to give the right answers and becomes aware of the power of questions.

> **CRITICAL QUESTIONS**
>
> - How can you draw on your own coaching behaviours to encourage pupils to become independently curious and tap into their intuition and imagination to enhance learning?
> - How do you protect the enlightened learner from the mixed messages of an inconsistent learning environment, where others remain focused on conventional teaching strategies and targets?

Society (transactional)

A combination of entrepreneurship and social responsibility means that schools are now seen as social hubs. The need to build strong business networks, as well as make a contribution to the local community, provides schools with an ideal outlet for the emotional and social development of their pupils. As well as building resilience and collaborative skills, volunteering, running community campaigns and getting involved with local projects develops an intellectual hinterland for young people that makes them aware of their surroundings and the wider issues that lie beyond.

Society (self-development)

Having their eyes opened to the wider world at an early stage introduces young people to the ideas of ambition and purpose: what they want to achieve and why. Developing a sense of valued contribution and acting on it is seen as a way of allowing young people to join, and impact, the wider social mobility debate.

Leadership (transactional)

Leadership skills are readily transferable to the behaviours and thinking needed by young people to transition into adulthood. The challenge for the school in the short term is to find opportunities for young people to use their learning and practise leadership in a school setting. In the longer term, leadership skills will support young people to effectively enter the workplace by aligning with the needs of employers, including: communication, project management, negotiation skills, judgement and decision making.

The case studies in Chapter 4 provide evidence that leadership skills are also transferable to academic tasks, having a positive impact on results, enriching the pupil experience and inspiring discretionary energy.

Leadership (self-development)

The idea that there is no template for leadership means that, despite its perceived exclusivity, leadership is a catalyst for inclusion in schools. A new set of expectations for leaders in an unpredictable and dynamic environment has widened the criteria that qualify young people for leadership roles. Along with those who already hold leadership responsibilities (head pupils, deputies and prefects), the new qualities of impactful leadership, disruption, challenge, originality and individuality mean that those from outside the academic mainstream are now seen as candidates.

Learning leadership is an ongoing process of self-exploration: what sort of leader am I? What are my leadership drivers? Why would anyone want to be led by me? What will my leadership achieve or change? These questions guide the young person towards an understanding of their qualities and their purpose. From this learning, a clearly defined personality emerges. Knowledge of self, at an early stage, allows young people to become confident about who they are and speak with both an authentic and authoritative voice.

> **CRITICAL QUESTION**
>
> - How might you encourage those pupils outside the school's mainstream leadership hierarchy to harness their potential and apply for a leadership programme?

Industry (transactional)

In the same way that learning to be creative is not just about more art lessons, learning about industry is not in the sole domain of economics and commerce. Focusing on preparing young people for the world of work signals a fundamental shift in learning, recognising the disparity between what is being taught in schools and what is needed in work. Young people need to be attracted to the idea of work, to develop a life-long work ethic that enables them to thrive professionally and make career choices that serve them well in later life. At a practical level, schools can provide access to work experience through their growing networks of commercial partners. Here, young people can learn about the professional mindset: taking personal responsibility for time management, performance, achievement and progression. However, pupils should also learn that they are entitled to have meaning and purpose, and to enjoy what they do in the future.

Industry (self-development)

Having introduced young people to the professional mindset, they must be prepared to navigate, emotionally and practically, the unfamiliar landscape of the workplace. To support them into work, they must learn advanced soft skills such as managing the expectations of others, resilience, empathy and rapport. Learning how to negotiate workplace politics is now an essential skill for young people at a pivotal time of generational movement in the economy. In other words, it is not enough to introduce young people to work; we have to support them to develop the soft skills and emotional intelligence to stay in work meaningfully.

Technology (transactional)

AI, virtual and augmented reality are all in the present; therefore, the learning focus on technology should no longer be focused on technological know-how but on problem-solving: how we put technology to work. Schools are already using technology to bring lessons to life, enhancing the learning experience. However, technology also has the potential to transform teaching, facilitating a move from passive to active learning. With more and more information available, young people need to be able to actively process knowledge, learning to act like researchers, making judgements about the validity and quality of data and aware of echo chambers and fake news. Technology will undoubtedly change the way we teach and much has been written and predicted about efficiency savings and freeing up the capacity of teachers. Preparing for a technological revolution in schools in this context misses the target; it is the impact it has on the way we learn that young people must take advantage of and teachers must embrace.

Technology (self-development)

The challenge facing young people is not to learn how to use the technology but to develop human skills and behaviours that differentiate them from AI, Chatbot GPT and the next technological innovations that will characterise the future world of work. In this way, technology is challenging young people to learn to think differently about their innate skills and apply them to the changing needs of work. They will also need to develop and access unfamiliar behaviours and thinking to enable them to have more autonomy over the way they work, making the right choices and developing self-motivation to take personal responsibility for active learning.

Well-being (transactional)

It may be controversial but in our general experience of working with young people (not just in schools), there is a real mistrust of well-being and mental health provision. Certainly, in less advantaged communities, vulnerable young people are underserved by limited access to specialists and tick-box strategies that signpost them to websites and literature. To really impact on mental health and well-being in schools, young people need to become active learners, identifying and calling out misconceptions and prejudices to be able to challenge stigmas and ignorance. A profound understanding of issues will also reinforce the confidence to make positive and independent personal choices.

Well-being (self-development)

Learning about the causes, misconceptions and issues around well-being means that young people are now well placed to play an active leadership role as relatable coaches, mentors and role models. Becoming involved in youth leadership projects like Ambassadors of Difference, delivered by the GreenWing Project, gives young people the opportunity to influence others and be part of a positive cognitive contagion. This dimension of learning invites young people to explore their leadership ambition, their values and ethics, and the contribution they want to make, impacting inclusion goals by positively reframing difference.

CRITICAL QUESTION

- As a secondary school teacher, how do you convince the school to integrate new learning dimensions into the current academic mainstream?

Further reading

Carson, S (2010) *Your Creative Brain: Seven Steps to Maximise Imagination, Productivity and Innovation in Your Life*. San Francisco, CA: Jossey-Bass.

Jamieson, M (2023) *Coaching Young People for Leadership*. St Albans: Critical Publishing.

World Economic Forum (2023) The Future of Jobs Report. Geneva: World Economic Forum.

References

Department for Education (DfE) (2023) Academic Year 2020/21: Longer Term Destinations. July 2023. [online] Available at: https://explore-education-statistics.service.gov.uk/find-statistics/longer-term-destinations (accessed 26 January 2024).

Institute of Student Employers (2022) *ISE Recruitment Survey 2022*. [online] Available at: https://ise.org.uk/page/ise-recruitment-survey-22 (accessed 26 January 2024).

Jamieson, M (2023) *Coaching Young People for Leadership*. St Albans: Critical Publishing.

Maslow, A H (1943) A Theory of Human Motivation. *Psychological Review*, 50(4): 370–96.

National Educatioin Union (2023) Educators Deserve Better: The Crisis in Teacher Pay and Supply. [online] Available at: https://neu.org.uk/sites/default/files/2023-06/NEU%20evidence%20to%20the%20STRB%20March%202023.pdf (accessed 26 January 2024).

UCAS (2023) *2023 Cycle Applicant Figures – 25 January Deadline*. February 2023. [online] Available at: www.ucas.com/data-and-analysis/undergraduate-statistics-and-reports/ucas-undergraduate-releases/ucas-undergraduate-applicant-releases-2023-cycle/2023-cycle-applicant-figures-25-january-deadline (accessed 26 January 2024).

Part 2
HOW TO COACH YOUNG PEOPLE IN SCHOOLS

Chapter 4

COACHING FOR THE NEW DIMENSIONS OF LEARNING

CHAPTER OVERVIEW

Having arrived at the new dimensions of learning, this chapter provides a practical guide for the coach as the facilitator of an alternative learning strategy. It systematically explains each dimension in the context of the classroom and introduces coaching models, ideas and strategies for delivery. In doing so, it stresses that new dimensions of learning are distinct because the knowledge they impart is part of a constantly evolving process to be shared with other young people through educators, role models, employers and leaders in the community and wider society. Each dimension embeds different ways of thinking and acting that are designed to be developed over a lifetime. To illustrate these points, it includes two case studies evidencing the transferability of coaching outcomes across dimensions and their adaptability to different tasks or situations.

How coaching can respond to the new dimensions of learning

Why and how is coaching the perfect fit for the new dimensions of learning? Having provided a logical explanation of their evolution, this section places the six dimensions of learning into a coaching context. The aim is to present coaching as the natural facilitator for the new unfamiliar outcomes it is anticipated young people will need to thrive in the future. Coaching is offered as a unique learning methodology with the capacity to perform a number of ambidextrous tasks, including:

- short-term academic targets in conjunction with long-term aspirations;
- tangible professional skills to thrive at work in conjunction with intangible emotional behaviours to survive in the 'political' working environment;
- cognitive skills to harness technology in conjunction with personal skills for differentiation.

In effect, coaching in schools is seen as the ability to simultaneously focus on the dual targets of enhancing academic achievement and enriching the student experience.

Using Table 4.1 as a reference, the new dimensions of learning are now discussed from the perspective of the coach (context and application). This is meant to be a fluid framework as there are clear overlaps between dimensions of learning and coaching. Therefore, it is envisaged that as the coaching process unfolds, the coach will be able to make judgements, depending on the specific context (desired outcome) of the coachees, to flex between different dimensions; for instance, coaching for creativity may be pivoted to focus on well-being (as a coping mechanism), society to leadership (as a focus for purpose) and so on.

Table 4.1 The new dimensions of learning and corresponding coaching foci

New dimensions of learning	Dimensions of coaching
Creativity	Curiosity and critical thinking
Society	Ambition, purpose and legacy
Leadership	Authentic to authoritative
Industry	Choices for purpose
Technology	Active learning and values proposition
Well-being	Awareness of self and others and active citizenship

Creativity

Many schools claim that they strive to teach creatively; but few teach creativity. At the same time, coaches who specialise in creativity adopt a similarly one-dimensional interpretation, generally focused on developing the coachee's artistic talent. We see coaching for creativity in schools, however, as generating a creative learning mindset for a new way of thinking. The heightened creative mindset will, in turn, provide a foundation for the other dimensions of learning, from which new ideas and possibilities will emerge. In *Coaching Young People for Leadership* (Jamieson, 2023, pp 48–51), creativity is discussed in the context of the qualification of youth to succeed to leadership roles. It is asserted there that young people are naturally creative because they are not afraid to take a chance and get something wrong; therefore, they are open to new ideas and experimentation. The late eminent educationalist Sir Ken Robinson (2006) argued that schools are designed to kill the natural state of creativity by hard-wiring pupils to strive to tick the right boxes or be marked down in the rigid assessment and evaluation systems that characterise educational targets. In effect, schools are preparing young people to become integrated into the blame culture that currently permeates the workplace and adult life in general.

How to coach creativity in the classroom

More generally, in the context of coaching, creativity serves two primary outcomes. Firstly, it is proven to improve mental health by increasing positive emotions and decreasing anxiety, stress and depression. Accordingly, it has become a general-purpose go-to tool for coaches to break unhealthy patterns. Secondly, it is utilised as a way of shifting the coachee away from entrenched mindsets and facilitating experimentation with new perspectives for game-changing strategies.

As a learning dimension, coaching creativity in schools is specifically about equipping young people to change the way they think about education by becoming active learners – making their own choices about learning. By nurturing curiosity, intuition and positive cynicism, young people can achieve a deeper level of knowledge by focusing on questions that count – what is not known – rather than answers – what is already known. To access creativity, we often use a version of the CREATES brainsets model (Carson, 2010) as a coaching/teaching guide. Designed by Harvard psychologist Shelley Carson, it identifies seven brain activation points for creativity:

1. connect;
2. reason;
3. envision;
4. absorb;
5. transform;
6. evaluate;
7. stream.

In our version (Figure 4.1), we substitute brainsets for mindsets (considered less scientifically proscriptive) and see them as seven cells, sequentially moving from one to the other to reach the ultimate creative mindset *streams.*

Figure 4.1 The seven destinations for coaching creativity

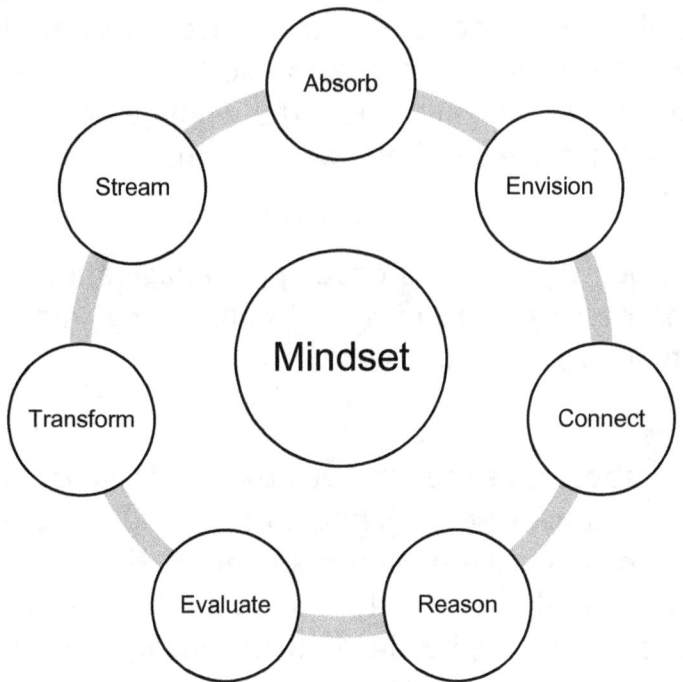

1. Absorb

This is the initial stage of coaching for a creative mindset. Using the Youth Leadership Coaching model (see Critical discussion point: Youth Leadership Coaching model on page 95), the absorb level forms part of the authentication phase of the process. It invites the young person to take a leap of faith into the unknown, using disruptive instincts to intelligently challenge conventional wisdom and apply new perspectives to experiences and information.

At this level, the coach is introducing the learner to the idea of independent and autonomous thought – thinking on their own terms.

2. Envision

Having laid the foundations for a creative mindset, this next cell gives the coachee licence to use their imagination to envision how things might be – the *what if?* scenario. This begins to move the coachee away from passive proscriptive learning.

At this level, the coach is developing imagination by positively harnessing disruptive and challenging instincts for curiosity to explore what is not known.

3. Connect

This cell rationalises the previous two by providing a structure for creativity, connecting uncensored experimental thinking to real outcomes and solutions. Here, the coach is encouraging the learner to make seemingly incongruent connections for a higher level of knowledge and multiple solutions, which simultaneously inspires greater interest in the project or task.

At this level, the coach is moving the young person from an operational to a strategic mindset, supporting them to think laterally about seemingly unconnected ideas to make surprising discoveries.

4. Reason

Reason and connection cells are closely related and effectively amount to the same outcomes. Where they differ is in the personality of the coachee. We think of reason as creativity for people who are not naturally equipped to explore and experiment with surprising ideas and notions. For them, creativity and creative outcomes are generated from trial and error.

At this level, the coach is making a safe place for experimentation by accepting the personality of the young person and enabling them to be creative on their own terms.

5. Evaluate

In practice, evaluation acts as the *project manager* for creativity. It is the practical stage of leadership when applied to a specific task or challenge. It requires the young person to assimilate knowledge and information and make decisions about direction, priorities and outputs. In academic terms, the young person is critically reviewing what they have found out and making judgements about how to best respond to the task: what is relevant and what is not; what is original and what is repetition. It is also a mechanism to ground extravagant creativity by maintaining steady focus on agreed targets.

At this level, the coach is working with the young person to develop the capacity for critical thinking. This process will enable the coachee to make judgements, prioritise and respond with effective decisions.

6. Transform

This cell is a coping mechanism for doubt and imposter syndrome. Regardless of age, we are all prone to experiencing moments of anxiety and self-devaluation at some stage during a creative project. The transform level supports the young person to normalise doubt and push through to a more positive state of mind.

At this level, the coach is developing the young person's ability to self-analyse, evaluating the worth of the contribution or impact they are capable of making. Often, this is focused on reinforcing their purpose.

7. Stream

In the Leadership Coaching Hierarchy (LCH) (Chapter 1, p 18) and *Coaching Young People for Leadership* (Jamieson, 2023, pp 106–10), we describe the pinnacle of youth leadership as being a state of unconscious competence. This is where the young leader's thinking, behaviours and actions come naturally and reflect the unique personality of the individual; in other words, their leadership has now become a way of life. Similarly, the stream cell represents the ultimate practical manifestation of creativity. It is when the young person's creativity is in full flow, to such an extent that their creative actions are almost subconsciously harmonious with the task so that they become lost in their work.

At this level, the coach is encouraging the young person to recognise their achievements and become aware of their ambition as an evolving goal (see Table 4.2).

Table 4.2 At-a-glance coaching toolbox for creativity (with reference to Figure 4.1)

Creativity levels	Coaching tools
Absorb	For curiosity
Envision	For imagination
Connect	For strategy
Reason	For a safe space
Evaluate	For critical thinking
Transform	For self-worth
Stream	For ambition

Society

As a learning dimension, society provides a practical opportunity to gain experiential and macro knowledge, introducing young people to the world outside the classroom. Here, the needs of all three stakeholders are met. So far, we have primarily focused on preparing young people for the workplace from the perspective of employers. Experience gained from working in a voluntary capacity provides a valuable introduction to the future workplace in terms of professional conduct, attitudes and behaviours, which differ from those in school, avoiding the cliff edge of moving from education to employment. It also equips the young person with the soft skills and emotional resilience needed to navigate the new challenges in the world of work.

At the same time, society, as a dimension of learning, invites young people to think about their personal values and the wider contribution they want to make. Generation Z, already in the workplace, has set the tone with expectations for a work–life balance that supports their physical and emotional well-being, as well as a focus on opportunities as opposed to jobs, seeking out employers with strong values and a sense of meaning or purpose. Learning in this dimension continues the evolution of workplace culture and is in the mutual interests of both employer and young person stakeholders. Finally, the goals schools have set themselves to become a social hub and make a wider contribution to the community are fulfilled. More importantly, the desired outcome to create brilliant human beings and send them out in the world to make a difference becomes an action as opposed to website rhetoric by focusing on the young person's ambition and the impact they can have – their legacy.

How to coach society in the classroom

The initial focus for the coach is to work with the young person in a leadership capacity to help them identify their authentic voice and their sense of purpose. To do this, we employ some relatable exercises around ambition, challenging the coachee to really think about what it is they care about and what they want to achieve. Initially, we ask them to explore their feelings around ambition, from which a number of nebulous concepts emerge: *I want to make a contribution; I want to have an impact; I want to change the world; I want to be rich and famous.* These notions help the young person to understand what motivates and drives their ambition. The coach is then charged with bringing meaning to these intangible concepts by connecting them to realistic outcomes and placing them in a context relevant to the coachee: *How will you make a contribution? In what area? What do you want to change and why?* Finally, the coach moves on to more specifically targeted questions as part of a possible career pathway: *Who currently does this and how can you get involved?*

Figure 4.2 A framework for ambition

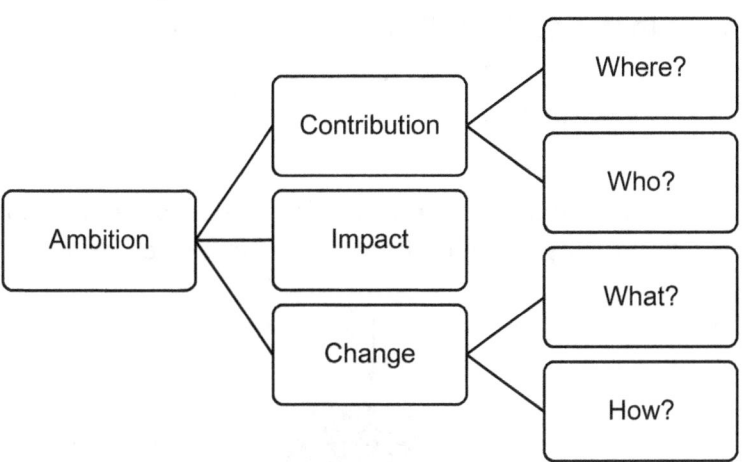

Figure 4.2 shows that by focusing on ambition challenges young people to take responsibility and make personal choices about their future. In the context of society as a learning dimension, the coachee is directed towards purpose and legacy: the long-term impact of what they do. Having crystallised their ambition, coachees become accustomed to the idea of positive entitlement to worthwhile and meaningful work.

Leadership

Leadership, as a destination for coaching young people, is discussed in Chapter 2 of this book and written about in detail in the first volume of this series: *Coaching Young People for Leadership*. Here, we use leadership in a transactional and developmental learning context. Transactionally, we are setting out to redefine leadership, create hundreds of new young leaders in schools and see young people leading young people as a catalyst for change. As part of a development strategy, leadership is used as a positive focal point and a gateway for inclusion due to its transitional, transformational and transferable qualities. More specifically, our work in this area proves that harnessing the components of a leadership mindset, as illustrated in Figure 4.3, equips the young person with the practical and emotional skills needed to thrive in the future.

Figure 4.3 The concept of coaching for a leadership mindset as a pathway to high achievement for future goals

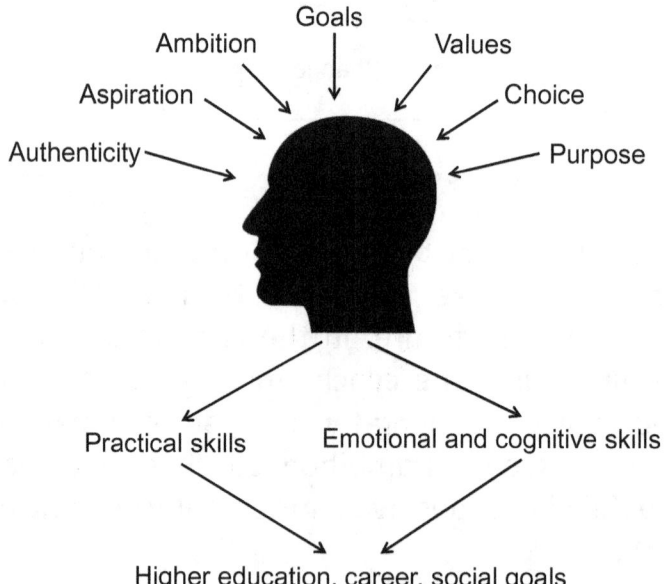

As a dimension of learning, the coachee is being supported to identify their authentic leadership voice, moving it along a learning continuum to develop their authoritative voice. Exploring the individual's leadership DNA gives them access to originality, creativity and purpose (the source of drivers and motivations), reinforcing their confidence to speak up and influence others. In the classroom, leadership learning acts like the conductor of the orchestra, pivotal to high performance, setting the intellectual tone and practical execution to achieve a given goal.

How to coach leadership in the classroom

As with all new learning dimensions there is a tendency not to think beyond literal interpretations. Therefore, *leadership* is either confined to a historical factual context or embedded in the conventional knowledge that we (and others) argue is no longer relevant. Schools are doing a good job of introducing pupils to hero leaders such as Rosa Parks and Martin Luther King Jr, and young people are responding positively to these curriculum role models. However, in our experience, they are limited to using their learning to recite facts and describe events. They are currently not required to think about leadership in terms of motivation, action and impact or, most vitally, their own potential to lead in the future. As a learning dimension, *leadership* stands out as the least relevant or relatable as it assumes a future leadership role that to many seems unlikely or unimaginable. Coaching makes leadership relatable to young people because it has the ability to connect it to the everyday events and mundane responses that are taken for granted. It does this in three ways. Firstly, it works within a broad-brush definition where leadership is accepted as meaning different things to different people. Secondly, it is actively inclusive by widening the criteria for leadership in terms of qualities, values and expectations. Finally, it personalises leadership by exploring the individual's aspirations and identifying realistic ambitions.

For the coach, focusing on recognisable leaders, historical or current, as an introduction to learning is a good place to start. Assuming leadership currently feels irrelevant to the coachee, the coach is able to begin the learning process in familiar classroom territory by talking about leadership and leaders. But here, the coach is actually eliciting the opinion of the coachee rather than testing the acquired knowledge of the pupil by moving to focus on motivation, action and impact.

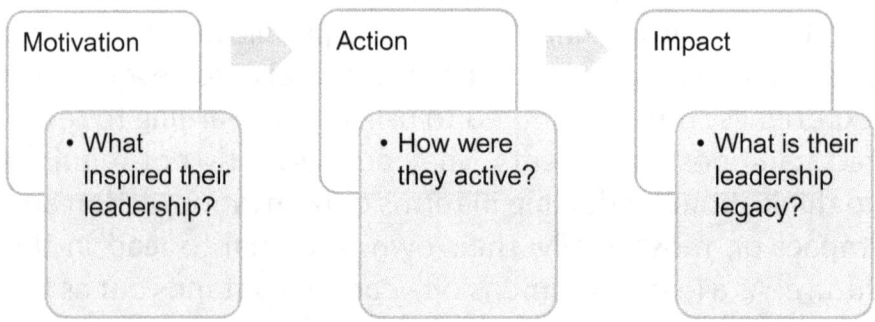

Figure 4.4 Introducing leadership as part of a hybrid (coaching and teaching) learning model

Using a simple three-stage model (Figure 4.4), coachees are encouraged to think about leadership as a logical sequence of emotions, responses and reactions. Stage 1, *motivation*, focuses on the drivers of leadership – why leaders do what they do – as opposed to the more conventional aspects of leadership learning – what they did and how they did it. Stage 2 focuses the coachee on leadership as an *action* – as a leader, you take action, and that action has an impact. This stage opens up discussions on two levels with the group. Firstly, the emphasis on reframing leadership as an action exposes the assumed passive relationship with privilege, entitlement and a *type* as unsustainable. Secondly, the introduction of a leadership counter-culture brings to life the unique energy (skills, instincts and values) of leaders and how this is harnessed to design actions appropriate to goals and personality: suffragette or suffragist? The final stage of the learning model, *impact*, expands the coachee's nascent leadership mindset to include the long-term effects of leadership. The coach is providing meaning to leadership by connecting motives and subsequent actions to resultant achievements. In this way, leadership comes alive as an emotional, physical and intellectual mechanism for change.

> **CRITICAL DISCUSSION POINT**
>
> **The youth leadership coaching model**
>
> The Youth Leadership Coaching model is a simple three-stage coaching system: authentication (*Why I am a leader and what type of leader will I be?*), development (*What are my unique leadership needs?*) and ambition (*What are my leadership goals?*). It was designed as a sequential set of steps to help the coachee map out and move along their individual leadership pathway. Each step is designed to perform a specific leadership development task. The first two focus on preparing the young person to think and behave like a leader, while the third step reinforces the sense of responsibility and privilege that accompanies leadership by centring on the leader's goals (see also *Coaching Young People for Leadership*, Jamieson, 2023).
>
> Using this model in the context of studying historical examples of leaders and their legacies enables young people to look at leadership in a completely different way, as a virtual reality from where they can view leadership as relevant and relatable.

CASE STUDY

Our time: legacy leaders for Bradford

Group: State school in Bradford, Key Stage 3 (11–14 years). Cohort of six leadership Year 9 candidates, each leading a group of six younger Year 7 learners.

Leadership role: Cultural Heritage Ambassadors

Partnerships: This was a collaborative project between the sponsor Historic England, GreenWing Leadership Coaching and a secondary school in Bradford.

Introduction: As a local legacy project, this programme was intended to coincide with Bradford's bid for City of Culture 2025 and to be used as a vehicle for application of youth leadership skills. As a case study, it demonstrates the interaction between new learning dimensions and coaching, the transferable skills of leadership and the learning benefits from integrating coaching into an educational context.

Proposal: The leaders, sometimes referred to as being 'intelligent disruptors' by school staff, were selected for leadership coaching based on a proven leadership track record or instinctive, currently unrecognised, leadership potential. Each leader was tasked with leading a team of six younger students. The three-day programme took the teams out of their usual school timetable to learn about local legacies of significant individuals. They were then challenged to plan, prepare and lead their own Bid for Culture, as part of a wider celebration of local legacies of impactful leadership within Bradford from a local, regional and national perspective. This culminated in a final celebration event to showcase Bradford's legacies to peers, school staff and other stakeholders.

Project description: The activity schedule followed the leadership coach's (in this case, GreenWing) framework for sustainability (Figure 4.5).

Figure 4.5 Schedule of activity

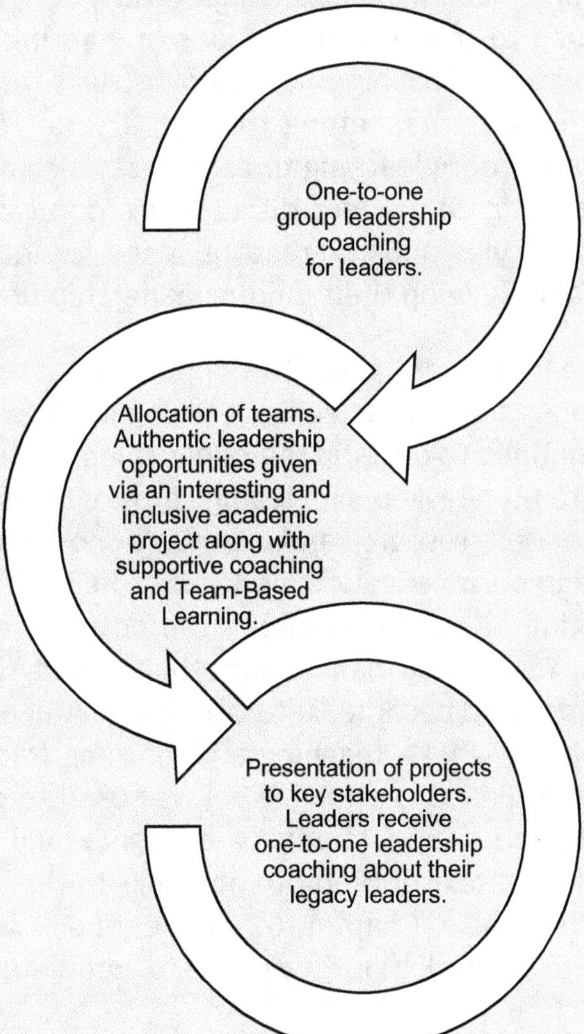

One-to-one group leadership coaching for leaders.

Allocation of teams. Authentic leadership opportunities given via an interesting and inclusive academic project along with supportive coaching and Team-Based Learning.

Presentation of projects to key stakeholders. Leaders receive one-to-one leadership coaching about their legacy leaders.

→

Day 1: The leadership cohort completed an intense programme of coaching, including one-to-one and group work, where they were introduced to a new vision of leadership (exploring the unique instincts and behaviours they had been selected for) and to the concept of coaching. In the context of learning, the nascent leadership mindset stimulated the group's engagement based on personal responsibility, choice and decision making, aligned to the new dimensions of learning. At this early stage, the coaching methodology was integrated into the educational setting through a series of more familiar classroom learning tools (quizzes, prompts and Q&A) to instigate a wider discussion around different leadership styles and to create a space for leaders to explore and develop their unique leadership brand.

Day 2: Leaders were given the opportunity to practise their conceptual and reflective learning in a live context and to continue to develop their unique leadership style. They were then tasked with leading groups of Year 7 historians to elect, research and organise a showcase event celebrating positive leadership legacies in Bradford and their lasting influence. In effect, the positive response from the Year 7 historians meant that leaders led their younger peers to become Cultural Heritage Ambassadors in their own right. A teaching and learning framework called Team-Based Learning (TBL) was used to develop all the learners' understanding of legacy and leadership in the context of Bradford and links to the national picture (see also Chapter 6). Some pupils were so engaged in the task that they chose to complete further independent research at home on their team's significant individual, one even taking photographs of place markers to use in their showcase piece.

Day 3: In the final workshop, all teams successfully delivered their showcase presentations on their chosen legacy leaders to their peers, teachers and representatives from Historic England. In conclusion, leaders attended a group debrief session, where the coach worked with them to interactively add meaning to their learning by connecting their leadership actions to the quality and positive experience of achieved outcomes.

Impact: Individual feedback from the Year 9 leaders was extremely positive. Headline themes included improved confidence, self-esteem, creative thinking, self-respect and self-belief (specifically in terms of individuality). More specifically, Table 4.3 is a snapshot of responses from a small sample of young leaders involved in the project in the context of learning dimensions and coaching outcomes.

The teaching staff who observed reported a marked difference between the attitude of the six leaders in a coaching setting and that of a classroom environment. They thought the individual leaders appeared more mature, engaged and focused during the programme. Furthermore, the careful management of Year 7 groups evidenced a positive attitude to authority (by being placed in a leadership role) and a real grasp of the kindness and respect needed to be a leader.

→

Table 4.3 Snapshot of leaders' feedback in the context of learning dimensions and coaching outcomes

Learning dimension	Impact as told by the leaders	Coaching outcomes
Creativity	'I got completely lost in the project. Suddenly, it was time to stop and I had so many ideas still running around in my head.'	Attaining level 7 of the leadership mindset: *stream*
Society	'Doing the project made me feel really proud of where I live – Bradford is an attitude!'	Connecting ambition, purpose and legacy as drivers for high achievement
Leadership	'I learnt so much about myself leading the group. It felt like what I had done made a difference.'	Leadership as an action
Industry	'I had to think about who was going to do what. I asked who was interested in doing certain things and then I gave them the work to do. It felt like they could choose what they wanted to do and then they all did brilliantly.'	Project management and empowerment through delegation
Technology	'Being a researcher means that you have to start by looking for questions – things that nobody knows. Then you go through all the information and make connections to get to the answers. It's a good way of learning because you are building knowledge for yourself and that makes it interesting.'	Active learning – focusing on what is not known
Well-being	'The best bit about being a leader is helping other people; that felt great. Especially when someone started quiet at the beginning and by the end was really enjoying contributing to the team.'	Awareness of others as an inclusion strategy

Leaders responded well to the coaching format: one-to-ones and group sessions. The concepts of coaching, leadership and leadership coaching were all enthusiastically embraced and the adaptability of the young people to switch from a more familiar classroom setting to an unfamiliar autonomous, creative environment was remarkable. The improvement in attitude, confidence, responsibility and focus on achievement was seen daily. By the end of the programme, all the young people were keen to continue working with a coach and become involved in further projects. Furthermore, many of the Year 7 learners wrote on their individual evaluation forms that they would like to be a leader in the future, highlighting just how inspirational peer leadership coaching can be.

The programme's success drew interest from the Department for Education and the Department for Digital, Culture, Media and Sport, and opened opportunities for the school to be recognised as a Champion Heritage School.

Discussion: The altered focus of having a choice reorientated the way the leaders approached the project, and they did so with responsibility. The headline insights from anecdotal evidence confirmed our impression that the leadership coaching experience was highly transferable to a very specific school project, by:

- unlocking discretionary energy of the leaders and their groups;
- producing project work of an exceptionally high standard;
- improving interest and engagement in an academic subject and a school activity;

→

- giving purpose to learning through the task having a 'real-life' local context.

From the debrief session, no two leadership experiences were the same and individuals reflected on different aspects of learning: time management, delegation, authoritative voice, project management and presentation. Thematically, behaviours and soft skills were deemed to be the most significant area of learning, specifically at the first two levels of the Leadership Coaching Hierarchy (self-awareness and awareness of others). However, positive feedback from all stakeholders and the production of high-quality outcomes evidenced the successful working relationship between coaching, leadership and the new dimensions of learning and was the overarching take-away from the project.

Throughout the three days, we observed how the leaders dealt with typical challenges associated with operational leadership: delegation, disruptive behaviour, clarity of purpose and meeting targets. More interestingly, leaders were introduced to the behavioural inhibitors of leadership: projecting authority among peers, imposter syndrome, separating leadership from friendship and managing difficult (authoritative) conversations. As part of the learning experience, leaders became aware that their unique leadership make-up produced blind spots and this helped them deal with behavioural challenges. For instance, leaders who styled themselves as friendly and approachable were also susceptible to people pleasing; those leaders who styled themselves as caring felt uncomfortable using their authoritative voice for fear of upsetting a colleague. At the end of the programme, all leaders had progressed and reported they had achieved personal milestones.

CRITICAL QUESTION

- At what stage should the coach or supervisor intervene on behalf of the leader when faced with disruptive behaviour from a team member during the project?

Industry

Industry, as a learning dimension, is an entry point for the coach to amalgamate transactional and developmental outcomes. As with all other learning dimensions, industry is not a one-dimensional subject, preparing young people to simply enter the workplace. Yes, it focuses on developing professional skills, but it sees those as tools rather than behaviours or ways of thinking. Referencing the Leadership Coaching Hierarchy (see Figure 1.4 on page 18), tools are only available to the coach once the authentic and authoritative voices (levels 1 and 2) have been identified; otherwise, they are unsustainable. Therefore, when the coach thinks about industry as a learning dimension, they are setting out to develop the coachee's work ethic and their workplace personality, including the wider values, motivations and purpose of the individual.

How to coach industry in the classroom

Transactionally, learning is straightforwardly focused on professional behaviours: conduct, attitude and presentation. Developmentally, the coach is working at a more complex level, helping the coachee to locate their work ethic – what drives them to perform. The drivers that define the young person's work ethic overlap with other learning dimensions, tapping into ambition, aspiration, values and ethics. Here, the coach is inviting the coachee to make a series of personal choices in these areas, to arrive at a meaningful sense of purpose to drive performance and embed a work ethic. This is a critical moment in the process as the coaching methodology explicitly emphasises learning as a choice in direct conflict with the conventional learning familiar to the coachee. Therefore, the coach must be prepared to work hard to create the credibility and safe space for the young person to begin to thrive in an alternative learning environment. It should also be noted that any accompanying teacher needs to be fully invested in the process and help manage the tensions between conventional and unconventional learning. In the two case studies in this chapter, the concept of learning as a choice is positively manifested in the discretionary energy unlocked in the performance of young leaders focused on an academic task. More generally, in the wider context of young people leading young people, it is highly relevant to how leaders impart learning to their individual groups and how a learning environment characterised by choice becomes a positive shared thought pattern among the group to enhance academic achievement.

The coach should remain cognisant of the challenge for the coachee to adapt from learning through teaching to learning through coaching. One way of supporting the coachee is to see the process as a transition from one to the other, facilitated by choice. Accordingly, the short-term learning around this dimension might focus on behaviours in the classroom initially to create future habits in the workplace. Therefore, disciplines such as time management, project management, planning and acquisition of quality knowledge are presented as an everyday choice: *Why do we choose to miss deadlines? Why do we choose not to prepare well?* This dramatically reorients the focus on discipline and performance and provides a basis for long-term sustainable solutions by building strategies that address core blockers.

A strong work ethic is underpinned by a real understanding of work as a multi-dimensional concept that does not only produce goods or services but has a wider purpose and impact. Working with the coachee in this way instils a sense of (positive) entitlement for them to expect to enjoy working, feel fulfilled and make a difference. In the longer term, this is a strong foundation for high performance in the workplace. In practical terms, the coach is also aiming to equip the coachee with the ability to navigate the politics of work. Again, there are numerous tips and hints about how to survive work; however, the coach might be best placed focusing on developing the coachee's authoritative voice to be able to effectively manage up and down the workplace hierarchy.

Technology

For teachers, it is predicted that technology will streamline procedures and free up time to refocus on teaching strategies. For pupils, it is about access to more information and independent learning. However, the technological revolution has implications for schools far beyond a radical change in educational processes. As a new dimension, it is not about learning how to use technology but learning to anticipate and adapt to its impact. This means harnessing soft skills to add value to a future workplace increasingly reliant on AI and moving from a passive to an active learner mindset.

How to coach technology in the classroom

The coach has two primary learning outcomes for the dimension of technology: developing the young person's capacity for independent thinking and instilling an understanding of the value they bring through a unique set of soft skills and behaviours. Firstly, taken to its logical conclusion, technology will transform schools by creating more space for learning while simultaneously generating a surfeit of easily accessible information. Essentially, this means the learner must develop independent thinking to prioritise information and exploit myriad sources to uncover new knowledge, transitioning from a learner to a researcher. Coaching research skills such as critical thinking, analysis and collecting data from surprising sources provides practical learning that is readily transferable to the workplace. Self-motivation, outside the direct instruction of a teacher or authority figure, reframes the school dynamic and the coach can serve the coachee by helping them acclimatise to unfamiliar autonomy. Again, the coach is reframing learning as a choice and encouraging the coachee to become an active learner.

Encouraging pupils to challenge perceived wisdom takes time and we must assume that coaching interventions in the classroom currently do not have the full attention of schools; therefore, time is a limited resource. Accordingly, the coach is looking for expedient strategies to implant the idea of independent thinking. To do this, we use several knowledge exercises, where the learner is required to build their own understanding of knowledge by following a logical learning pathway to make meaning. Table 4.4 is a template that enables the learner to respond to a topic or question by considering knowledge in three ways: what we know, what that means and what we need. The evidence column is deliberately open to individual interpretation and asks the young person to think hard about the current context in terms of the impact of what is known. It should be expected that this level of knowledge is limited to specific areas of personal interest and it is important the facilitator/coach does not overthink the content but holds fast to the principal outcomes of the exercise: developing a new process for independent thought and investigating what is currently not known.

Table 4.4 Template for independent thinking and knowledge building

Evidence	Forecasting	Outcomes
Trends	Scenario 1	?
Influencers	Scenario 2	?
Variables	Scenario 3	?
Contingencies	Scenario 4	?

Secondly, it is not technological competence but how the young person differentiates themselves from the technology in the future that counts. Accordingly, somewhat counter-intuitively, technology requires the coach to work hard on the coachee's soft skills, emotional intelligence and authentic self. An understanding of these will help the young person realise their worth and the contribution they can make as a human being in both the workplace and society. Table 4.5. is a value proposition template we use to guide the young person's self-reflection and then connect innate values to external contexts: specifically, a future workplace increasingly characterised by technological advancement.

Table 4.5 Template for unique value proposition

My values	My unique value proposition
What are my strengths?	
What are my values?	
How am I performing?	
Where do I belong?	
What is expected from me?	
What do I expect from myself?	
My Value	

The values table is effectively used as a set of prompts and it is expected that the coachee is guided by these to give some structure to personal reflection outside the classroom as part of the developing habit of self-awareness. It is important to be able to connect individual values to a value proposition (a relatable understanding of what they have to offer) as a means to articulate worth. This requires another level of thinking to construct meaningful relationships between seemingly unconnected skills and outcomes, supported by a deep-level understanding of self. The final *My Value* row represents the unique personality of the individual from a combination of all responses.

Well-being in schools

A strong commitment to young people's well-being is an unequivocal statement of intent from schools; however, it is clear that, in the eyes of most young people, the self-help culture for well-being and mental health care in schools is not effective.

Personal plans for emotional and physical success are generally limited to compilations of web-based information, while access to one-to-one interventions is extremely restricted and often off-the-shelf or highly impersonal. Most schools do not have the space, time or capacity to look beyond the statutory requirements in place to define their delivery of health and RSE (relationships and sex education) learning. Coaching is focused on teachers, already beyond capacity, to act as well-intentioned but underqualified expert counsellors. First and foremost, it is not our intention to criticise schools but merely to point out that they are under-resourced and, despite being passionately committed to young people's well-being, much of what is made available misses the mark. Chapter 10 of this book discusses in detail the potential psychological impact of coaching on schools and the limitation of well-being strategies. As a dimension of learning, the coach's focus is on changing the way young people think about well-being, challenging prejudice and removing stigmas to create a positive cognitive contagion as part of a wider strategy for inclusion.

How to coach well-being in the classroom

Well-being is the least understood and most underserved of the learning dimensions. In coaching for well-being, the coach must do two things. Firstly, they must accept that they are probably not qualified experts in the field and therefore their approach must recognise their limitations. Secondly, they must look to contribute beyond the constant background noise around young people's mental and emotional health that currently pervades schools. These two provisos mean that the coach is directed towards a different approach to well-being that focuses on awareness and leadership rather than the individual's needs, which are subsequently served as part of a well-being action cycle. On this basis, our model (Figure 4.6) is based on the premise that young people should play a more active leadership role in well-being and mental health care in schools, and in doing so will physically and emotionally benefit from their actions.

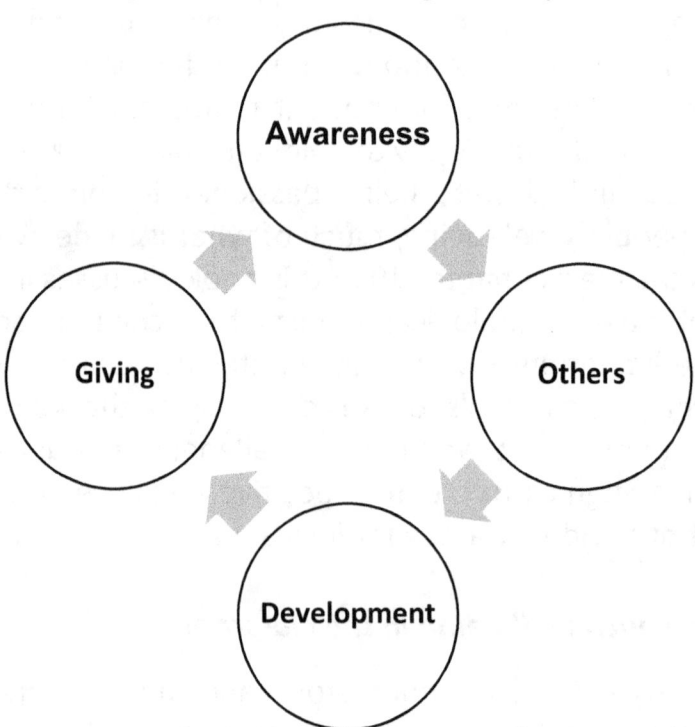

Figure 4.6 The well-being action cycle

The initial focus of the coach is on leadership development, specifically levels 1 and 2 of the Leadership Coaching Hierarchy model (self-awareness and awareness of others), to develop the coachee's authentic (true to values) and authoritative (true to purpose) voices for an acute awareness of well-being and its potential impact on themselves and others. Here, the coach is developing the young person's curiosity to acquire knowledge, both practical and emotional, to have the confidence to make intelligent interventions. In this way, the coachee develops a deep-level understanding of well-being which equips them to not only empathise with others but act effectively to support them and reframe difference positively. The development cell represents well-being as a learning activity, both intellectually and physically, to effectively take action to support and give to others. Reinforcing the coachee's leadership purpose gives them the courage to speak out, speak up for others and include them. In turn, this has a positive impact on their own sense of well-being and self-worth.

> **CASE STUDY**
>
> **Ambassadors of difference**
>
> **Group:** State school, Year 7 and Year 8 students.
>
> **Leadership role:** Role models
>
> **Partnerships:** This was a collaborative project between specialist teachers and GreenWing Leadership Coaching, and a secondary school.
>
> **Introduction:** As a social communication intervention, it was intended that this programme would complement work being carried out by specialist teachers in communication and interaction, as well as being used to channel youth leadership skills in a different way. As a case study, it combined well-being, leadership and society learning dimensions as a strategy for inclusion to achieve the long-term goals of the school.
>
> →

Proposal: The ten leaders were chosen by the specialist teachers because they already belonged to an existing leadership group. Each of the students had a social communication difference, whether this was a diagnosis of autism, ADHD, sensory differences or some social anxiety. Three members of the group were also looked after children (LAC). The group, made up of students from Year 7 and Year 8, had established a circle of resilience and friendship. They sat together in the school canteen and protected one another from an environment which would overwhelm them in isolation. Interestingly, this group was innately respectful about the school environment and authority and were considered role models for good behaviour. But there was a lack of self-awareness and awareness of each other (their authentic voice), which prevented them from being able to empathise and effectively support others, and to have the self-worth and confidence to make interventions and lead others. This was seen as a legitimate entry point for leadership coaching, as part of the wider purpose of the project to purposefully probe general assumptions made about social communication differences to do with group work and empathy.

Project description: This programme took place over a period of six weeks, where the students were released from one of their lessons to participate in the sessions. Students received a group leadership coaching session, where they looked at identifying their own strengths, differences and values. They then looked at their own leadership styles and shared these with each other. It was important that even though these were personal reflective tasks, sharing them with the group created a sense of safety, belonging and self-respect. The process of sharing also ensured that the students' individual needs did not overwhelm the focus on leadership and respect for others' differences. Team-Based Learning and a unit on 'Respect' were then used as a vehicle for application of group leadership skills as well as validating well-being as a learning activity.

Impact: In the penultimate session, the groups were tasked with creating and justifying a meme for 'respect', which could be displayed for others to see in school. Here, the impact of the coaching was clearly observed, as the prospect of expressing their authentic and authoritative voice, as well as their leadership actions, no longer scared the students. All the students wanted the sessions to continue, and some took copies of their team's memes home so that they could create a more professional version for display as they entered the *stream* stage of the creativity mindset. In the final session, GreenWing, as the coaching provider, delivered a one-to-one online debrief coaching session with each of the leaders to complete the well-being action loop. This session focused on how the leader would go on to use the knowledge and experience they had acquired to make their own unique positive difference to others.

Discussion: This project demonstrated the transferability of tangible leadership outcomes and intangible leadership thinking, as an effective alternative

→

approach to inclusion and the wider well-being strategy in schools. The coaching team faced a number of new practical and environmental challenges specifically in delivering the programme weekly with a group of diverse leaders, for example: the room was not consistent, access to resources was not always dependable and there was some absence due to unforeseen circumstances. In addition, the leadership cohort itself was unique and the coaching model had to be cognisant to the differences of the group while not allowing individual needs to overtake the overarching foci on well-being and inclusion. Despite some challenges, the motivation to contribute to the group became stronger throughout the process and the altered focus of *choosing to be involved* meant that the individuals became personally invested in the promotion of inclusion. Finally, various longer-term leadership outcomes were discussed with the group, thematically celebrating difference, including active citizenship, knowledge forums and mentoring schemes.

CRITICAL QUESTIONS

- How can the transferable outcomes of leadership coaching practically create a culture of inclusion and acceptance of difference in your school?
- How can coaching add personalised learning in the mainstream classroom in your school so that learners do not miss out?

References

Carson, S (2010) *Your Creative Brain: Seven Steps to Maximise Imagination, Productivity and Innovation in Your Life*. San Francisco, CA: Jossey-Bass.

Jamieson, M (2023) *Coaching Young People for Leadership*. St Albans: Critical Publishing.

Robinson, K (2006) Do Schools Kill Creativity? [online] Available at: www.ted.com/talks/sir_ken_robinson_do_schools_kill_creativity?language=en (accessed 26 January 2024).

Chapter 5

WHO GETS COACHED AND DISTINCT LEARNING PATHWAYS

> **CHAPTER OVERVIEW**
>
> This chapter sets out the criteria for who gets coached and investigates the distinct reactions of the two different types of leadership candidate: developmental and reorientation. From the process of integrating different types into the leadership cohort, a new profile of candidate emerges: the activist. Finally, it describes how leadership, coaching and the new dimensions of learning interact so that the whole becomes greater than the sum of its parts.

Who gets coached: misconceptions, assumptions and misdirections

The concept of leadership coaching in schools is greatly misunderstood and, where adopted, misdirected. In Chapter 1 we discussed the incidental relationship between coaching, as a development strategy for teachers, and the unspecified positive knock-on effects to pupils, as a symptom of an obdurate education system using conventional thinking to elicit radical change. Having gone on to make the argument that leadership coaching should be directed towards pupils, a second casual assumption needs to be dispelled around who gets coached. It is generally assumed that leadership candidates are drawn from an existing student hierarchy of high achievers. However, we see this as a convenient truth that underserves both leadership and young people. The reimagined vision of leadership and the new dimensions of learning have now widened the scope of coaching, placing those deemed to have raw potential (usually excluded) alongside those with recognised credentials (usually included).

The discussion around who gets coached is often complex as it encompasses conceptual as well as tangible key outcomes aligned to the school's overarching strategy. To cut the Gordian knot, we generally work to two guiding principles: timing and personality.

Timing: looking for pivotal moments and the right frame of mind

It should be expected that schools will have their own agendas, prioritising different key outcomes for target groups; however, coaching is most impactful when applied at pivotal moments and where there is space for creativity and vision.

Pivotal moments are identified as transitional rites of passage: physical, emotional or cognitive shifts in the young person's life leading to adulthood. They are seen as seedbeds for the development of long-term behavioural habits and patterns of thinking, and an obvious entry point for the coach. However, designated pivotal moments can also inhibit the coach's work when they coincide with defining exams. Here, the principle of best interest is in play – investments in time and energy from the coachee are designed in the best interests of a primary goal or a mission-critical task – reducing the creative space of the young person by drawing attention predominately to impending exams. Under these circumstances, coaching becomes a transactional engagement, focused on achieving short-term outcomes at the expense of the longer-term visionary aspects of leadership.

Therefore, in one pilot programme where we were working with the school's senior student leadership team (Year 13) and those designated as their potential successors (Year 12), we found that the Year 13 coaching programme struggled to gain momentum and meaning. The leaders from this group clearly found it difficult to imagine the long-term outcomes they wanted to achieve, mainly because they were preoccupied with the immediate imperative of exams. Accordingly, our focus was limited to supporting coachees to carry out their leadership responsibilities at a time of intense academic focus. In contrast, the Year 12 cohort, free of exams and energetically anticipating leadership in 12 months' time, were experiencing a creative hotspot and were highly receptive to new ideas. This meant we were able to offer a balanced programme, moving through all three stages of the Youth Leadership Coaching model (authentication, development and ambition) focusing on short-term targets (in this case, application for senior leadership roles in Year 13) and long-term ambitions.

COACHING TIP

When considering timing and pivotal moments for coaching interventions, the school and the coach should be aware of the principle of best interest. In other words, it is not sufficient to make judgements solely on a transitionary phase for a young person; the coachee also needs to be in the right frame of mind.

Personality

At the initial scoping stage of a coaching programme, the common misconception, embedded in conventional school wisdom, is that candidates are self-selecting by being high achievers, earmarked for future leadership responsibilities or already in situ.

When we explain our expectations of the personality of candidates, schools are simultaneously sceptical and enthusiastic. Sceptical because they are being asked to consider candidates who are currently not only outside of the academic mainstream but appear to deliberately contradict it. Enthusiastic because these same candidates are seen as problematic and any alternative practical solution to prevent them from being cut adrift is welcomed. The logic of including non-conformist personalities is spelt out by two tenets of the coaching offering: the focus on leadership and the two distinct approaches, development and reorientation.

Why schools should focus on leadership

Leadership is one of the most overused words in a school's lexicon. Like other key words or phrases, such as mental health, well-being and emotional intelligence, leadership, either through casual usage or semantic satiation, has lost meaning and practical purpose. Therefore, despite the great weight of literature and theory around leadership, very little is known about the potential impact of its essential transferable and transitional constituents when applied to young people in the classroom – until now. Having put theory into practice, our assertion is that the qualities and behaviours of leadership, facilitated by coaching, will not only support young people to make good learning choices but positively harness innate instincts and personality traits to make great life choices. The capacity to employ an exclusive focus (leadership) to deliver a wider strategy for inclusion (those with unrecognised counter-intuitive behaviours that would normally disqualify them) is explained below using the leadership ecosystem (Figure 5.1).

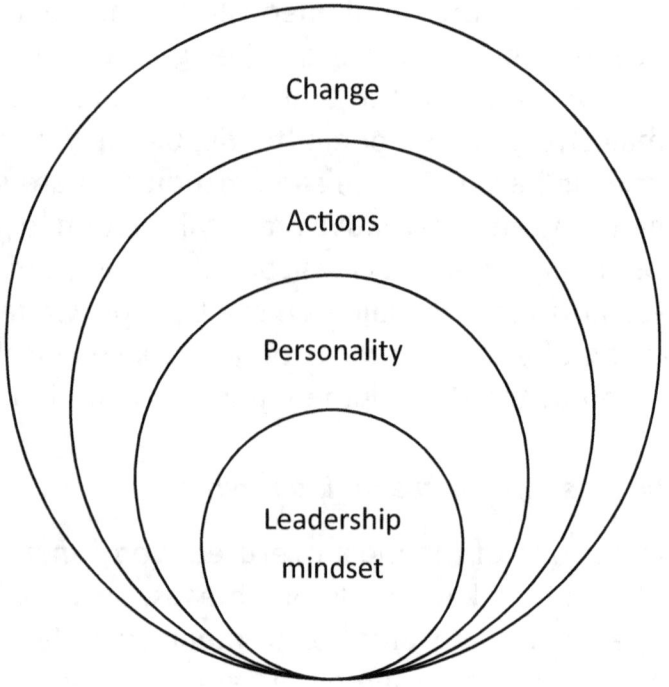

Figure 5.1 The leadership ecosystem encompassing contrasting personalities

In the ecosystem, the leadership mindset, comprising the character, values, drivers, instincts, motives and ethics of the individual, acts as the catalyst for the unique personality of the leader. The interaction between mindset and personality allows the leader to make sense of non-cognitive characteristics such as self-motivation, curiosity, imagination, disruption, engagement and intuition. The leadership mindset acts as a filter for the personality and does not judge or discriminate between so-called positive and negative personality traits. These personality traits are harnessed by the coach to inform distinct attitudes to cognitive and behavioural functions, like learning and relationship building. As the coach develops the young leader's personality, they are effectively handing over control to the leader of the choices they make for the actions they take. In turn, these actions go on to effect change at personal, peer, community and society levels.

When working with schools, it is important for the coach to explain this process: leadership as a system of complex and unique fields that interact to bring about increasingly ambitious goals. In the context of the classroom, developing non-cognitive behaviours creates new skills for learning, assisting young people to flex between short-term targets, such as an academic task (motivation and persistence), and long-term goals for wider ambitions (aspiration and purpose). In terms of inclusion, this model provides a structure for integration, arguing the case for perceived negative personalities by framing leadership as an energy to be harnessed and reoriented to inform choices about future directions of travel. More generally, leadership is presented as an enabler of individuality in an environment designed for conformity and a catalyst for independent thought and creativity.

The challenge is to bring theory to life. Essentially, the coach is asking the school to break the shackles of conformity and create a safe space for pupils to do the same. The persuasiveness of the coach at the selection (of candidates) process is a key determinant of the level of effectiveness of the overall programme. Accordingly, coaches should be prepared to work hard to forge meaningful relations with schools – connected by partnerships rather than contractual obligations. A partnership mentality invites the coach to become part of the school, aligning values, outcomes and personalities to ensure shared purpose. It also means that the design of the programme is a collaborative effort, removing suspicion of coaching as a challenger to conventional learning structures.

> **COACHING TIP**
>
> The first practical step along the way is to support the main sponsor (partner teacher) to make judgements on selection that are both subjective and instinctive, including personalities that may well elicit raised eyebrows from colleagues. The absence of a written criteria to follow and the reliance on unfamiliar autonomy mean that most sponsors are initially tentative over selection. The coach should be aware of sponsor inhibitions and work to support and guide them through the selection process, tapping into instincts, gut-feel and even a hunch to inform choices. It is usual for the sponsor to seek feedback after the initial one-to-one introductory sessions from the coach about the quality of their selections. Positive feedback elicits a satisfied *I knew it* or *I told you so* response, albeit tinged with some relief.

CRITICAL QUESTIONS

- How would you justify your selection of a reorientation candidate to a colleague?
- What is the tone of your justification?
- As a coach, would you be prepared to work with a school where a partnership mentality could not be achieved?

Distinct approaches for different outcomes

Despite myriad personalities and the idiosyncratic nature of leadership, coaching young people is predominately focused on two distinct, but not mutually exclusive, categories: developmental and reorientation. Figure 5.2 illustrates the characteristics of the two types of leadership candidate in secondary schools and the space occupied by coaching.

Figure 5.2 Who gets coached? The two types of leadership candidate and the space occupied by coaching

Developmental
- Recognised leadership potential or already in a leadership role
- Self-acclaimed leadership credentials
- Exemplary track record in the academic mainstream

Reorientation
- Unrecognised leadership potential
- Self-assumed lack of leadership credentials
- Currently outside the academic mainstream and marked down as an underachiever

The space occupied by coaching

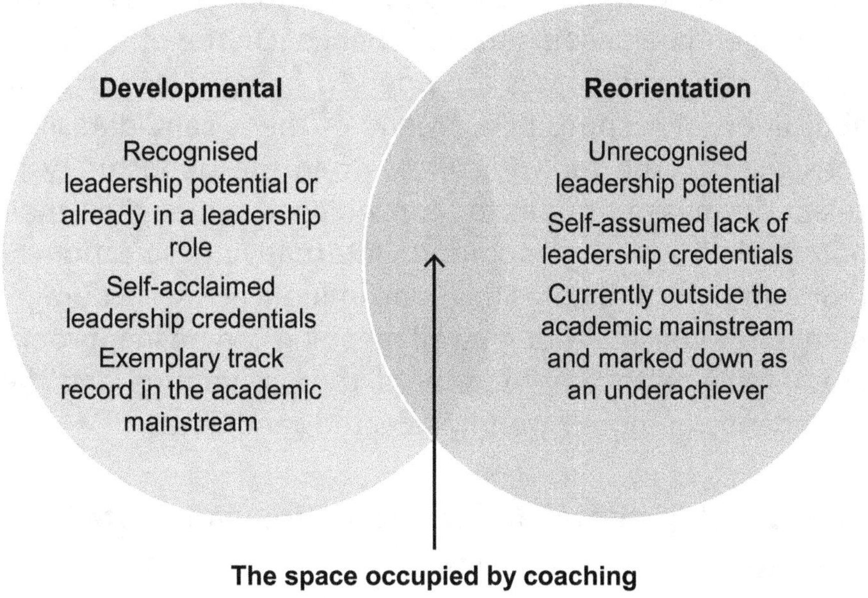

In short, developmental candidates see themselves and are seen by others as having explicit leadership credentials. These candidates are usually self-selecting. On the other hand, reorientation candidates are generally from outside the academic mainstream and perceived negatively or as problematic. These candidates are selected for their potential at the sole discretion of the sponsor.

Both types have selection blind spots of which the coach and the sponsor should be aware. Due to the positive go-to relationship they have with the school, developmental candidates are often selected as a matter of course. This lack of imagination discourages those from outside the inner circle from applying for leadership roles under the impression that selection is a fait accompli. Furthermore, the continuous selection of developmental candidates potentially stultifies the leadership mindset and perpetuates conventional thinking and behaviours to stall change. On the other hand, reorientation candidates are open to being selected as an abdication of responsibility. Many of these candidates are consigned to the *too difficult box* and the opportunity to select disengaged pupils for convenience rather than their potential is a real temptation. Alternatively, selection of reorientation candidates might be influenced by encouragement bias, which although well meaning can be inappropriate, damaging to the integrity of the programme and the attendance of more carefully selected candidates.

How developmental and reorientation candidates react to leadership coaching

At the introduction and authentication stage

At the initial coaching one-to-one (the beginning of the authentication stage of the Youth Leadership Coaching model), the developmental candidate exudes confidence –

they understand why they have been selected and are looking forward to the experience. Many developmental candidates provide well-rehearsed responses using the tone, content and body language that has so far served them well during their school careers. As we explain more about the programme, one of our key challenges is to unsettle the candidate from delivering a masterclass in how to respond to perceived authority, creating a safe space for them to explore unfamiliar non-conformist ideas without fear of blotting their copybook. Reorientation candidates are similarly hardwired to take up a default position when responding. They initially assume that their inclusion in the programme is remedial – they are here for behavioural and attitudinal correction. In contrast to their developmental colleagues, their body language is negative and reluctant, and their responses to initial questions are often monosyllabic and generally uninformative.

The contrasting reactions of developmental and reorientation candidates set the tone for the coach as they begin to integrate the coachees into the leadership group. One of the early challenges for integration is for the coach not to make impulsive judgements based on first impressions. Despite the coach's skill in constructing open questions, the reorientation candidate is habitually defensive, putting up barriers. In contrast, the developmental coachee is more familiar with positive interventions and settles quickly into the rhythm of the session. The coach should beware of casually comparing the two: either overvaluing the contribution of the developmental candidate or underestimating the apparent reticence of the reorientation candidate.

> **COACHING TIP**
>
> As part of the later evaluation process, it is helpful to record first impressions to assess the impact of the coaching against the individual progress of the leader. An awareness of behavioural and mindset movement from the very beginning of the programme will enable the coach to factor in subjective judgements into a more formal objective assessment framework.

Integrating developmental and reorientation candidates into the leadership group

From the perspective of the developmental candidate, becoming part of a mixed group disrupts their sense of a steady state where they are rewarded with positive opportunities for conforming to conventional rules and standards of behaviour. Ironically, this embedded instinct to comply with the standardised version of good behaviour that characterises schools places the developmental candidate outside the new leadership mainstream. This version of compliance, it can be argued, means that the young leader is complicit in the ways of outdated leadership thinking and out of touch with new expectations, goals and attitudes. Therefore, as coaches, we will derive more valuable insights by studying the developmental candidate's blind spots rather than their obvious attributes. These blind spots include the perception of a leadership template into which they strive to fit, a compulsion to conform, box-ticking and complacency (see Table 5.1).

Table 5.1 Why developmental candidates find themselves outside the new leadership mainstream

Developmental candidate's blind spots	Characteristics of blind spots
The idea of a leadership template	A catalyst for complying with outdated leadership thinking
Conformity	Inhibition to express leadership creativity
Box-ticking	Passive leadership that is risk averse in pursuit of a *clean* leadership CV
Complacency	A go-to relationship with leadership that perpetuates the steady state and stalls change

We found that placing developmental candidates alongside reorientation peers negated many aspects of these blind spots in a single stroke. Specifically, the developmental candidate was challenged to not only accept but become actively involved in the new ways of leadership. For them, the trade-off for already having a strong sense of why they had been selected for the programme was to recognise, include and, most importantly, treat with respect the disruptive and unconventional attitudes of their new colleagues.

In contrast, with the integration of reorientation candidates, the coach is looking to work with the unconventional and surprising qualities of the candidate – despite themselves. We observed that reorientation candidates disregarded much of the early work done in the introductory one-to-one coaching session and quickly defaulted to negative classroom behaviours when introduced to the group. Here, the blind spots of the young leader are more basic and refer to bad habits picked up as a result of being disengaged with school (see Table 5.2).

Table 5.2 Why reorientation candidates struggle at first to transition into the leadership group

Reorientation candidate's blind spots	Characteristics of blind spots
Credibility	Transition from an unsponsored to a sponsored profile
Application	Breaking the habits of a self-fulfilling prophecy of underachievement
Attention span	Focusing on unimagined targets

The coaching challenge to build and maintain credibility (for the project, coaching as a development methodology and qualification of the candidate) is exacerbated by the limitations of the coach as a visiting external consultant. The lack of continuity means that the reorientation candidate is likely to experience confusion, especially in the change of tone and approach when leaving the leadership group and returning to the classroom. The candidate is suddenly thrust back into an environment that continues to perceive them negatively, undoing their progress with the coach towards self-affirmation. From here, the coachee struggles to manage the tension between negative and positive mixed messages and resist the dominant fall-back position to act up when returning to the group. The coach should also be aware that, unlike developmental members of the group, reorientation candidates have probably never imagined their future in terms of leadership. Therefore, attention spans revert to the same level as in the classroom, not because of a lack of interest in the subject but because leadership and success are nebulous concepts that previously have not applied in that environment. In short, the coach should anticipate the transitional challenges for the reorientation candidate (what they *now* expect from themselves and what others outside the group *still* expect from them), especially during the early stages of the programme, and be prepared to accommodate them.

To greater and lesser degrees, the problems with integration and, more specifically, transition for both types of candidates are threefold: consistency, scepticism and shared progressive thinking. Firstly, access to the coach is necessarily inconsistent and momentum, particularly with reorientation candidates, is constantly being interrupted. Furthermore, in three-quarters of the schools in which we work, the leadership group is disrupted by internal contingencies, deemed to take priority. This means that candidates can be moved to an environment that is less conducive to coaching, be pulled out of the group to attend a school event or have limited input from the sponsor (partner teacher) due to strained capacity and resources.

It could be argued this is the everyday way schools have to operate, living from hand to mouth with scant resources and unsustainable workloads for teachers. On the other hand, this is also symptomatic of a half-hearted investment in time, money and intellect from the school. This absence of unwavering commitment from schools fosters scepticism among teaching colleagues who, through poor communication and a lack of ownership, fail to buy in to the programme and return candidates to their predetermined positions in school society once they leave the coaching bubble. Finally, coaching and the new dimensions of learning are currently victims of the principle of best interest. The intense pressure of the curriculum and the assessment regime that accompanies it leave schools with little space to explore progressive ideas around learning and development.

> **COACHING TIP**
>
> To aid a smooth transition into the leadership group for both types of candidates, the coach should adopt familiar (to the classroom) interactive content, such as quizzes and case studies. As the group sessions progress, candidates become accustomed to the pace and tone of the work and the coach can move seamlessly to prompts and questions to elicit energetic and challenging debate.

> **CRITICAL QUESTION**
>
> - Without long-term access to the coach, how do you avoid the mixed messages from outside the coaching bubble and keep up positive momentum, especially for reorientation candidates?

The emergence of the activist candidate

Without wishing to complicate our two-dimensional taxonomy, a third, hybrid candidate emerged from the group: the activist. Essentially, we still classify the activist as a developmental candidate; however, despite their place in the mainstream, they share some of the disruptive instincts of reorientation candidates. Being characterised as highly articulate and intelligent, the activist has a naturally authoritative voice (they are listened to), which gives them leverage to challenge conventional wisdom and authority without the negative connotations that accompany reorientation candidates. As part of the leadership coaching methodology, they will remain as developmental candidates, but as we examine the different development and learning pathways of fully integrated groups, they assume their own distinct identity.

Different development and learning pathways

Having arrived at new dimensions for learning and introduced leadership and coaching as their facilitators, let us look at how they interact and whether the whole is greater than the sum of its parts. Reactions to learning dimensions are typical; therefore, to avoid listing repetitive themes, we have taken an in-depth look at one particular example dimension. Focusing on creativity, we set out to observe the different reactions of candidate types when applied to a specific task.

Table 5.3 Different reactions to a learning dimension (creativity) when applied to a specific task

Creativity levels	Developmental reactions	Reorientation reactions	Activist reactions
Absorb	Reluctant to tap into non-conformist instincts.	Suspicious about legitimising non-conformist instincts.	Engage with self-expression and disruptive non-conformist instincts.
Envision	Deliberate move from passive to active learning by adapting conventional learning energy.	Natural move to reframe challenger instincts to seek out interesting questions.	Energetic move to challenge and seek out provocations.
Connect	Comfortable and confident with creative mindset, using questions to arrive at a deeper level of knowledge.	Less confident in seeking out insightful questions outside the academic structure and in the context of a task.	Highly confident in using independent thinking and making surprising connections.

Reason	Welcomed as a safety net for unfamiliar creative licence.	Testing is seen as a refocus on standard outcomes and achievement.	Accepted as a checks and balance system for unbridled creative thinking.
Evaluate	Engages with critical thinking for high achievement against given outcomes.	Tension between outcome management and people management.	Enthusiastic critical thinker placing pressure on judgements.
Transform	Confident about progress as a leader and to achieve a given task.	Accepting of progress as a leadership personality but needs reassurance.	Clearly connected to purpose and confident about achieving goals.
Stream	Leadership responsibility increases engagement in project and enhances academic results.	Leadership responsibility greatly increases interest in project and changes approach to learning to improve academic results.	Leadership responsibility confirms purpose and passion for project and enhances academic results.

Using the CREATES framework, Table 5.3 records the leadership development pathway of the candidate through the three stages of the Youth Leadership Coaching model (authentication, development and ambition) in the context of an academic project. The graph (Figure 5.3) plots the progress of candidates along their coaching-type pathways.

Figure 5.3 Distinct development and learning pathways of different candidate types

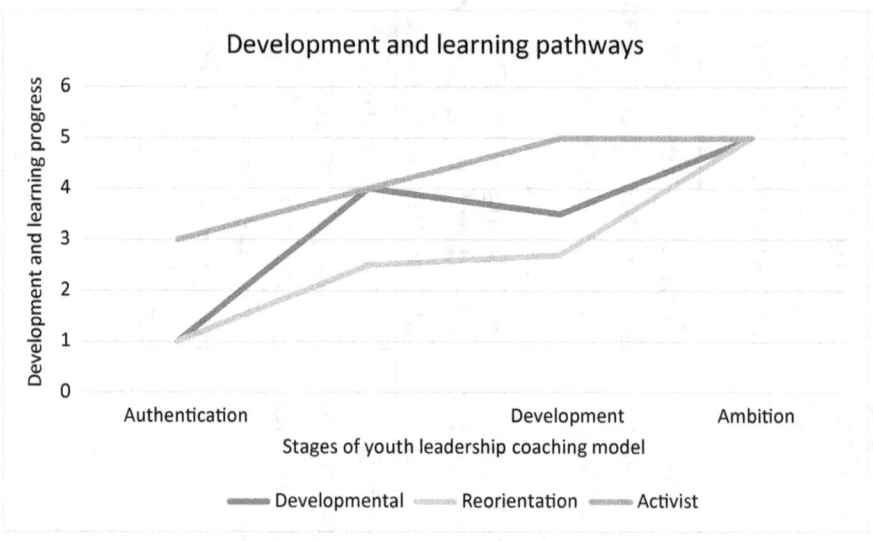

The key for Figure 5.3 (Table 5.4) shows the component parts of authentication, development and ambition stages in terms of the Leadership Coaching Hierarchy model and a selected learning dimension (creativity), to add clarity to the graphic.

Table 5.4 Key for Figure 5.3

Youth Leadership Coaching model	Leadership Coaching Hierarchy	Creativity levels
Authentication	Self-awareness	Absorb
	Awareness of others	Envision
Development	Tools	Connect
		Reason
		Evaluation
		Transformation
Ambition	Unconscious competence	Stream

For different reasons, developmental and reorientation candidates start at a fairly low point at the authentication stage. We found that developmental candidates struggled to break with character and access their authentic voice, specifically their underlying challenger instincts. Reorientation candidates, moreover, were inhibited by negative stereotypes serving as self-fulfilling prophecies for underachievement.

Developmental candidates were most confident at the development stage, where tools and reasoning provided a structure for them to follow and a natural space in which to thrive. Figure 5.3 records an irregular blip in progress, reflecting the gradual transition from structured to abstract ideas, before resuming a steady rise. In contrast, reorientation candidates flatlined at this stage, seeing a more structured phase of learning as a return to the classroom and reverting back to negative behaviours. A relatively steep incline towards ambition is then apparent, reflecting a positive transition towards more abstract concepts.

Both developmental and reorientation types arrived at their ambition destination at the same time. In terms of learning, the ambition stage is an amalgamation of the tangible and intangible outcomes of leadership coaching. Here, development and learning have responded to the leadership ecosystem (Figure 5.1), with the nascent leadership mindset shaping the coachee's personality to make choices about non-cognitive behaviours (motivations, discretionary energy and purpose) and operational actions (project management, delegation, people and time management). The ambition stage acts as a leveller between the two types of coachee. For developmental candidates, there is a sense of destiny fulfilled, while reorientation candidates feel a sense of achievement in spite of the negative generalisations that often unfairly hinder them. Not unsurprisingly, given their characteristics, developmental candidates generally express ambition in terms of a realisable outcome, while reorientation candidates are inclined towards more abstract goals.

With regard to the combined impact of leadership (as a focus), coaching (as a facilitator) and the new dimensions of learning (as a destination), a snapshot of headline findings is encouraging. In 90 per cent of cases, schools reported that learners (including developmental types) exceeded usual levels of academic achievement, while positive personal development in 85 per cent of learners, including confidence, visibility and engagement, was also recognised. During the learning process, we noticed increasing levels of concentration and application to a task, resulting in 100 per cent of learners achieving a level of unconscious competence (stream) as they went about their work.

Is the activist candidate a model leader or an anomaly?

Activists are effectively restless developmental types. Energy of purpose distinguishes the activist, which, combined with high academic achievement, accelerated them along their developmental and learning pathway (Figure 5.3). The activist generally has a strong understanding of self, ambition and their potential to make a difference, and they are already at an advanced level at the authentication stage. Their innate confidence and sense of self-worth gives them the capacity for independent thinking and clarity of purpose to challenge conventional practice; in other words, the activist comes across as the acceptable face of non-conformity.

The activist is unlikely to experience peaks and troughs as they progress along their leadership pathway. At the development stage they are able to apply academic discipline to clarity of purpose, not only to access tools and ideas but to adapt them and put them to best use. Finally, the combination of self-worth and purpose drives their ambition, instilled at the beginning and crystallised at the development stage (explaining the flatline in Figure 5.3 as reaching clarity of purpose rather than dwindling motivation).

We do not consider activists as anomalous, as they are generally rooted in developmental types, although they are in a minority. At face value, they encapsulate the perfectly integrated group; however, having a foot in both developmental and reorientation camps has its challenges.

COACHING TIP

We generally talk about ambiguity negatively, but in the context of coaching tools it can be put to good use. Ambiguity resulting from different personalities in a group can be harnessed to lighten the weight of ideology, inviting nuance and multiple interpretations to move theory into practice.

CASE STUDY

The challenges for the activist

The activist faces an ambidextrous challenge to balance developmental and reorientation characteristics. As part of a scheduled check-in with a leadership cohort who had completed an intense coaching programme six months earlier, we carried out 20-minute individual sessions to evaluate the impact of the programme and provide continuous support for the young leaders.

Cas was the original activist candidate: authentic, authoritative and ambitious. So, when we reconvened, we did not expect to hear that she had recently been playing truant and skipping important classes as GCSEs loomed. It occurred to us, albeit fleetingly, that perhaps we had misjudged Cas and got carried away by the aura of leadership that she emanated. Having dismissed this notion, we began to look for more scientific reasons to explain Cas's lapse. In doing so, we reminded ourselves that Cas was still only 15 and the expectations we had placed on her were high and possibly unrealistic. We were also cognisant that the coaching she had responded to so positively was perhaps a distant memory, clouded by the prospect of defining exams. What we came to realise as we continued to talk to Cas was that the activist candidate does not come without practical challenges. Unlike singularly defined developmental and reorientation candidates, the activist is a hybrid and is challenged to balance discipline and disruption (Figure 5.4).

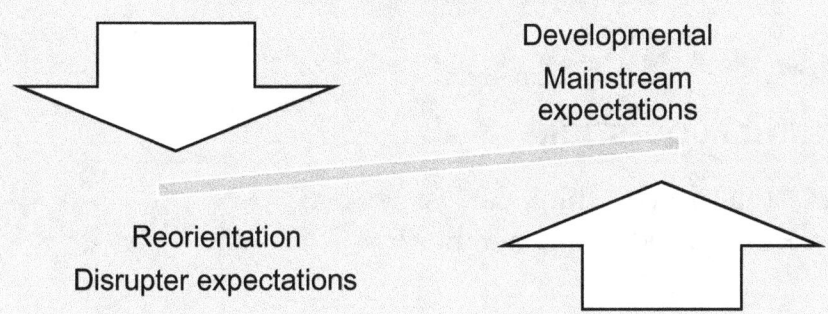

Figure 5.4 Balancing the expectations

It is highly likely that when the scales are weighted towards a dominant type, behaviours will reflect the imbalance. In this case, Cas's reorientation profile was dominant, which meant that she was out of kilter and adopting a negative attitude.

We booked a follow-up session with Cas to help her balance the scales. We began that session by exploring ambidextrous tools to help her, but in the course of our work Cas opened up about her reasons for truanting – she was missing lessons because of the bullying behaviour of others and the lack of support and action from those in authority. Cas's balancing act was of a more existential

→

nature: managing the tension between the responsibility of being an activist leader and the day-to-day commotion of being a 15 year old. However much we expound the extraordinary leadership potential of young people, we should always remember they remain young people and face the normal challenges of young people. Cas, who has spent much of her school career speaking up for others, had experienced a debilitating sense of humiliation and injustice, and her response was to walk away from confrontation and remove herself from the situation.

CRITICAL QUESTIONS

- What do you think Cas' issues are?
- How would you coach her?

Chapter 6
TEAM-BASED COACHING

CHAPTER OVERVIEW

Having discussed how leadership coaching complements academic and personal development, this chapter explains how an embedded coaching culture can usher in other high-impact learning interventions. It specifically details how Team-Based Learning (TBL), established as a way to accelerate engagement, achievement and attainment of learners, can work in concert with coaching to get the best out of individuals and groups of learners. It introduces the Leadership Coaching Team-Based Learning (LCTBL) model as a refined version of TBL and a new dimension to coaching, showcasing a three-phase cyclical model:

- team-based coaching;
- team-based leadership development;
- team-based learning and leadership application.

Finally, it provides a case study, across three different secondary schools, to illustrate how this model can improve social communication flow, mutual accountability and faster assimilation as well as learning.

Optimal learning

Before discussing how coaching can boost high-impact learning, it would be helpful to define what we mean by optimal learning and why it is important. According to educationalists, 'best' learning is thought to be reached when we process information for ourselves (via active, collaborative and experiential learning) rather than being passively spoon-fed knowledge. It manifests as a learning state of unconscious competence or *stream*, when we become completely lost in the learning process, and is facilitated by intrinsic motivation (natural curiosity), a love of learning, enthusiasm and commitment. This high-level engagement in learning assists our memorisation of information and our ability to develop schemas (a bit like internal filing systems), which help us acquire and access knowledge more quickly. Optimal learning therefore covers the construction of knowledge, the development of transferable skills and, importantly, a passion for life-long learning (see Figure 6.1).

Figure 6.1 The characteristics of optimal learning

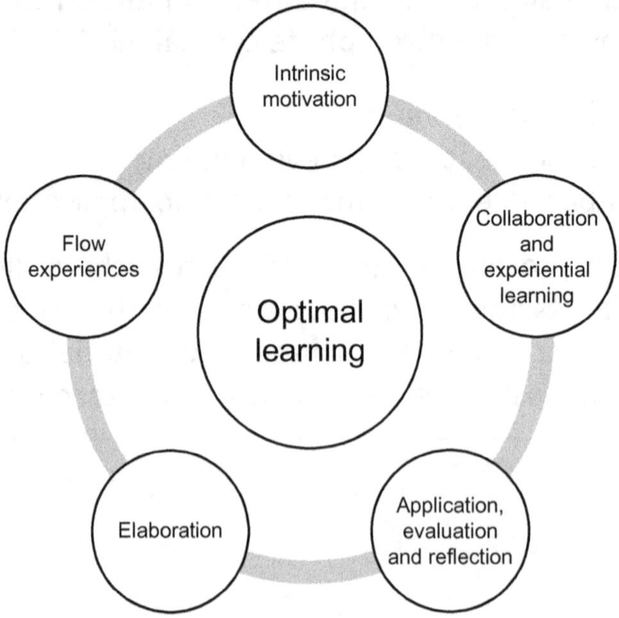

In Chapters 3 and 4, we proposed six new dimensions of learning and their corresponding coaching foci. These dimensions are fundamental for learners' personal development and ability to engage with optimal learning. In this section, we explain how coaching can open the door for the successful implementation of other high-impact pedagogies, connecting new dimensions to optimal learning approaches while simultaneously accommodating the 'knowledge-rich curriculum' that schools now must follow.

A knowledge-rich curriculum versus optimal learning

The thinking behind a knowledge-rich curriculum goes back to the early 1980s with American literary analyst and professor E D Hirsch (1983) and an emphasis on cultural literacy. Hirsch discovered that if learners do not have 'common knowledge', they are deprived of the necessary basis for factual knowledge to enable them to become expert learners. Despite being a logic for a different time, Hirsch's theory continues to be espoused by educational administrators – in 2021, the Secretary of State for Education denounced advice from experts in the field that encouraged schools to teach *twenty-first century skills* including creativity, teamwork and problem-solving. Two years later, the political dial appears to have moved 180 degrees, heralding a new direction for schools. In 2023, the Times Education Committee published their report contradicting the knowledge-rich curriculum, implicitly endorsing the new dimensions of learning.

Without wishing to throw the baby out with the bathwater, we accept that Hirsch's logic still stands, to some degree, despite the passage of time and recent enlightened views. Therefore, we are not arguing against the value of mastering shared knowledge but for a balanced approach between new knowledge and skills. Although we agree that an updated curriculum for cultural literacy and knowledge is integral to education, we certainly do not agree that 'generic skills' are unnecessary. What value is this *powerful knowledge* if learners are not also taught the skills of when and how to apply that knowledge in the real world?

The argument for a knowledge-rich curriculum is reliant on, and enabled by, the redundant criteria by which we currently evaluate success in schools: good grades and good behaviour. Politicians are adept at being selective when arguing a point, using examples from carefully controlled school environments that sit at the top of league tables with exemplar teachers. We would argue that these examples are tendentious and, far from justifying a knowledge-rich curriculum, strengthen the case for optimal learning. We fundamentally agree that if knowledge is not at the core of any educational model, then it does not really fit in the educational paradigm. However, under the purview of leadership, we assert that knowledge can be updated and redirected to enable young people to make informed choices and navigate their unique life's pathway, to choose how they impact the world.

The impact of leadership coaching on optimal learning

If TBL is to be used as a dimension of coaching, it is important that we connect the two. Using four of our prompts from the Youth Leadership Coaching model – *Why am I here? What is my unique leadership style? What are my unique leadership development needs? What are my leadership goals?* – we applied these to learning to produce a sequential set of metacognitive (the way we think about thinking) steps to help a young person map out and move along their optimal learning pathway.

Figure 6.2 Leadership coaching prompts reimagined for learning

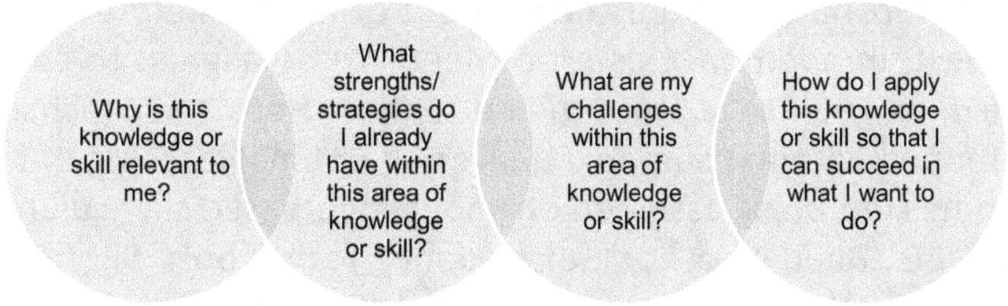

- Why is this knowledge or skill relevant to me?
- What strengths/strategies do I already have within this area of knowledge or skill?
- What are my challenges within this area of knowledge or skill?
- How do I apply this knowledge or skill so that I can succeed in what I want to do?

In Figure 6.2, each question is designed as a specific meta-cognitive step. The first focuses on getting the learner to engage with the task on a personal level. The second and third focus the learner on their self-awareness – strengths and blind spots – to inform strategies to achieve a learning task. The final question helps learners put their plan into action, applying their learning for immediately actionable and relevant outcomes. Connecting coaching to optimal learning methodologies brings the process alive and equips the learner to thrive. Coaching fulfils the basic and psychological needs of the learner to enable them to develop the self-esteem to put to good use the tenets of optimal learning: autonomy, motivation, purpose and, especially, mastery.

Trying to teach my dog French

A knowledge-based curriculum is not designed to meet basic and psychological needs and barely scratches the surface in the context of the potential impact of optimal learning. But coaching in schools is at a nascent stage, at best a curiosity, eliciting scepticism, at worst, a threat to the steady state to be treated with suspicion. This means that secondary schools need proof of impact before they invest. In addition, this proof needs to be aligned to curriculum goals to capture their attention. Here, the coach is trapped within a paradox: delivering optimal learning outcomes but being assessed on knowledge-based curriculum targets. Building a book of evidence for schools will take time. Furthermore, we accept that it is not sufficient to, in the meantime, simply take the view that schools should be prepared to take a leap of faith on the basis that the current system is failing. But articulating the fault lines in a knowledge-based curriculum contributes to the wider debate around change in education, where young people can experience creative and purposeful learning to acquire powerful knowledge to bring about positive social change and social equity. As succinctly stated by a colleague from a leading UK university when we were co-facilitating a conference at the beginning of 2023:

> *I taught my dog French. Every night I taught him French. I went through every word in the French dictionary. Covered the contents back to back. I was a brilliant teacher. But he still can't speak French ...*

At this time, coaches must find the energy to coax schools into welcoming a coaching culture. In our experience, there are two clear routes: a Trojan horse programme – an externally commissioned project that fits within the curriculum and is conditional on facilitation by a leadership coach – and a seemingly more structured and established pedagogy that appears less arcane to the school sponsor, such as TBL.

> **CRITICAL QUESTION**
>
> At the beginning of every school year, pupils are given a learning journey map, outlining content to be covered and its relevance to the national curriculum. As a learning enabler, this map is limited, acting as a timetable or a tick-box form to mark progress.
>
> - What would be the impact of a personalised learning journey, designed by the individual and supported by a coach, applying the four questions in Figure 6.2?

Introducing the Team-Based Learning model

Team-Based Learning (TBL) was originally developed by Larry Michaelsen (Michaelsen and Sweet, 2012). Its first use was in business schools with the aim of increasing learners' critical thinking. Since then, it has been widely implemented in the health profession over the last decade and is becoming a popular flipped form of teaching and learning within higher education across many subjects, where it has had huge success in increasing engagement, motivation and attainment of learners, and reducing gaps between different groups of students. Its impact in these areas has seen a push for its use in secondary school education where it is having similar success. The reported increase in knowledge acquisition, engagement and, interestingly, empathy has excited educationalists, who see its potential as a proactive and cost-effective way of reducing the ever-increasing attainment and employment gaps in the UK.

TBL is a framework of active collaborative learning, which has a specific sequence to encourage optimal learning

(Figure 6.3). It differs from other types of pedagogy in its focus on generating independently functioning teams, creating small groups within a bigger group (autonomy). Effectively, what this looks like in the classroom is five to six groups of students all working simultaneously (and competing against each other) on structured tasks. These peer support groups and the collaborative learning that takes place are facilitated (rather than didactically led) by a teacher (or coach). The sequence of tasks is so specific, and the tasks themselves intentionally chunked and scaffolded, that although the students perhaps do not realise it, they are also being explicitly taught social communication skills, turn taking and effective collaboration, as well as how to apply and evaluate concepts to micro and macro missions relevant to them.

Figure 6.3 The sequence of events as they take place in TBL

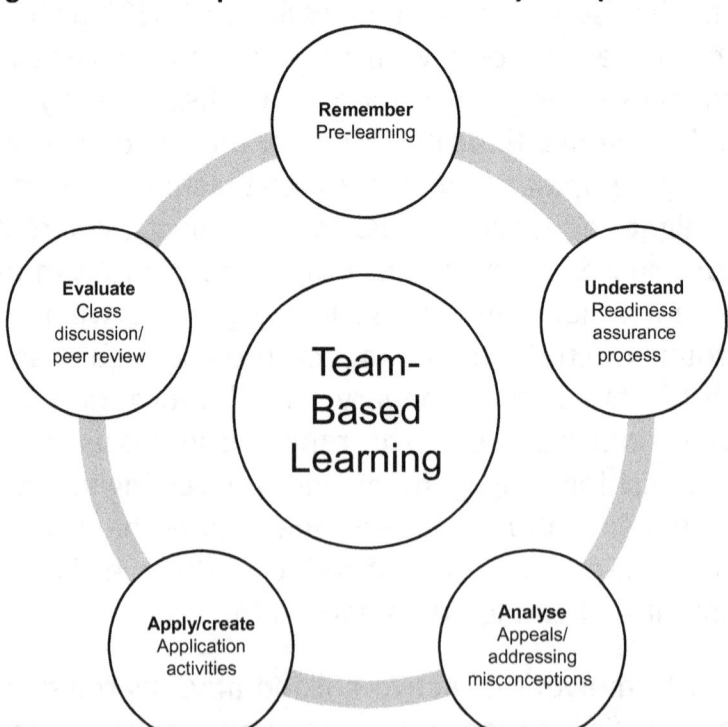

How Team-Based Learning works

- The incentive to engage with the pre-class content (autonomy) comes from a readiness assurance process, including individual and team quizzes (and sometimes very popular scratch cards) to foster immediate structured discussion, debate and peer learning that is also fun (motivation).
- Learners receive immediate feedback on team performance, allowing a focused class discussion and specific time to address misconceptions.
- Learners then apply their new knowledge to solve authentic, real-life problems and make team decisions during discussion and debate (mastery). The application tasks, based on real-life situations, help motivate and engage learners and develop their knowledge and understanding of the world around them (purpose).
- The final key component of the TBL sequence is peer evaluation, which is added to the learners' marks and therefore also adds to their accountability (crucial to its effectiveness).

The application tasks use a '4-S' model: a *significant* problem (which is relevant to the learners), the *same* problem (to encourage questions and debate), a *specific* choice (a limited choice of the best answers to urge critique and justification) and *simultaneous* reporting (to promote accountability and formulation). This model ensures that time in the classroom is spent on focused application tasks (which ensure that students work at a higher level of cognitive and metacognitive learning) rather than just knowledge transmission, promoting deep or optimal learning and knowledge acquisition as opposed to surface learning.

Introducing the Leadership Coaching Team-Based Learning (LCTBL) model

In TBL, we now have a recognisable (to schools) high-impact pedagogy to which we can connect leadership coaching and introduce a classroom culture that combines a knowledge-rich curriculum and optimal learning. Perhaps unimaginatively, we have called the resultant model Leadership Coaching Team-Based Learning (LCTBL). The dynamics of the LCTBL model are illustrated in Figure 6.4.

Figure 6.4 The dynamics of the LCTBL model

- Team-based coaching: identifying primary strengths and responsibilities
- Team-based leadership development: candidates develop strengths and behaviours as part of a leadership team
- Team-Based Learning and leadership application: candidates put leadership skills to work academically and/or socially

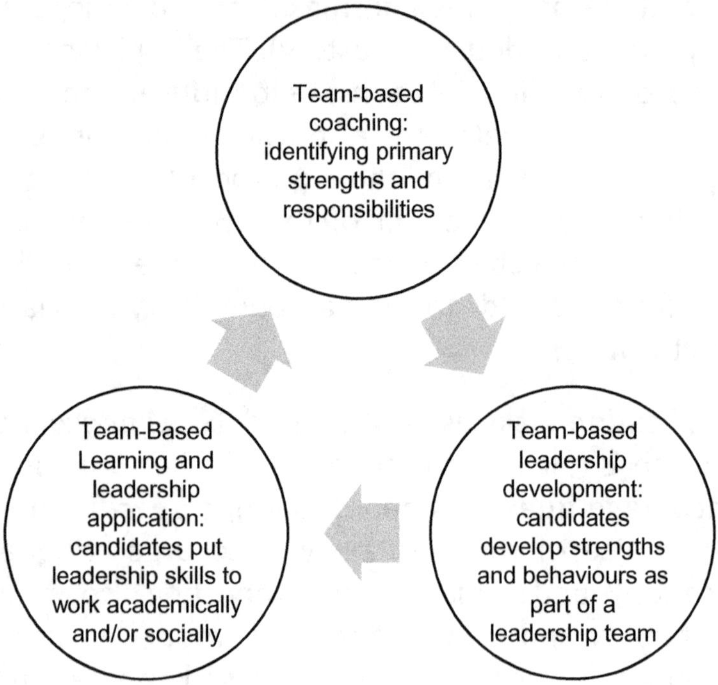

In effect, each team has a leader (not to be confused with a boss or micro-teacher, which would not work with the theory of TBL). Each leader receives one-to-one leadership coaching prior to a TBL session (this one-to-one dedicated support is ongoing throughout the project to continue to develop the young leader's behaviours, thinking and sense of responsibility). The individual leaders then participate in a group leadership workshop to practise the TBL sequence and contribute as part of a leadership co-operative, developing the confidence to model 'esteem' and 'self-actualisation' to their designated team when the time comes. The leaders are then allocated mixed-ability teams and a live leadership opportunity to practise leading with their authentic voice, recycling the leadership coaching they have received to instil this ethos in others – young people leading young people. From the perspective of the leadership coach, using TBL as a framework delivers an immediate impact on the coachee at individual, peer and societal levels, negating one of the main criticisms of coaching in schools, that it is a slow-burning intervention and difficult to evaluate.

In Figure 6.5, the leaders and their teams are set an academic task. Their coaching work provides them with an active learner's mindset, which allows them to challenge and question the task rather than report what is already known. Independent thinking enables the leaders to make decisions about the direction of the project, always with the outcome in focus. The space created by the new mindset encourages the leader to let their team experiment creatively with new ideas. The Team-Based Learning model supports and structures active collaborative learning and helps the leaders gain confidence in their roles. Using leadership skills for project management, the group refine the task before finally delivering it in the format of their choice.

Figure 6.5 How leadership coaching combines with TBL to enhance academic achievement and enrich learning

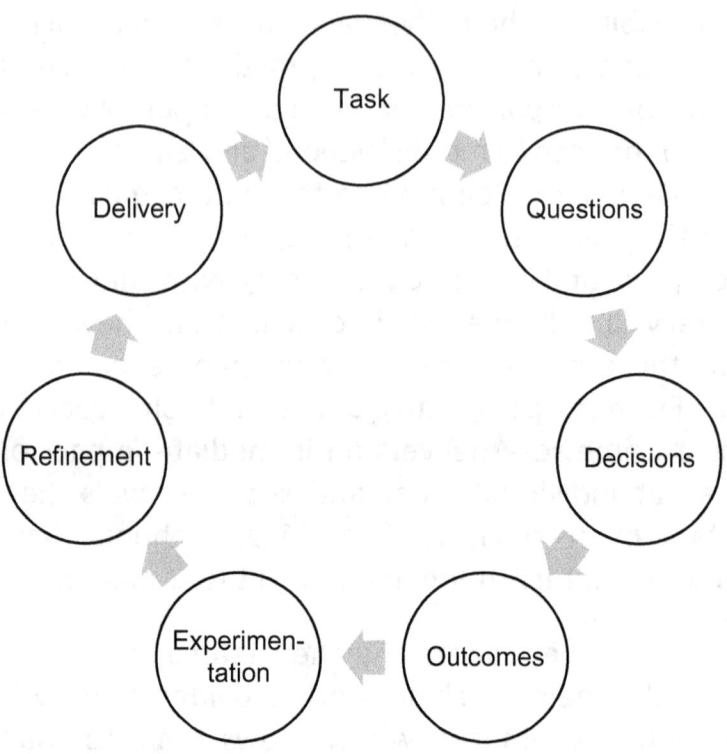

CRITICAL QUESTION

- As a teacher, how do you manage the tension between a knowledge-rich curriculum and optimal learning?

CASE STUDY

Our time: active citizenship

In partnership with Leeds Beckett University, we used the LCTBL model to deliver an active citizenship project in three different secondary schools. Working with over

85 young people, we co-created learning resources for an Arts and Humanities Research Council social history project on the letters of Richard Cobden. Year 9 leaders received coaching to lead Year 7 and Year 8 students on history and citizenship tasks, to produce their own active citizenship campaigns about current relevant issues to them, and to enter a competition with the History of Parliament Trust, as well as to inspire other young people across the UK to participate.

Groups: Three state secondary schools, Key Stage 3 (11–14 years), cohort of six leadership Year 9 candidates each leading a group of four to six younger Year 7/Year 8 learners.

Leadership role: Active Citizenship Emissaries.

Partnerships: This was a collaborative project between the sponsor Leeds Beckett University (funded through the Arts and Humanities Research Council), GreenWing Leadership Coaching and three very different secondary schools in Leeds, Rochdale and Bradford between April and June 2023.

Introduction: *The Letters of Richard Cobden (1804–65)* online project aims to use the collection of transcribed Cobden letters to promote the values and practices of active citizenship to secondary school pupils and channel youth leadership skills. Developing teaching materials in partnership with staff and school pupils, the project aimed to increase awareness of the relevance of Cobden's life and ideas to a modern democracy. As an end

→

goal, the sponsor had set a non-traditional essay-writing competition with the History of Parliament Trust, incentivising young people to enter and influence others to get involved.

Outcomes: To demonstrate the versatile nature and transferable skills of leadership in a classroom context and the value of creativity for optimal learning.

Proposal: Pupils were selected for leadership coaching based on a proven leadership track record or instinctive, currently unrecognised, leadership potential (developmental and reorientation types). GreenWing would use the LCTBL model to deliver an active citizenship project in three different secondary schools (working with over 85 young people), which had the overall aim of co-creating learning resources. GreenWing's workshops would achieve this objective by delivering citizenship teaching resources based on the Cobden letters and gauging how pupils responded to these, so that the resources can be further refined. Leadership coaching (individually and as a group) would be woven into the project, focusing on the six Year 9 pupils in each setting to support them to lead small groups of Year 7 or 8 pupils, develop campaign materials related to the workshop content and present their completed project to the external sponsors and school staff.

Project description: This project used the same GreenWing model for sustainability (Figure 4.5) and schedule of activity as used for the legacy leaders project case study in Chapter 4.

Project diary

Day 1: The leadership cohort completed an intense programme of coaching, including one-to-one and group work, where they were introduced to a new vision of leadership (exploring the unique instincts and behaviours they had been selected for) and to the concept of coaching. Within the realm of active citizenship, the leaders engaged in a wider discussion around different leadership styles and were given time to explore their own unique leadership brand. Additionally, the coaches facilitated a workshop about Richard Cobden's leadership and active citizenship style, using the methods of TBL.

Day 2: Leaders were given the opportunity to practise their conceptual and reflective learning in a live context and to continue to develop their authentic leadership voice. They were tasked with leading groups of Year 7 or Year 8 historians to organise and create an active citizenship campaign about a subject or a cause they felt passionate about, simultaneously cascading leadership behaviours and thinking down to their younger peers, so that they too would become Active Citizenship Emissaries in their own right. TBL was used to develop all the learners' understanding of history, citizenship and reform through time, creating links to the current national and global context. The LCTBL model ensured focus, enjoyment, engagement and, importantly, socialisation through its step-by-step process.

At this stage of the project, we began to observe a number of unusual events and encouraging behavioural

→

developments. Firstly, in the absence of constant supervision, leaders were using coaching methodologies to inspire, guide and support their teams. Secondly, some of the Year 9 leaders became immersed in their leadership roles, setting up Snapchat groups so that their team could further discuss and plan their campaign outside school hours. Thirdly, leaders exhibited a mature attitude to the responsibility of their role; for instance, at one school, one of the leaders knew that she wouldn't be in for the first 30 minutes of the day, so she prepared some supporting material and left guiding questions for her team. Finally, members of the Year 7 and Year 8 groups were taking on their leader's enthusiasm for the task and volunteering discretionary support and creative ideas, such as creating branded team stickers for all team members to wear during the presentation of the campaign.

Day 3: It had become apparent to us that Day 2 was a pivotal stage in the LCTBL process, with all participants moving into an optimal learning space. The teams had not only acquired knowledge, but they were able to use their unique strengths and skills to apply this knowledge. On the final day, teams were busy finalising their presentations. Left to their own devices, these were highly creative, including: online quizzes, delivering podcasts, writing letters, creating dramas and devising leaflets and posters. In addition, the ideas for wider societal change that accompanied their projects were diverse and innovative, formed with the clarity from the challenging logic of inexperience, ranging from (in the example of educational reform) the aspirational – providing access to wider cultural history – to the practical – the importance of reducing the hidden costs of education.

In the final workshop, all teams successfully delivered their active citizenship campaigns to their peers, teachers and representatives from Leeds Beckett University. Real 'Assessment for Learning' then took place, using a secret ballot to vote for the best campaign and self and peer reviews about how well each learner had contributed to the learning that took place within the teams. The younger learners were also given the opportunity to feed back by identifying three words that they would use to describe their leader's style.

In conclusion, leaders attended one-to-one coaching sessions to explore their personal experience of leadership and its impact on their learning and academic goals. A final group debrief session was then held, where the coach worked with the leadership team interactively to add meaning to their learning by connecting individual and collective leadership actions to the quality and positive experience of achieved outcomes. The leaders were also asked to complete anonymous evaluation forms so that they could process their thoughts about the programme and feedback.

Impact: 100 per cent of the leaders said that they would like to continue with the leadership coaching in the future. Individual feedback from the Year 9 leaders was extremely positive. Headline themes included improved confidence:

> *It felt amazing to actually lead a group of people; to know how you help and inspire people feels really fulfilling. It has made me so much more confident in everything I do.*
>
> A, Bradford

→

Enjoyment and engagement in learning as a relatable choice they could connect to future ambitions:

> *I learnt how people have made a difference in the past and how I can make a difference now – and also what I want to make a difference about.*
>
> G, Rochdale

An awakening of personal aspirations and purpose to challenge bias and exclusion:

> *I want to inspire and influence people to speak out against what they think is wrong and make the world better for everyone, especially people who are discriminated against or mistreated for being different.*
>
> J, Rochdale

And active leadership in the school – young people leading young people:

> *Inspire more people to step into a leadership role; the only thing they have is the school council that people say isn't effective or just isn't something they want to get involved with.*
>
> M, Leeds

This is just a snapshot of responses, but perhaps one of the most insightful comments (to the purpose of the project) came from a teacher who had not been directly involved in the project, perfectly encapsulating the impact of coaching on reorientation types and the paradoxical world of the classroom in which they find themselves:

> *X was absolutely buzzing about the project and his role in it; he just wouldn't stop talking about it – all through his detention!*
>
> Head of History, Bradford

COACHING TIP

The coach should be constantly aware of contingencies and be prepared to act with agility and crafted resourcefulness. One of the leaders at the school in Bradford missed the beginning of the second day of the programme. It was clear that this was due to personal circumstances. Unfortunately, the learners from his team had already been reallocated to other teams and it would have been too disruptive to move them again. It would also have been unfair to deselect him from his leadership role. He had impressed so far at his one-to-ones and in the group workshops where he had successfully harnessed his natural hyperactivity and impulsiveness to contribute at a high level. Accordingly, a different leadership opportunity was offered to become a part of the coaching team to offer floating support to all groups. This allowed him to have more movement around the classroom and a varied role, which suited his leadership personality. It became quickly established that he was very technologically able, putting organisational systems into place and, as the day progressed, his confidence grew and he thrived with his responsibility, showing initiative and exceptional communicational skills with his peers. When the headteacher came into the classroom for the presentations, she remarked on

→

the difference in his focus and his peers applauded him for the help, support and guidance that he had offered throughout the workshops.

Takeaways: Delivering the same programme in three different schools provided us with an opportunity to compare and contrast as part of a wider evaluation process (see Chapter 8). Although some of the learning resources were adapted to the varying levels and needs of a distinct cohort, the programme was delivered and received differently in each school, generally reflecting the standing of the particular school. Despite these differences, some clearcut themes emerged.

- One of the main takeaways from discussions with the leaders was that they really appreciated the time and the opportunity to be coached; to feel that their voice was heard and that they were given space to discuss not just their strengths but their challenges and blind spots. The opportunity to receive ongoing one-to-one coaching during the project clearly accelerated their real-time constructive development.
- All the learners enjoyed working in teams, and by the end of the three-day workshop strong friendships and alliances had developed within the groups. This was not always what they expected to happen. However, because social communication skills are modelled and coached by the leaders, supported by the coaches, the teams become independently functioning where the learners become reliant on each other's strengths rather than seeking out staff.

- The transformation of all the teams, in all three schools, was phenomenal. The pivotal transformational moment was recorded at midday on the second day at all the schools. Leaders and their teams would get halfway through the optimal learning sequence, where they had already developed a strong sense of intrinsic motivation, collaborated with team members and other leaders, and practised, evaluated and reflected on their optimal learning. At this time, we noticed that their energy levels dropped dramatically – they became distracted, tetchy and hungry for lunch. However, after lunch when they had had some time to reboot, reflect and evaluate for themselves, and then were given the freedom to elaborate on the task, they became lost in the learning experience and in their own bubble. This discretionary energy carried on overnight, as the teams chose to work at home (as opposed to doing homework), stretching their learning and using their individual talents for the benefit of their team. They came back on the third day as leaders of their own learning with the aim of showing off their projects, their teams and arguing for a cause that truly mattered to them.

Evidence of impact: and we have a winner ...

One of the Year 7 students participating in this project won the National History of Parliament essay-writing competition and his Black Voices Matter Library Campaign is now being endorsed for implementation by Leeds Beckett University.

> **CRITICAL QUESTIONS**
>
> - What could happen if your school took leadership coaching seriously?
> - How could the LCTBL model work in your school?
> - How would you use coaching questions to help a young leader access and articulate a cause that really mattered to them?

Further reading

Darby, S, O'Hanlon, D, Casterton, S, Harding, N, O'Brien, A-M, Quinn, G, Urmeneta, O and Tweddell, S (2023) Improved Learning Outcomes and Teacher Experience: A Qualitative Study of Team-Based Learning in Secondary Schools. *Social Sciences & Humanities, Open,* 8(1): 100590.

References

Hirsch, E D (1983) Cultural Literacy. *The American Scholar*, 52(2): 159–69.

Sweet, M and Michaelsen, L (2012) *Team-based Learning in the Social Sciences and Humanities: Group Work That Works to Generate Critical Thinking and Engagement*. New York: Routledge.

Chapter 7
COACHING LEADERSHIP FOR LEARNING

CHAPTER OVERVIEW

This chapter takes a detour to explore the parallel relationship between leadership and learning. It concentrates on the transformational powers of leadership on the learner and the transitional challenges of integrating youth leadership into the academic mainstream. It sees leadership as inextricably woven into the coach offering as the facilitator of a new way of thinking about learning.

Introduction

Most schools reference youth leadership as a primary value and espouse its transferable skills as part of their overarching manifesto. However, schools' attempts to promote youth leadership miss the mark for two reasons. Firstly, they capture a leadership theory that contributes to the steady state rather than one that envisions new horizons. Secondly, they have a one-dimensional vision of leadership that includes exemplar students but excludes those outside the academic mainstream. Not only does this narrow the field for candidates, but it also inhibits leadership thinking and limits future opportunities to familiar unimaginative roles. This chapter sets out to resolve the practical implications (for the future of young leaders) of the systemic failure of schools to evolve their thinking in this area. It focuses on the conflicting relationships between contradictory personalities and cultures that need to be managed and brought together to create an environment in which young leaders can flourish and move forward.

Do young people actually want to lead?

The intellectual lodestar for coaching young leaders is to usher in a new vision of leadership, but if we are to accept that young people are generally excited by the challenge, we should also recognise that some will be reluctant to step into the current leadership vacuum characterised by distrust and disillusionment. Therefore, we should not simply assume that young people, having completed a phase of coaching, will want to continue along a leadership pathway. At the design stage of our early pilots, we anticipated that a number of candidates would either decline the invitation to enrol or opt out at some stage during the programme. What we did not anticipate was that this would be such an inappreciable number. Our data shows that only 2 per cent of coachees who signed up to our programme did not complete the course, mainly due to choosing to prioritise critical exams.

Analysis of the data from our feedback surveys suggests two reasons for such high engagement: selection and induction. Careful selection of candidates predicated by a shared understanding of criteria (between the coach and the sponsor teacher – hereon referred to as the coaching partnership) meant that most were naturally open-minded and receptive to both coaching and the idea of leadership. As a starting point, a positive frame of mind was reinforced by a rigorous induction process including introductory town-hall presentations and the dedicated one-to-one space provided by the authentication stage of the Youth Leadership Coaching model.

However, staying the course is not sufficient evidence in itself of the transformative powers of leadership. Nor does it justify the presumptive logic that candidates will want to continue along a leadership pathway or have crystallised their ambition to be able to visualise a future leadership role. Accordingly, we designed post-programme questionnaires, surveys and debrief interviews with the wider philosophical debate about leadership in mind (see examples below). Rather than asking predictable questions to elicit predictably positive responses, we were curious about changes in attitudes and aspirations from the perspective of future leadership imagined, focusing on decisions, judgements and choices. In this way, coachees were being invited to respond as leaders rather than participants, practising with the developing leadership mindset by connecting conceptual ideas to practical outcomes, in order to articulate a point of view and influence others.

Questions for young leaders

How has your thinking about leadership changed in terms of:

- your unique style?
- the role you would like?
- what you would like to achieve?

> *I think I respect people and that's why they listen to me. Some teachers just yell and don't listen – I'm not like that.*
>
> C, developmental coachee, 14

> *I want to make a difference in any job I do, using my experiences to help others.*
>
> Y, reorientation coachee, 15

> *I don't know what I want to achieve yet; I guess it's always changing and that's a good thing. I think once I've got to where I'm aiming for, I'll be thinking about the next goal.*
>
> M, developmental coachee, 16

What difference has a leadership mindset made to you?

> *Leadership is not what I first thought – being in charge! Having a leadership mindset means that leading is not something I consciously do; it's become more a way of life. If I'm thinking too much about it, I'm probably not doing it right. So, it's changed the way I do everything – sometimes only small things, but others revolutionary – the way I communicate with people, the way I learn, the way I make sense of all the effort I put into my school work. It's really interesting because leadership teaches you to be the same person – true to yourself – but with a completely different outlook.*
>
> F, developmental coachee, 17

How should youth leadership be promoted in your school?

> *I would say one thing – take it seriously! Two things – take us seriously! If you want to improve*

things, then talk to us, give us a voice and listen. Helping us to help you.

A, reorientation coachee, 16

Leadership should be promoted as a school code of conduct. It covers values, behaviours, results... everything we do in school. It should not be a badge for good behaviour, but something – a way of acting – that you expect from yourself and from others.

D, developmental coachee, 16

What arguments would you present to convince your school to invest in leadership programmes for pupils?

Leadership is a way of connecting you to school values and goals. If you are serious about all the stuff you say on the website then you need to take leadership as an action seriously. Otherwise, it's just the same words – keeping on saying it won't make it happen.

J, reorientation coachee, 15

Leadership is a thought process; it's not just being Head Girl or a prefect, it's a way of making positive things happen by getting pupils to contribute differently.

S, developmental coachee, 15

If nothing more, coaching gives you a new set of skills to help you achieve better academic results by getting you to really think about the way you learn ... because you're making your own choices not just doing what you're told.

K, reorientation coachee, 14

> *We talk about well-being and mental health all the time; learning to be a leader is a way of positively impacting on young people by giving them purpose and getting them to look forward. It is the knock-on effects of leadership that you [the school] are investing in.*
>
> R, reorientation coachee, 15

Despite being focused on the impact of a specific coaching programme, feedback can also provide useful insights for schools. The clear subtext from our data is that schools are engaged in *gesture leadership* – statements of good intent that tap into the educational zeitgeist but with no significant impact – and young people see right through it.

In other more practical areas, headline findings revealed that 90 per cent of candidates (post programme) considered themselves leaders and felt ready to take up a leadership role in the immediate future, while 85 per cent of candidates wanted to continue with some form of leadership coaching. All candidates stated that they preferred coaching sessions to regular lessons and believed they learnt more efficiently through active engagement with the subject. Over 75 per cent said that they intended to continue researching the particular project they were studying and would encourage others within their original leadership teams to assist.

Reliability of data: considering context

We acknowledge that the reliability of these figures can be questioned due to the fact that they are limited to self-reporting anecdotal evidence or short-term observation of impact. Furthermore, we were conscious, as we collected data, that ingrained attitudes and behaviours relating to codes of conduct and school targets remained influential in responses and observations – it was felt the coachees still wanted to please the coach and give an answer they believed was the right one rather than an authentic one. In Chapter 8, we present a rigorous evaluation framework for a more reliable measurement of impact; however, we should not discount these subjective snapshots and their contribution to a more formal evaluation system.

Because coaching is not prescriptive and leadership is idiosyncratic, reliability is constantly being called into question. Furthermore, the contractual nature of the business of coaching means that evidence is often tendentious, flattering the coach and exaggerating the progress of the coachee. That being said, one of the main reasons for unreliability is that coaching, highly sensitive to context, is subject to acontextual interpretation. Coaching in the classroom adds yet further layers of contextual complexity. For instance, reorientation is seen as part of a wider preventionist social strategy, the coaching context for which contradicts the exigency for short-term success, measured against conflicting criteria demanded by investors – there is a low tolerance for experimentation and failure. But it is in the context of coaching as a vocational transaction (as opposed to financial) that sees it at its most vulnerable, where the coaching partnership is susceptible to subtle distractions, specifically in making headstrong judgements about the future direction of travel for the young leader. The emergent expectations of the coaching partnership, given licence through a vocational context, can be a kind of coaching hubris and to move forward, these need to be managed.

Designing an environment for future leadership: Part 1 – managing expectations

To create an environment in schools for youth leadership to thrive, we should recognise the various personalities of those involved. This means that, either as individuals or as part of a support group, we must be able to predict the potential fallibilities of the actors and how they might play out in a setting defined by incompatibilities. In practical terms, this involves managing expectations resulting from assumptions, familiar role plays or the personalised agendas that characterise schools, specifically coaching hubris.

The hero coach and avoiding coaching hubris

Coaching hubris is one component of a wider agenda to manage expectations when moving candidates into future leadership roles. Generally, when we think about managing expectations, we refer back to the early work spent building credibility with the candidate at the *authentication* stage through to the final *ambition* stage – putting theory into practice. But, in a vocational coaching context, we should not overlook the expectations of the coaching partnership as potentially derailing the relatability, realism and relevance essential to any coaching intervention. First of all, what exactly do we mean by *coaching in a vocational context*? A vocational context is best described as having a High-Church quality: uncompromised by financial gain, emphasising pure motives that best serve the young person, often taking place in underserved or overlooked groups. It is when coaching is seen as a good deed that the coaching partnership and the sponsor must beware of self-appointed hero status: what we are describing here as coaching hubris.

Coaching hubris is defined as the instinctive characteristics of the hero coach manifest in overconfident assumptions and passive controlling behaviours – in other words, the coach's belief that they know best. Given the benefit of the doubt, it is passed off as the well-meaning over-enthusiastic expectations of sponsors, teachers, parents and coaches, as part of the caring contract between adults and young people. At its worst, it can be debilitatingly overbearing and patronising, capturing the space between outdated established leadership and new thinking by perpetuating existing hierarchical status. In a vocational context, the coaching partnership is frequently challenged to examine their personal motives, not just for quality assurance but because of the potential to misdirect the ambitions and aspirations of young leaders in their care. As part of this self-reflection, the coach should be aware of a number of potential psychological bear-traps (all versions of accepted psychological phenomena) when working with young people at school.

Cognitive bias: pushing instead of guiding

Coaching hubris is our collective term for various cognitive biases in leadership coaching in schools, where the coach's actions and thought patterns are consistent with the perceived dominance of their status, enabled by the expectations of the young person. This can lead to a lopsided intervention with the coach typically expediting solutions, making moral judgements on behalf of the coachee, being dismissive or working to their own agenda. In effect, the coach is pushing the young person in a direction of their (the coach's) own making rather than guiding the coachee along their (the coachee's) chosen pathway. The following iterations of coaching hubris, discussed below, have been observed throughout our work in the classroom: countertransference, ambition projection, saviour complex, illusory bias and a life lived vicariously.

Countertransference

Countertransference occurs when the coach transfers their own personality traits to the coachee, shaping interactions and responses during the session. The coach is influenced by the young person's status, background or behaviours and they coach using assumptions and subjective judgements based on their own experiences. For instance, where a young person has difficulty expressing themselves at the authentication stage, the coach may provide prompts to encourage a positive dialogue. This in itself, especially due to the limited time that the coach probably has with the coachee, is not necessarily problematic; however, it becomes an issue when the coach is deemed to be putting words into the coachee's mouth. It also occurs when the coach, with minimal relatable knowledge of youth issues, draws on their own experiences as a parent or adult and increasingly adopts the controlling behaviours used in those contexts. As the coach is engaged with future leadership destinations for the young person, countertransference can result in pushing the coachee towards goals that they are unsuited to or which are not in their best long-term interests.

COACHING TIP

Disciplined self-awareness is a way of dealing with countertransference, recognising you are becoming over involved, over sharing (personal details), or over sensitive to suggestions and advice that are either ungratefully received or rejected out of hand. Along with acute self-awareness, the coach is best served by being purposefully unaware of the coachee's background (unless necessary) to develop a trusting relationship uncluttered by the past – defining young people by their future not their past.

Ambition projection

Ambition projection is defined as the coach's unqualified conviction that the coachee seeks a particular outcome, which in reality represents their own beliefs, standards or expectations. In the context of helping young leaders to move into leadership roles, ambition projection can occur when the coach attributes their own aspirations and pursuit of personal goals to the coachee.

COACHING TIP

As with countertransference, an acute sense of self-awareness allows the coach to recognise ambition projection and put in place boundaries. Using the Leadership Coaching Hierarchy model, the coach might remove themselves from a level of unconscious competence

→

> and spend some time acting deliberately with conscious competence as a way of self-supervision, slowing down the process to avoid subconsciously jumping to conclusions.

Saviour complex

Saviour complex characterises the hero coach. It occurs when the coach is attracted to the perceived vulnerability of the coachee and migrates from a supportive to a saving role. Here, the coach can be guilty of trying to fix the coachee, suggesting solutions rather than eliciting choices. In terms of future leadership roles, the young person can feel overburdened by unsolicited suggestions of how to change their lives for the better (particularly in the case of reorientation candidates) rather than being guided towards making their own moral choices.

Illusory bias

There is a fine line between positive encouragement and counter-productive cheerleading; when that line is crossed, illusory bias occurs. As a psychological phenomenon, illusory bias refers to the disparity between self-reported competence (higher) and actual competence (lower). In our coaching context, we experience a kind of transferable illusory bias, where the coach overestimates the capabilities or ambitions of the coachee, effectively setting them up to fail by encouraging them to aim for unachievable targets. The selection criteria, often instinctive in the case of reorientation candidates, accept that there is no template for leaders and that leadership achievements can range from modest to grandiose. Therefore, the coach is working with unique leadership personalities and varying levels of ambition and ability; accordingly, they need to be adaptive to the individual and weight achievement sensibly and with sensitivity.

A life lived vicariously

Usually, living vicariously is attributed to parents projecting their own dreams onto their children. Negative manifestations include helicopter parenting (exerting extreme positive control over children), prioritising the needs of the parent over the child and excessive criticism when unowned targets are not achieved. To a lesser extent, coaches and teachers can exhibit these traits, and both should remember that, as young people develop under their professional watch, they are seeking out their unique identities and that to allow them to so do is a fundamental tenet of both coaching and teaching.

Throughout our work we have experienced examples of all of the above. The prevalence of psychological traps reflects not only the vocational context of the coaching but the various involved relationships that distinguish coaching in schools from other forms of leadership development. Accordingly, it is when these relationships cross over and new behaviours, attitudes and thinking have not been fully grasped that confusion occurs. In short, the coach should steer clear of handing out career guidance, while the teacher or parent should remember that when adopting coaching behaviours, reverting back to default positions of authority sends out mixed messages. A lack of self-awareness of potential personality fault lines is one of the main reasons that schools are restricted to leadership gestures.

Leadership gestures: what schools already do

It can be argued that schools already provide a number of creative outlets for youth leadership, but these are designed within the confines of existing hierarchical thinking and generally one-dimensionally focused on developmental candidates – more opportunities for the same faces. They are not designed in response to a dedicated programme of leadership coaching and are, therefore, disconnected from the wider debate around young people and their role in a leadership reset. Nevertheless, some schools have purposefully placed youth leadership at the heart of their values, promoting active participation in school strategies, specifically around mentoring younger students, ambassadorial duties and as part of a school union. The clear aim of these schools is to provide students with a voice and an opportunity to make a contribution outside the classroom, creating relatable role models and focusing various leadership groups on specific areas – young people leading young people. But an examination of the level of support offered to young leaders reveals that, however enlightened and well intentioned, youth leadership in schools is generally limited to gestures and rhetoric.

It is symptomatic of the lag in leadership thinking in schools that training and development remain focused on pastoral staff and teachers, confined to cost-effective, mainly online resources. The notion that a 45-minute pre-recorded training seminar is sufficient preparation to design and co-ordinate a youth leadership strategy contradicts the statement commitment to young leaders from schools and providers and supports the claim that both are engaged in gesture leadership. The half-hearted commitment to investment (financial and intellectual) in youth leadership means that strategies are built on shifting sand and are stubbornly out of touch with new thinking. Unsurprisingly, they are predestined to miss the target. To identify, develop and fulfil the ambitions of young leaders, schools must go beyond gesture leadership by dismantling existing systems and integrating new ideas, combining coaching (as a new way of learning), leadership (redefined for a new generation) and the application to new dimensions of learning (outcomes for the future). It is only after this has been achieved that future leadership roles will take on real meaning and cease to be gestures.

Designing an environment for future leadership: Part 2 – managing a clash of leadership cultures

Having studied the personalities involved in creating a positive environment for future leadership, we should turn our attention to the institution, characterised by the fallout from a clash of leadership cultures. In essence, we are talking about managing the aftershock from introducing unconventional leadership into an ultra-conventional leadership system.

How to create the right environment for leaders to move forward

In partnership, the coach and the school are striving to create a leadership environment that acknowledges structures in place, but with enough elasticity to flex into creative counter-intuitive spaces to allow the new vision of leadership to blossom. In our experience of working with schools to create such an environment, we arrived at seven guiding principles: positive, safe, development, inclusive, relevant, balanced and active (Figure 7.1).

Figure 7.1 The seven guiding principles for partnerships to follow for the design of a workable hybrid leadership environment in schools

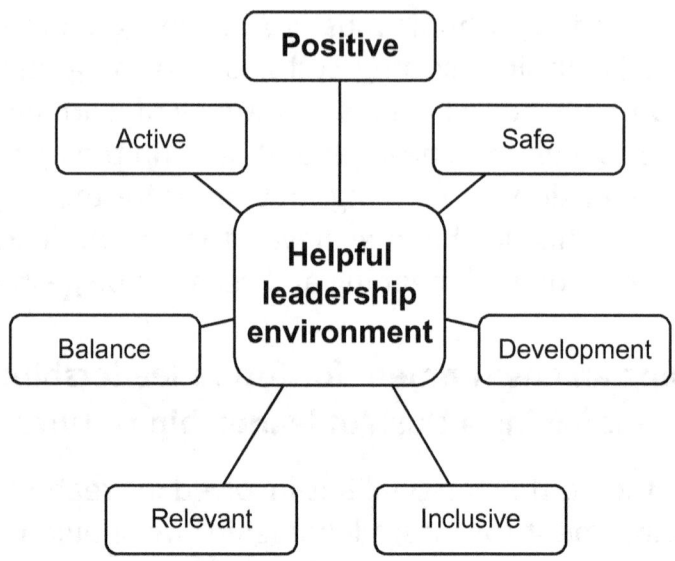

The seven cells are not sequential but subordinate to the primary function, *positive*. This means that, as a working model, building positive relationships with different actors emerges as foundational to the design of an environment in which youth leadership can blossom.

A positive relationship: primary function

A generative leadership environment is dependent on three positive relationships working in concert: pupils with teachers, pupils with their peers and teachers with the curriculum.

Pupils with teachers

Developing leadership in young people is a process of intense identity exploration and inward focus. We can only imagine the instability of young people at a pivotal age being caught between two worlds – an identity that is diminishing and one that is barely imagined. It is how teachers respond to this state of flux that underpins the positive leadership environment. Managing our personal motivations to see young leaders succeed is part of the coaching methodology; however, for teachers, coaching is not part of their contract with the institution. Unlike the coach, managing personal hubris, the teacher is managing the institutional expectations of the school. The two tensions amount to the same thing: pressure that can both inspire and weigh down the young person.

For teachers, there is less room for manoeuvrability and reflection to achieve longer-term development outcomes. Therefore, combining the prospect of infinite possibilities with academic targets is like oil and water, often resulting in unthinking positive encouragement as a reflex action. Being constantly told that anything is possible increases the burden of expectation on the coachee, while striving for high achievement becomes ambition by proxy infused with institutional goals.

> **COACHING TIP**
>
> To build positive relationships, teachers can accept developmental instability, focus on realistic goals and make informed judgements about exactly when to intervene. Inadvertent anxiety resulting from expectations for high achievement can be negated by the teacher, creating a sense of normality around experimentation, transience and failure as part of the growth phase.

Pupils with peers

To express themselves without inhibition, young leaders need to have positive relationships with their peers. We have found two main causes for why young leaders can become distracted from their leadership pathway: negative peer pressure (generally affecting reorientation candidates) and positive peer detachment (generally affecting developmental coachees).

We define negative peer pressure as *fitting in*, eliciting inauthentic, anti-social or unhealthy behaviours. In these instances, we observed a sense of jealousy or suspicion towards some candidates as changes in interpersonal relationships triggered negative social emotions. In accepting that negative emotions arise from a perceived threat to a valued relationship, we noticed that this was exacerbated when one side is unexpectedly labelled superior. Alternatively, we recognised that a small number of candidates deliberately detached themselves from their peers as a statement of self-affirmation. This we saw as positive peer detachment: conforming to standardised definitions of good behaviour and feeding off a close cabal of like-minded colleagues to achieve school targets. These candidates were characterised by others as aloof and superior, but seemingly took the negative attention they attracted in their stride.

As candidates, this second group is instantly recognisable to the coach as more mature, confident, aware (of their abilities) and regularly referencing family members as role models. Their innate self-assuredness, often generated from a strong family unit constantly reinforcing self-belief and long-term ambitions, means they are comfortable to acknowledge personal unpopularity in some school settings and see others as jealous of their status. At first glance, these candidates are outstanding examples of developmental coachees, but as the programme progresses, exposure to unfamiliar counter-intuitive behaviours and thought processes reveals a fragility to which the coach must be sensitive. Suddenly, they find themselves refocused on different targets for excellence and often struggle to integrate into a leadership group of mixed personalities, some of whom they would shun under other circumstances. Here, reorientation candidates have a head start as they are already familiar with distraction techniques, albeit in a negative context, and simply have to reframe their natural disposition rather than unlearn inherent disciplines and attitudes and re-evaluate criteria for success.

> **COACHING TIP**
>
> In terms of negative peer pressure, reinforcing the coachee's self-awareness and sense of purpose helps the coachee rationalise the behaviour of others to make positive choices and overcome distractions. However, where the candidate is aloof and distances themselves from peers, the coach should be conscious of helping to integrate them by carefully managing the dynamic of the group. The coach should also remember that, where a competitive element is introduced into the programme, these candidates are unused to coming second and unconventional criteria for success can heighten any sense of isolation, unfairness or perceived bias towards less-deserving peers.

Teachers with the curriculum

To create a rich environment for emerging leadership ambitions to thrive, teachers are challenged to build a positive relationship with the curriculum to accommodate active learning, new dimensions of learning and the entrenched attitude of some colleagues. In this sense, the curriculum does not only refer to a knowledge-rich agenda for teaching but the institution of education.

We accept that schools are a high-pressure under-resourced setting to experiment with new ways of learning and creative notions of leadership. As such, teachers may find it difficult to find the space or energy to instigate innovative concepts outside the curriculum which are not currently valued or assessed. At the same time, we do come across a minority of teachers in senior positions, especially where the school has not invested financially and the coaching is in the gift of an external sponsor, who, by not taking the programme seriously, undermine all those who participate.

CASE STUDY

Failing to read the room

Having spent a day and a half with a cohort of young leaders working on a particular project, we carried out a midway debrief session as a group. In this session, we discussed the individual leaders' progress, specifically their developing style of leadership, any challenges and emerging blind spots. As part of this discussion, the coach was facilitating a conversation around the fine line between leadership strengths and weaknesses, specifically *influence* versus *manipulation*. At this point, the headteacher, who had previously been anonymous, paid a visit to the group.

Picking up on the group's conversation but without the benefit of context, the headteacher's one contribution was a reference to how she used manipulative tactics to get teachers to do what she wanted. This may have been intended as a humorous throwaway; however, it landed badly with the group as a basic admission of poor leadership, undermining the positive relationship that had been built over the past couple of days. The headteacher's glibness, far from being witty, showed ill-judgement and a lack of respect for the work of the group and the authority of the partner teacher. It also cast a shadow over the future development of the group as leaders once the programme had ended – for the programme to achieve long-term goals, the teacher would need to ensure a level of intellectual investment from senior colleagues. In the immediate term, the coaching partnership would need to rebuild trust and credibility as a result of an unthinking joke from a senior authority figure who had spared no more than two minutes for the project.

CRITICAL QUESTION

- How would you manage senior school leaders who are not truly invested in the project and build a positive relationship?

> **COACHING TIP**
>
> In essence, the coach is supporting the teacher to create a hybrid learning environment for an overall positive relationship. To create such an environment, we use the model in Figure 7.2, which is designed to accommodate both the knowledge curriculum and the new dimensions of learning by focusing on five key areas: design, connect, rhythm, interact and feedback.

Figure 7.2 Coaching foci for a hybrid learning model to build positive relationships

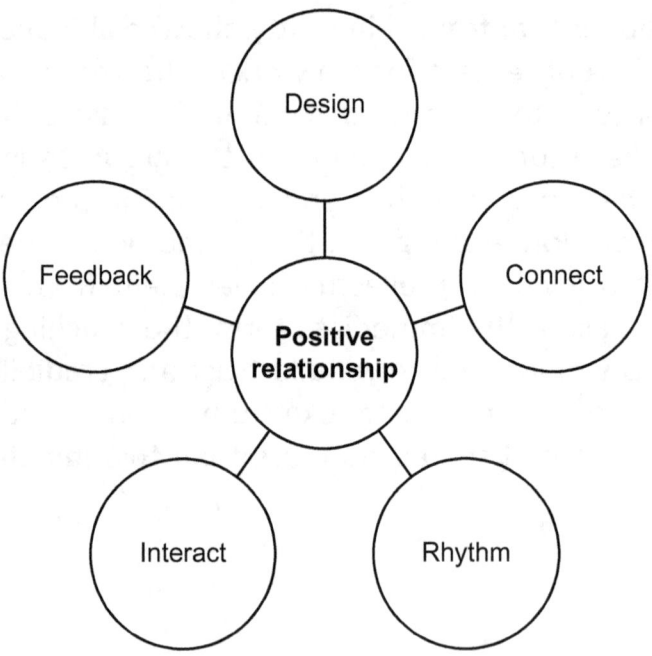

At the design stage, the teacher is using leadership activities to trigger independent thinking and enhance academic achievement. To provide relevance, surprising new knowledge and lines of enquiry resulting from an active learner's mindset then need to be connected to existing school goals. To underpin these two stages, the teacher is required to consider the rhythm of their teaching and the structure of lessons, removing some content to make space for interactive case studies, quizzes and discussion. As part of the interactive learning process, the teacher naturally becomes more involved with learners, guiding their thinking and encouraging them to challenge conventional knowledge. Finally, the teacher is constantly eliciting feedback to give ownership to the learner over future design to complete the loop.

A safe space

For some young people the leadership spotlight can be destabilising or confusing. For young leaders to grow and develop, there is a responsibility to make them feel comfortable in their new surroundings. But creating a safe space is a two-way street. Encouraging young leaders to experiment and reassuring them that making mistakes is essential to their learning is asking them to take a leap of faith in full view of their elders and betters, requiring buy-in from all sides of the positive relationships described in the previous section. Different candidates have different psychological and emotional needs which have to be accepted before creating a safe space to explore future leadership options. The reorientation candidate will still be processing the reframing of disruptive negatively criticised behaviours as part of a positive characteristic of a counter-intuitive reimagining of leadership. Moreover, developmental candidates are hardwired to avoid failure, closing off avenues for creativity and experimentation. Therefore, it is not sufficient for the coaching partnership to simply state that a safe space exists; they must constantly reinforce the message by challenging the limiting beliefs of the candidate.

In practical terms, we achieve this in schools through normal coaching techniques, focusing on the individual's psychological limiting beliefs and potential blind spots. Creating a safe space is a gradual process but once established can become contagious, to those in the leadership group and those being led, and a defining part of unconsciously competent leadership. It is from this safe space that the candidate can flex their leadership mindset and visualise future roles.

An agenda for development

By definition, leadership coaching is developmental as opposed to remedial, as it sets out to develop, rather than alter, the natural character traits of the coachee (the authentic voice). It specifically does not start from a basis that sees the coachee as flawed, acting as a function for change to remedy instinctive behaviours by adopting standardised examples of excellence that are neither natural (to the coachee) nor necessarily aligned to the new vision of leadership. Personality mimetic isomorphism (mimicking exemplar leaders by replicating behaviours and attitudes) undermines the environment and corrupts the young leader's progress. Accordingly, the coach and the school must remain connected to the development agenda to create meaningful opportunities for young leaders.

> **COACHING TIP**
>
> One way of sticking to a development agenda is through connectivity. In Figure 7.3, the four orbs represent connection points for coaching focus. It is taken as read that the coach will have an understanding of these as part of a development agenda and adopt their own

methodologies to ensure that the coachee remains connected. What is not so certain is the natural environment in which the coach and the young leader operate. It can be argued that navigating the institutional barriers to coaching in schools is part of the overarching fundamental requirement to build positive relationships. However, a development agenda is a key tenet of coaching and justifies its position as an essential element of a helpful environment for young leaders. A primary focus on development ensures that the coach is constantly prompting the coachee and, more vitally, the school to maintain connection with the overall vision of the project.

Figure 7.3 The connection points integral to a development agenda

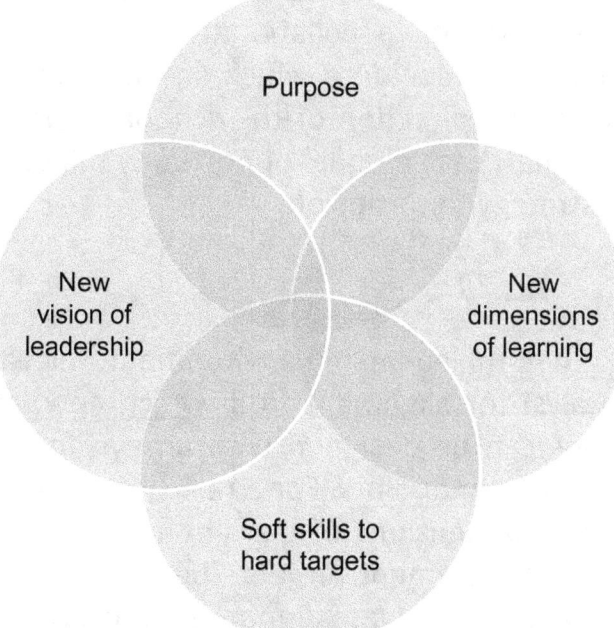

Inclusivity

Having convinced the school to include reorientation candidates as part of a leadership coaching cohort at the beginning, the coaching partnership is then challenged to see this through to the end of the programme, specifically in the design of future leadership opportunities. This means not only diverting the school from defaulting to placing obvious candidates in existing roles, but selecting counter-intuitive candidates (by reputation) for creative and innovative leadership opportunities that have yet to be imagined.

Accepting that leadership is not a template but a collection of diverse thinking, attitudes, values and ambitions means that anyone concerned with future outlets for youth leadership should be prepared to stretch current realities to accommodate both developmental and reorientation candidates in the design of future opportunities. This implies that the school must embrace wider change, as such an approach depends on a collaborative environment constantly generating new ideas which, in turn, will guide the long-term cultural direction of the school. In practice, the school might harness an equal opportunity mindset as part of a wider strategy for inclusion.

Relevant

As part of a helpful leadership environment, relevance provides a catalyst for alignment from which new leadership opportunities can be designed with an eye for both present and future standpoints. For a relevant environment to exist, the new dimensions of learning must be aligned to measurable establishment targets, thereby satisfying both progressive and steady-state demands. In this way, focusing on relevance acts as a device to effectively incorporate new thinking into existing entrenched mindsets, where the coach and the school are actively engaged in negotiating a hybrid learning and development environment that accepts change as evolutionary (as opposed to revolutionary) and dispels suspicions of coaching as a subversive force.

At another level, relevance means that the true ambitions and aspirations of the young leader are respected. By committing to relevant goals, future leadership roles take on real meaning to candidates and are seen as both realistic and relatable. In our experience, relevance, relatability and realism reinforce young leaders' energy to invest in a programme of development with no tangible short-term outcomes. By staying true to the candidate's goals, future leadership roles play to the individual's strengths and are more likely to be created (to exploit strengths) rather than seen as shoo-in applications to situations vacant.

Balanced

If *relevance* recognises the need to steer a steady course between the establishment and the visionary, balance is the navigational mechanism that makes it happen. Ambidexterity (balancing short-term known targets with long-term unknown goals) is the coaching tool and leadership skill that can deliver a workable environment to explore future leadership opportunities. Ambidexterity works on two levels: for the individual leader and for the school. It allows the young leader to make space through personal time management to stay connected to their leadership vision while balancing immediate academic and personal imperatives. At the same time, seeking to achieve personal balance in their lives means that the young person is actively practising leadership disciplines, specifically in judgement, decision making and prioritisation – making choices between what's important and what's urgent (Figure 7.4).

Figure 7.4 An ambidextrous view of time management for a young leader – important versus urgent

A balanced environment has the capacity to accommodate and encourage new ideas within a rigid structure, assisting the evolution of learning and development. By adopting an ambidextrous approach, the school is making a commitment to the real goals of young people and the new dimensions of learning.

Active

One of the key themes for this book (and its predecessor, *Coaching Young People for Leadership*) is that for any leadership outcome, the leader must take action. Therefore, unsurprisingly, the leadership environment in schools is an active one, where actions are needed to deliver the seven guiding principles of a helpful leadership environment. An active environment is not to be confused with *active learning* but refers to the actions – negotiation, compromise, alignment, communication, empathy, decision making, judgement and choice – needed to bring the prospect of leadership futures to life. Without deliberate actions taken on behalf of all parties, youth leadership is in danger of withering on the vine.

Leadership end goals

This chapter has deliberately avoided providing a convenient list of current outlets for youth leadership in schools, however quirky, imaginative or topical, as representative of the future for young leaders. Its priority has been to design an environment in which young leaders post coaching can continue along their leadership pathway – leadership as an action rather than a status. The helpful leadership environment is built upon positive collaboration and we can see that, in the future, roles will emerge from shared thinking involving all stakeholders. In this way, new dimensions of learning and active learning methodologies become integrated into the system, making a compelling case for an education rethink, as the needs of all stakeholders are met, testing the obduracy of a system that hitherto has confined change to the *too difficult box*.

Chapter 8
EVALUATING THE IMPACT OF COACHING

> **CHAPTER OVERVIEW**
>
> This chapter defines evaluation as the third critical stage of the coach–school relationship. Often overlooked and underestimated, characterised as overly complex and unrelatable, this chapter makes the case for evaluation being an essential part of the coaching programme. In doing so, it explains the four functions of an effective system: producing important data for financial accountability, connecting diverse stakeholders to a shared vision for education, and providing strategic insights into both learning and leadership. Using two case studies to illustrate versatility, the chapter explains how to direct soft skills to hard targets and provides yet more evidence of the potential of coaching as a positive accompaniment to learning.

Introduction: why evaluation gets overlooked

Evaluation is an administrative afterthought, generally consigned to *AOB* status on the coaching agenda. Admittedly, organisations and coaches share a common interest in financial accountability to balance the books or sell their wares but, on the whole, evaluation is overlooked and underestimated. However, when we consider the vast investments organisations make in the recruitment, development and retention of talent as they strive for leadership excellence to achieve competitive advantage, eschewing evaluation makes no sense. In our experience, evaluation is the poor relation in any coaching programme for two reasons: organisations are simply not interested and neither are coaches.

In their book *Evaluating the Impact of Leadership Coaching* (2022), Jamieson and Wall explain the reluctance of organisations to evaluate their coaching investments, in terms of four influencers: primary goals, evaluation status, multi-generational leadership pools and organisational context. Firstly, they argue that primary goals dominate the evaluation agenda and corral resultant data towards short-term targets, ignoring long-term goals. Secondly, that evaluation status reflects the immiscible environment and the tension between operational and strategic stakeholders. Thirdly, they suggest multi-generational leadership pools represent a demographic perfect storm in the workplace. Finally, they see the organisational context as synonymous with the unique cultural and political sensitivities at play in the organisation. If we then overlay the idiosyncratic nature of leadership, it is perhaps not surprising that evaluation is yet another task confined to the too difficult box.

If evaluation is to be taken seriously, coaches must play their part. Research carried out for the European Mentoring and Coaching Council (Wall et al, 2017) found that 90 per cent of coaches taking part expressed a negative attitude to evaluation, ranging from conceit and casual disregard to tendentious marketing advocacy. Many coaches believed that the coaching intervention was sufficient in itself and needed no further justification; others did not think it their place to *interfere in organisational politics*, while those who did attempt to evaluate impact produced incredulous self-serving rates of returns on investment (RoI), thereby entirely undermining the process.

Exploring influencers and commissioning research makes sense in a general organisational setting, and in the context of scholarly or practitioner interest in formulating an evaluation model. However, as a practical starting point for this chapter, the evaluation conundrum is best encapsulated in the following hypothesis: leadership coaching is a recognised spearhead strategy into which vast sums of money are invested. And yet, at a time of intense financial scrutiny and an abundance of theory, evaluation remains of little interest to investors; this suggests that evaluators are prepossessed with developing evermore ingenious systems rather than making evaluation a compelling proposition by arguing its relevance and potential. Accordingly, we set out to make the case for evaluation as part of a learning reset and show how a relevant and relatable system can be integrated into an educational setting.

Why schools should be interested in evaluation

In our book *Coaching Young People for Leadership*, the final chapter presents the case for evaluation of impact. In that book, we claim that evaluation needs to be seen as integral to any youth leadership coaching programme and, without it, the motives behind any investment (financial or intellectual) are brought into question. To encourage organisations to take evaluation seriously, we also accepted that they need to be incentivised to invest further time and effort into a time-consuming and complex function. Accordingly, we asserted that an effective evaluation mechanism serves two masters: financial accountability and strategic vision – was the investment value for money and what insights can we act on to ensure the future health of the organisation and those within?

Figure 8.1 The dual functions of evaluation

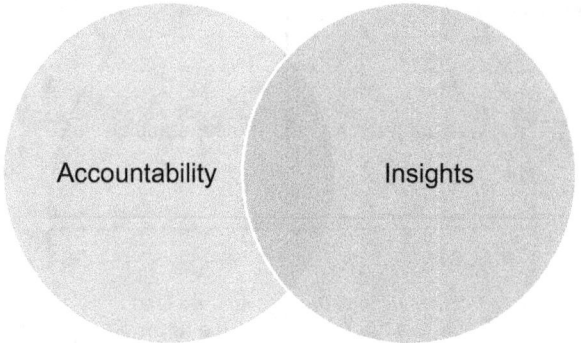

When we applied evaluation directly to the impact of coaching in schools, we found a more complex environment, specifically the gap between espoused values and actual evaluation targets. However, one of the main points of interest was the potential destination of strategic data. There are myriad questions from both sceptics and zealots, setting out to test or prove coaching as either yet another fad or a ground-breaking learning phenomenon upon which evaluation insights can be focused. But it is the worldview questions resulting from the ambitious nature of coaching, as a catalyst for radical change in the way we think about learning and leadership, that evaluation data can inform. Accordingly, we refined and expanded the functions of evaluation (Figure 8.2) to include local and worldview targets to ameliorate perplexities, convince schools to take it seriously and contribute to the wider debate around education and youth.

The four dimensions of evaluation in education

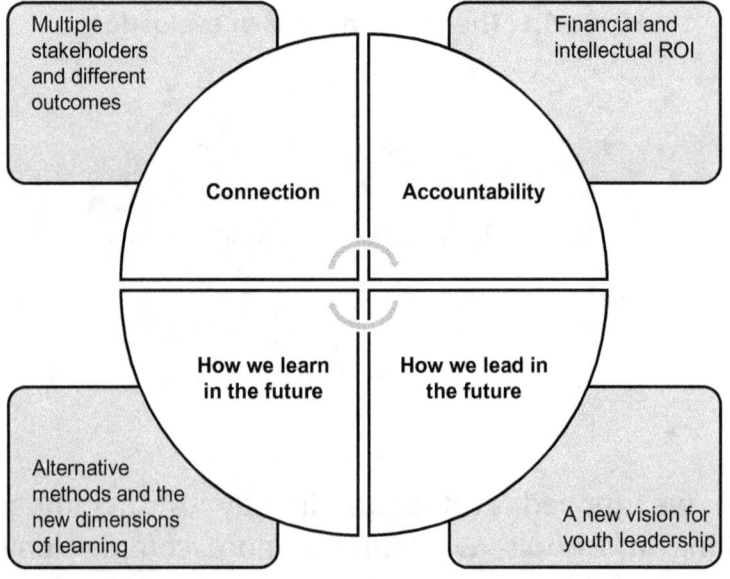

Figure 8.2 The four dimensions of evaluation in the context of coaching in the classroom

Connection

Evaluation is an opportunity to unravel the complexity of multiple stakeholders and interested parties by connecting diverse outcomes and motivations. Essentially, evaluation has the potential to bridge the gap between the current curriculum and the new dimensions of learning while acting as a balance mechanism to ensure a non-disruptive transition between the two.

Accountability

Financial and intellectual accountability are primary destinations for evaluation data. The interests of sponsors, partners, parents, schools and, primarily, young people are all served by evaluation. However, unlike other organisations, investors should be encouraged to focus on the non-cognitive changes seen in coachees rather than a short-term financial justification. Coaching in schools is at an embryonic nascent stage and evaluation should be focused on a return on intellectual investment at this time.

How we learn in the future

In this area, evaluation is setting out to answer the question: what is the impact of coaching on academic achievement and the learning experience? In practical terms, evaluation data can facilitate the integration of coaching as a legitimate learning companion to teaching and challenge current perceptions and systems for education. More specifically, data provides evidence of positive improvement of attitudes to learning across developmental and reorientation candidates triggered by coaching, including originality, independent thinking and critical analysis, all of which are transferable to the future workplace.

How we lead in the future

Leadership, constantly evolving, is seen as a moving target for evaluation. Focused on a new vision of leadership, evaluation insights challenge assumptions about young people, evince emerging leadership qualities and inform strategies about inclusion and well-being. In the wider sense, data informs the germinal theory of young people leading young people as a strategy to address youth issues across society.

How to evaluate the impact of leadership coaching in schools

Designing a framework for evaluating impact

Now that the evaluator has caught the attention of the school, a system can be designed. The starting point for any evaluation design is that it is assumed to be unique (to the individual and the school). Here, the coach's relationship with the school enters its third and final critical phase. By now, the coach will have built a fairly strong partnership with the school based on values, culture and outcomes. These conceptual values correspond with the practical stages of the coaching programme: inception, delivery and evaluation (Figure 8.3). At the inception stage, the coach is working with the school to align with broader values and aspirational goals. Once this has been achieved, the coach, in partnership with the school (teacher), is using an understanding of the school's culture and working environment to navigate barriers and deliver the programme. Finally, at the conclusion of a programme, the coach is focused on the school's tangible targets and outcomes to evaluate and disseminate evidence of impact.

Figure 8.3 The three critical stages of the coach–school relationship

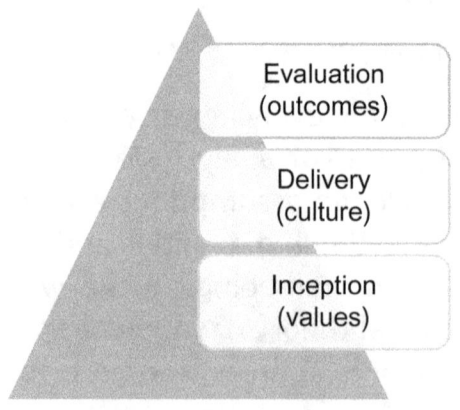

This final stage of the relationship calls upon a profound understanding of all three dimensions (values, culture and outcomes) as working parts of an evaluation framework. Designating impact points for evaluation to existing school targets is a relatively straightforward process; however, dissemination of relatable and useful resultant data requires a nuanced overview. For this overview, the coach is often looking to convince the school to look beyond financial accountability and conceive new criteria for success which are more complex – in other words, how to measure potential?

The premise for designing an evaluation framework in schools is to be able to provide evidence that soft skills outside of academic disciplines are capable of working inside the system to simultaneously achieve desired existing outcomes and enrich the student experience. This begins with a dedicated meeting with the school to discuss a single-item agenda: agreed outcomes. At this meeting, targets are defined within the context of the personality of the individual and aspirational goals of the school. To design an effective evaluation framework, the evaluator must first understand the evaluation context by distinguishing between different types of candidate and goals. The following two diverse case studies illustrate different approaches to evaluation in action.

CASE STUDY

Developmental leadership candidate

- **School:** Secondary comprehensive faith school (all boys) in London
- **Leadership candidate profile:** Head boy – developmental leadership candidate

→

- **Values:** Alongside a commitment to education, that every student understands their place in the community and wider society
- **Culture:** Combines the secular with the religious
- **Outcomes:** Accountability and insights (Table 8.1)

Table 8.1 Framework for evaluation outcomes

Accountability outcomes	Insights
Personal achievement	Assessing the impact (positive or negative) of leadership coaching on academic results. Assessing the impact of coaching as a learning methodology. Accumulating data for long-term career progression.
School goals	Does coaching, specifically leadership skills, transfer to school values and goals?
School targets	How does coaching impact on tangible school targets (short term and long term)?
Coaching	Can we evaluate and produce an RoI for the impact of leadership coaching on *potential*? Is this the most effective time for a coaching intervention?

Understanding the evaluation context

In this case study, we are setting out to evaluate the impact of a developmental leadership coaching programme on Sam, who at the end of Year 12 was appointed head boy for his final year. His inclusion in the programme (comprising six other members of the school's student senior leadership team) was suggested as a way to provide support for the role and help balance extracurricular responsibilities while working towards career-defining exams. As part of the appointment process for a school officer, Sam was invited to a meeting with the headteacher and head of sixth form to discuss his personal ambitions, along with the expectations of the school, for the year ahead. In summary, these comprised the following.

- Establish a stand-alone sixth form as a recognisable entity in its own right within the school.
- Establish and lead a mentoring culture throughout the school.
- Establish an advisory council to meet regularly with a reciprocal teacher group to discuss internal issues and new ideas.

He was then introduced to the leadership coach at a subsequent one-to-one introductory session. As part of a future evaluation framework, desired outcomes were agreed at this session and an individual coaching plan was designed to include anticipated development foci (Table 8.2).

→

Table 8.2 Sam's leadership coaching plan

Designated responsibilities	Impact points	Soft skills	Leadership coaching focus
Head of school duties	Impact and (short-term) legacy	Authentic voice	Personal leadership brand
Scholar	Academic achievement	Judgement Curiosity Active learning	Ambidexterity for time management and decision making
Establish sixth form identity	Culture change Events Wider contribution to school	Creativity and strategic innovation	Collaborative leadership Empowering delegation Vision and implementation
Establish a mentoring culture	Mentoring system Recruitment and development of mentors	Emotional intelligence	Developing coaching behaviours
Establish advisory council	Communication and organisational	Authoritative voice	Managing up Project management

Designing an evaluation framework

The tenure of Sam's leadership role is realistically two terms, during which he will have had regular coaching one-to-one sessions and at least three leadership group sessions with the other members of the cohort. This assumes the final term is preoccupied with exams and succession planning. Accordingly, the evaluation process begins towards the end of the second term. At this time, Sam was asked to complete an evaluation data collection form (Table 8.3).

This form has evolved from the leadership coaching plan. It reflects designated responsibilities in real terms as actual outcomes, while impact points in the original plan are now assessed as demonstrable impact in the context of evaluation of the impact of coaching. The final column connects the impact of coaching to an existing school target.

Creating value dimensions

Table 8.3 represents Sam's experience of coaching and is confined to qualitative anecdotal data, specifically reaction and learning dimensions. To arrive at value dimensions, the coach collaborates with the school to identify impact points as a basis to connect coaching foci to coachee performance. These outcomes are then aligned with school targets and eventual assessment of value (to the school). In this way, soft skills facilitated by coaching are connected to hard targets with the potential to be monetised (Table 8.4).

→

Table 8.3 Sam's completed evaluation data collection form

Actual outcomes	Demonstrable impact of coaching	Contribution to a school target
Visibility, achievements and initiatives	The coaching has helped me understand the personality of my leadership. This means I have enjoyed my time as head boy because I've been free to express myself as a leader rather than play a part. I have also learnt that leadership is an action and this has helped me to drive the new initiatives that were on my agenda. I think when I look back, I'll be proud of what I achieved as head boy.	To create happy, confident and respectful adults who will thrive in the future and make a positive contribution to wider society.
Academic progress	Having a coach was really helpful because juggling my duties and preparing for exams was something I was worried about. The coaching helped me make good choices about time management and gave me the confidence not to feel insecure about handing over my responsibilities to concentrate on revision.	Ofsted reporting and rating.

Evaluating the impact of coaching

To establish a distinct sixth form culture	The coaching was split into two sections: operational and strategic. Working on project management and organisational skills was a good basis for what we went on to achieve with this goal. Most importantly, the strategic thinking work we did really helped me to collaborate with the team for new ideas and delegate effectively.	To raise the profile of the school and attract new students to the sixth form.
To create a mentoring framework	I was able to transfer a lot of the coaching behaviours and thinking into the mentoring project. I think we have created something that will work well in the future because we have established some basic rules – not everyone is suited to being a mentor (careful selection) and those that are need to be supported and coached.	To promote inclusivity throughout the school. To provide an effective well-being and mental health support strategy.

→

Table 8.3 (Continued)

Actual outcomes	Demonstrable impact of coaching	Contribution to a school target
To represent pupils and liaise with staff	Coaching completely changed the way I thought about communication – on so many levels. The idea about using authentic and authoritative voices allowed me to get the best out of the team. But the ability to adapt communication to the needs and expectations of others meant that I was able to successfully (I think!) manage up and down. The meetings with teachers and student representatives we have held have a completely different vibe to anything else we do in school. It is like we've created a new dynamic where members of the group are all expected to listen with respect no matter what your status is outside the forum. This means we are engaging in conversations about new ideas rather than asking for permission.	To listen to the wider representative voice of the school to understand the needs of students and produce relevant initiatives.

Table 8.4 Creating value dimensions

Impact point	Coaching dimensions	Demonstrable impact	Contribution to a school target	Value dimension
Student	Ambidexterity. Judgement. Time management. Communication. Learning behaviours.	Exam results and university placement. Positive feedback from peers and teachers for head boy duties.	School league tables.	Ofsted rating. Teacher retention. Student recruitment. Student destinations (higher education and employment).
School	Project management. Collaboration.	Successfully established distinct sixth form culture, including: sixth form	Attract new students to sixth form.	Reputation and status.

→

Table 8.4 (Continued)

Impact point	Coaching dimensions	Demonstrable impact	Contribution to a school target	Value dimension
	Creativity and innovation. Commercial mindset.	fellowship scheme, business networking breakfast forum and TED talk discussion groups including external experts.	External partnerships and opportunities.	Student recruitment.
School community	Coaching behaviours for leadership. Organisational skills. Delegation. Running meetings. Authoritative voice.	Set up mentoring framework. Ran mentoring workshops using external speakers to develop mentoring behaviours, support future mentors and safeguard mentees. Formed student advisory panel with rotating membership	Inclusion, well-being and mental health strategies. Innovation and initiatives.	Higher attendance levels. Higher attainment.

			Sponsorships and commercial networks.
		across all academic years. Held regular forums with teachers to discuss issues and put forward new ideas.	
Wider community	Public speaking. External networking. Commercial and strategic mindset.	Invited to speak at external education forums: *How a mentoring culture in schools is good for your mental health.* Interviewed for article about career networking in schools.	Raise school profile in the local community. Student engagement.

→

The final phase of evaluation involves the retrieval of strategic data. Table 8.5 corresponds with the original framework (Table 8.1) for evaluation outcomes, revealing evaluation to be a rich source of strategic insights. In the framework, findings from the evaluation process are placed in the context of agreed impact points and interpreted as strategic data. In this case study, an additional coach impact point has been included for the benefit of the coach and future programme design (Table 8.5 is incomplete and the strategic data column contains prompts for the school and coach to work to).

Table 8.5 The destination of strategic data

Impact points	Areas for strategic data
Student	Enhancing academic achievement.
	Enriching the student experience.
	Student leadership.
School	Reputational standing and status.
School community	Mental health, well-being and inclusion strategies.
	Student issues and needs.
Wider community	Commercial strategies and partnerships.
	Careers advice, preparation and placement.
Coach	Advocacy for coaching as an accompaniment to learning.
	Design of future programmes.
	Evolving vision of youth leadership.
	New coaching methodologies and techniques.

Evaluating the Impact of Coaching

In this study, the school was able to use Table 8.4 as a framework to monetise the impact of the coaching on school targets for the purposes of financial accountability and future learning and development projects. At this stage, the coach stepped back from the evaluation process and financial assessment remained confidential and in-house. The coach then returned to the school for a final debrief session to disseminate and discuss strategic data.

CASE STUDY

Mining for valuable insights

- **School:** Secondary state school
- **Leadership candidate profile:** Year 10 reorientation leadership candidate
- **Coachee context:** Outside the academic mainstream and poor disciplinary record
- **Criteria for selection:** Intelligent disruptor
- **School outcomes:** Remedial (Table 8.6)

Understanding the evaluation context

Asif is in Year 10. He is considered to be a disruptive influence in his year group and disengaged (when he attends) in classroom activities; accordingly, his academic record is poor. Having discussed the counter-intuitive qualities of leadership candidates with the coach, his class teacher put him forward as a candidate

→

for reorientation coaching, describing him as an *intelligent disruptor*. His selection raised eyebrows among other teachers and this general scepticism was reflected in his coaching plan (Table 8.6).

In terms of evaluation, the focus is on correction and remedial outcomes that contribute to the school's record and Ofsted rating where there is a significant financial implication (for instance, Ofsted analysis puts the average cost of alternative provision for a student at £18,000 per year, while wider research (TES, 2017) suggests that the long-term cost to the taxpayer of excluding a child is up to £370,000). The impact points in this case study reflect areas of concern rather than responsibility (as with the developmental candidate in the previous study). As setting impact points is the school's prerogative, the coach and the coachee (in stark contrast with developmental candidates) are bystanders at this stage. This means that the coach and the school can sometimes find themselves at loggerheads and there is a requirement to re-prove the concept of coaching as a legitimate accompaniment to learning. Here, the coach is challenged to close the gap between the school's natural negative instinct for correction and the positive coaching methodology based on reframing and development. In this case, the coach uses the evaluation process, interpreting data in terms of the hard currency of school targets, relating non-cognitive skills to remedial outcome as part of a wider reorientation (as opposed to prevention) strategy while at the same time confirming the young person's potential and their leadership status (Table 8.7).

Table 8.6 School impact points and coaching targets as part of a prevention strategy for Asif

Impact points	Coaching dimensions	School targets
Attendance	Purpose	Full attendance
Punctuality	Time management	Positive attitude to timetable
Extracurricular	Social intelligence	Contribution to school activities
Curricular	Focus	Achievement points
Learning progression	Curiosity	Improved engagement
Absenteeism	Positive decision making	Zero truancy

CRITICAL DISCUSSION POINT

Reorientation versus prevention

Coaching Young People for Leadership (pp 96–7) discusses different perceptions of prevention, as a strategy to eradicate youth issues. Many of the charities, institutions and schools with whom we work, due to limited capacity, scant budgets and a default instinct to firefight, view *prevention* as a safety net – to catch a young person when they fall. The idea that prevention is characterised as a last resort before a catastrophic event accepts that outcomes are evaluated in terms

→

of reduction targets in problem areas such as exclusions, addiction, anti-social behaviour and poor mental health. This means that *prevention* can become a self-fulfilling prophecy because we miss opportunities to harness disruptive energies and reorient young people positively, empowering them to make positive choices to change their lives.

Alternatively, from the coach perspective, reorientation is a development strategy, as opposed to a remedial one. By accepting the personality traits of the young person and reframing these positively, the coach engages with the individual at a pivotal time, giving them responsibility over the choice of their future direction. Facilitated by a focus on leadership, young people are encouraged to reorient intrinsic behaviours, attitudes and assumptions to avoid catastrophic events by choosing a different pathway. Figure 8.4 shows the distinct characteristics of the two approaches.

Figure 8.4 Distinct prevention (left) and reorientation (right) characteristics

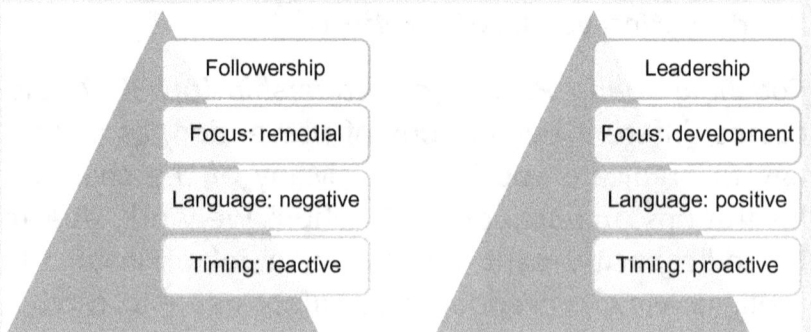

Table 8.7 illustrates the effect of coaching on Asif and on school impact points and the positive outcomes achieved by switching to a reorientation mindset.

Table 8.7 Qualitative data – impact of reorientation coaching on school targets

Impact points	Reorientation (leadership) coaching dimensions	Demonstrable impact (of coaching) on school target
Attendance	Awareness of others – how do my actions affect my colleagues? Self-awareness – what are my transferable skills?	I had to miss a morning of the coaching programme because of something at home. Normally, I would've just skipped the day and probably dropped out altogether. But I owed it to the others to carry on and when I turned up, I could tell they were surprised – they'd split my team up and given them to the other leaders. So, I got a different role, working with the coaches and going around the groups and helping out where I could – it was brilliant.
Punctuality	Awareness of others – what does my attitude to others say about me?	I was never on time; it was like my trademark. I now think being on time is an attitude; it's about being respectful. I respect the others on the programme so I'm always on time – even early – my teacher can't believe it.

→

Table 8.7 (Continued)

Impact points	Reorientation (leadership) coaching dimensions	Demonstrable impact (of coaching) on school target
Extracurricular	Self-awareness – why would anyone want to be led by me? Awareness of others – what do those in my team need from me?	We've started this leadership club and I help Miss organise the group and work with the younger kids as a kind of coach. They really get a lot out of it and I feel that I'm inspiring them to become future leaders.
Curricular	My leadership style – how do I motivate others?	For the project, we set up this Snapchat group so we could carry on after school. Some of my group were working on a drawing for the presentation … one made stickers and badges for the team.

Learning progression	Tools – using choice and judgement to achieve my goals Tools – taking responsibility for my learning Tools – original thinking and powerful questions	I don't enjoy lessons so I'm going to say that coaching is much better because it's interesting. But when I look back at what we achieved and the presentation we made, I think I actually learnt a lot more about the subject – more than I would've in class.
Absenteeism	Communication – finding my authoritative voice Awareness of others – others' motivations	The reason I truanted was because others were making personal comments about me in class. So, not only was I being bullied, but I was being punished for being bullied! As a leader, I have learnt to try to understand why people act the way they do rather than just react. This made me feel more in control and I spoke to Miss about it and she had no idea about what was going on. It wasn't like grassing but more like finding a solution together.

→

In this case study, the coach has applied leadership to the coaching dimensions in Table 8.6 to deliver a reorientation programme for Asif. In this context, the impact of coaching is remarkable and, even though the school can draw financial evaluation data by connecting Asif's improvement against the impact points and targets in Table 8.6, to overlook and disregard the reported qualitative data would be myopic. Here, the evaluation process emphasises resultant insights and, in the case of Asif, these are more usefully focused on the individual's progress rather than the school's strategic direction (as with the developmental candidate in the previous case study).

CRITICAL QUESTIONS

- As a teacher, how can you use the positive evaluation data attached to a reorientation candidate to capitalise on their potential in practical ways?
- What does the school's/coach's attitude towards evaluation say about them?
- As a coach, would you be prepared to work with a school that showed no interest in collaborating for evaluation? Explain your answer.

Unexpected data

As evaluators, we are also interested in informal evaluation data. This data is generally anecdotal but, nevertheless, gives us valuable clues as to the impact of coaching in the classroom. These clues are generally non-cognitive behaviours such as confidence, motivation and curiosity, of which we should be consciously aware. What we are looking for is evidence of change, both in attitudes of the school and the leadership candidate. For instance, a number of teachers with whom we partner go on to train as coaches as part of their continuing professional development, simultaneously helping to integrate coaching as an accompaniment to learning. Others set up leadership clubs and forums for pupils to provide real-life leadership experiences. Young people who have been through the programme express a keen interest in continuing coaching and actively seek out leadership opportunities, both in the school and externally in various clubs, societies or initiatives. Changes in attitude to social responsibility, taking on voluntary work and generally becoming involved by engaging with the wider world may not be easy to monetise, but they are treated joyously, as hard evidence by coaches of the impact they have had.

Further reading

Jamieson, M (2019) *The Evaluation of Leadership Coaching through a Lens of Ambidexterity*. University of Chester. [online] Available at: https://chesterrep.openrepository.com/handle/10034/622941 (accessed 26 January 2024).

References

Jamieson, M (2023) *Coaching Young People for Leadership*. St Albans: Critical Publishing.

Jamieson, M and Wall, T (2022) *Evaluating the Impact of Leadership Coaching: Balancing Immediate Performance with Longer Term Uncertainties*. London: McGraw-Hill Education (UK).

TES (2017) Excluding a Pupil 'Costs Taxpayer Up to £370k'. 10 October. [online] Available at: www.tes.com/magazine/archive/excluding-pupil-costs-taxpayer-ps370k (accessed 26 January 2024).

Wall, T (ed), Jamieson, M, Csigás, Z and Kiss, O (2017) *Research Policy and Practice Provocations: Coaching Evaluation in Diverse Landscapes of Practice – Towards Enriching Toolkits and Professional Judgement*. Brussels: European Mentoring and Coaching Council.

Part 3

HOW TO EMBED A COACHING CULTURE IN SCHOOLS

Chapter 9
MAKING SPACE FOR LEADERSHIP COACHING IN SCHOOLS

> **CHAPTER OVERVIEW**
>
> This chapter suggests how coaching can be practically embedded into an educational setting as part of an integrated learning experience and an aid to conventional school targets. It recognises the incongruence between an unfamiliar free-style development methodology and a rigid structured educational setting as a source of complexity and challenge for any coaching partnership. It argues that teachers and learners operate within a dysfunctional environment and, to accept an alien culture, the coach has to work within the system not against it. More specifically, an examination of the current environment reveals three systemic barriers to be overcome: time, transience and intransigence. Breaking these down, the chapter identifies and addresses five key characteristics of dysfunction and suggests practical frameworks as a basis to enable schools to make space for coaching as a companion to teaching. Finally, it discusses the space needed for teachers to adopt and use coaching behaviours to ensure that the coach's work has durability, long-term impact and the school has ownership of the design of any future leadership coaching culture.

The current environment

To make a compelling case for schools to accept youth leadership as a primary focus and coaching as a method of delivery, we must first investigate the current learning environment to understand systemic challenges and barriers. Embedding a leadership coaching culture in schools is a pinch-point for this book, where unconventional theories and conventional realities are set on a collision course. Here, the tension between the steady state and a new vision of learning is stretched to breaking point and it is how the coaching partnership can flex between these different points of view that will determine the success, or otherwise, of our project. In simple terms, we are asking schools to make the time and space for a left-field concept in an environment where it would not naturally be welcomed. From our experience, there are three barriers that characterise the current learning environment and inhibit schools from embracing a leadership coaching culture: time, transience and intransigence.

Why teachers struggle to manage time

Are teachers poor time managers? This is an intentionally provocative question designed to open up a wider discussion around the environment within which they operate. In our experience, teachers are no better or worse than most professionals at managing their time; what they are is time poor.

From a coaching perspective, we interpret time management issues at their source: lapses in professional judgement or the inability to prioritise important goals over urgent targets. In most instances, organisations are highly receptive to expeditious leadership behaviours as they clearly contribute to a primary goal. Furthermore, leaders in these organisations generally work within a flexible structure that expects them to exercise some latitude in the pursuit of strategy. Schools are distinct because they do not have this flexible structure built in; teachers are not afforded the same leadership status as, say, a middle manager in other sectors, and accordingly there is very little emphasis on personal leadership development programmes to support strategic autonomy. In other words, teachers are expected to work within a rigid system and to a strict timetable, focused on primary goals of which they have no ownership and disconnected from their original (vocational) purpose. As part of the collateral damage from being time poor, becoming disconnected from purpose is one of the most common reasons for low morale in teachers we work with:

> *I became a teacher to make a difference, but I simply don't have the time to do anything more than the bare minimum. Each year, I make a list of new academic year's resolutions that try to capture the enthusiasm I once had – the motivation. I have all these ideas when I have the time and space in the summer holidays – anything seems possible.*
>
> S, Leeds

Institutional transience trumps discretionary efforts

If lack of time ownership restricts autonomy and removes teachers from their purpose, institutional transience reminds them that they also have a lack of strategic ownership, restricting their creative space and negating the discretionary efforts they are prepared to exert. Evidence that teachers are abandoning the profession in record numbers (DfE, 2022) illustrates that time and space afforded by school holidays to renew energies and motivation have their limitations. Returning to school in September, there is the realisation that time spent during the summer months preparing and planning exciting new activities is wasted as timetables change, classes get moved and new operational non-learning initiatives are enforced. The systematic shifting sands upon which teachers are required to work make it impossible for them to plan ahead and they are resigned to churning out the same lessons and schemes of work, as schools seemingly prioritise operational detail over creative learning partnerships.

> *There's a drive for equality with all learners getting the same content and experience. Then there's the uniform, Progress 8, Attainment 8, SEND, LAC, PLAC, behaviours and attitudes, equipment, punctuality ... this leaves no space to expand their [pupils'] minds, to discuss an interesting topic, to develop learning skills in different ways.*
>
> L, London

Curriculum intransigence

Despite the moving targets resulting from institutional transience, teachers are restricted by an obdurate learning environment that slavishly adheres to a knowledge-rich curriculum. Schools, with the exception of some independent or free schools, generally strive to standardise learning by offering the same curriculum and the same experience. Thematically, this book has alluded to schools setting out to create *generation sameness* – young people who have the same qualifications and interpretations of knowledge as a result of being passive participants in the school curriculum – in contrast to the requirements of independent thought and originality needed to thrive in the future.

> *Secondary school education is shackled to its Victorian foundations and unfortunately the government response is to add more hours to the school day – where other organisations are becoming more and more flexible about working hours – and do more English and maths. That isn't school improvement; it's just going around in ever-decreasing intellectual circles.*
>
> A, Manchester

A dysfunctional environment

To navigate the institutional landscape to make space for experimentation with new learning ideas, schools need a very deliberate shift in mindset and behaviours. They must first accept that the three inhibitors described above are a result of a dysfunctional environment. In supporting schools to make space for coaching, we use an adapted version of Lencioni's Five Dysfunctions of a Team model (Lencioni, 2002), expanding the original focus to encompass the overarching operating environment within which their professionals have to perform (Figure 9.1).

Figure 9.1 The characteristics of a dysfunctional environment and resultant inhibitors

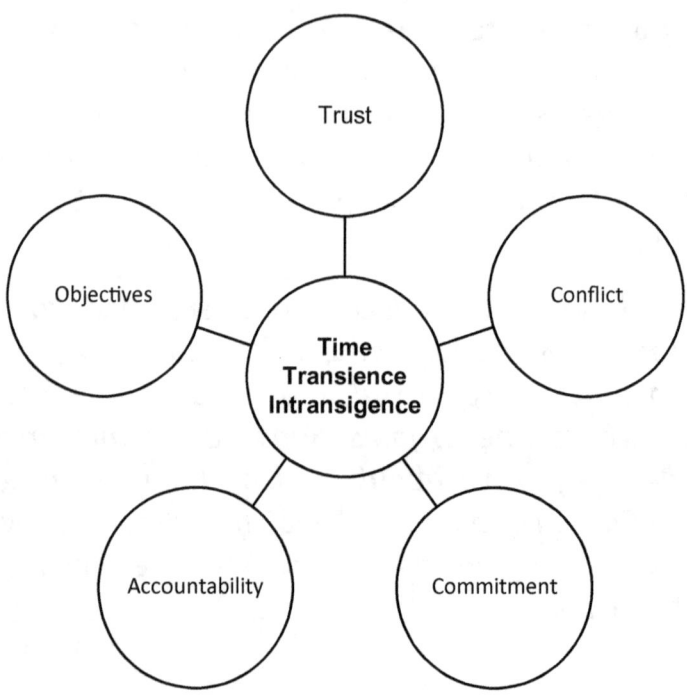

In our version, we focus on the operating environment's impact on professionals rather than the idiosyncrasies and insecurities of the individual as part of a team blocker.

Trust

In our research and in informal conversations with teachers, there is a sense that a lack of trust pervades the current education system. The rigidity of structures and the constant flow of new legislation create untenable demands on teachers' time and restrict creative space. Instead of guidelines, professionals are subject to highly systemised rules and regulations, while inflexible boundaries discourage discretionary energy. The environment is seemingly designed from a negative viewpoint emphasising control over freedom of expression. This implicit lack of trust in teachers is not only time consuming but demoralising.

Conflict

When trust is absent, conflict, or more relevantly, fear of conflict, characterises an environment striving to capture a steady state with no drive to innovate or move forward. The hierarchies in schools and the opaque criteria for promotion find teachers more inclined to toe the career line than pursue positive conflict with colleagues. Here, the environment is designed to accommodate conformists over challengers (as with pupils). Furthermore, without the benefit of coaching investments, where personal insecurities can be negated by professionalising behaviour, teachers can be overly sensitive to what they perceive as criticism from others and, in turn, are inclined to avoid conflict with colleagues. In this environment, innovation is stilted and major issues are gossiped about in corridor conversations rather than explored in formal strategy meetings.

Commitment

Teachers are vocational careerists and the current environment ensures that, for most, it is only a matter of time before they become disconnected from their original purpose through the intransigence of the curriculum and/or the system. Unrelatable transient targets and goals that are not germane to the original ambitions of teachers (why they joined) mean that they are disengaged in a shared outcome and lack real commitment. An environment where there is a lack of commitment is a basis for underperformance; however, it is the fallout from teachers' diminishing morale and low motivation that means nothing is likely to change and the steady state is maintained.

Accountability

The dysfunctional environment is a contradictory space for accountability. Trust, conflict avoidance and a lack of commitment to a common cause mean that schools operate in a blame culture and accountability becomes skewed and irrelevant. There is little appetite to hold the system to account, challenge systemic fault lines or champion new ideas and actions. Where there is a disconnect from goals and purpose, accountability criteria become meaningless except at a tick-box level. At the same time, standards and values are accepted as rhetoric to which no one can be held.

Objectives

Despite mission statements, manifestos and charters, the characteristics of a dysfunctional environment undermine the school's primary goals. In other words, it is not the clarity of intention, as it so often is, that results in inattention to objectives, but the lack of ownership and belief that means teachers are disloyal to the cause. In this context, no amount of management tools or KPIs can negate the lack of emotional connection to objectives.

In essence, the dysfunctional environment is unwelcoming to the vocational careerist who thrives on autonomy, trust, consistency and strategic agility. It is also a citadel for the steady state, protective of familiar principles and suspicious of change. It is the dysfunctional environment against which teachers and coaches must steel themselves if they are to make space for a leadership coaching culture in schools.

How to make space for a leadership coaching culture in schools

Given a dysfunctional environment, how can schools make space for a new vision of leadership and an unconventional (to pupils) development methodology? At first glance there would appear to be two choices: change it or work with it.

Changing a dysfunctional environment: the impractical solution

In its original form, Lencioni's model is designed as a potential roadmap for coaches to follow when working with leadership teams. Its overarching purpose is to tackle the root causes of organisational politics and reorient failing teams so that the sum of the whole is greater than its parts. As with many coaching models, it is hierarchical, meaning that each level needs to be completed before moving on to the next. This format allows the coach to compartmentalise individual issues and guide the group to find singular solutions that contribute to the whole. Its popularity with coaches and organisations alike is down to its immediate relatability, as well as its capacity to simplify complex political issues by isolating them and placing them in the wider context. However, in schools the leadership authority is fractured, inasmuch as education practitioners have minimal influence on primary goals and direction of travel, and the system is an unwieldy behemoth. The coach simply does not have the capacity or, more importantly, the remit to work with the individual groups of protagonists (Figure 9.2) as a way of embedding a leadership coaching culture.

Figure 9.2 An impractical solution – the span of coaching needed to influence culture in an individual school

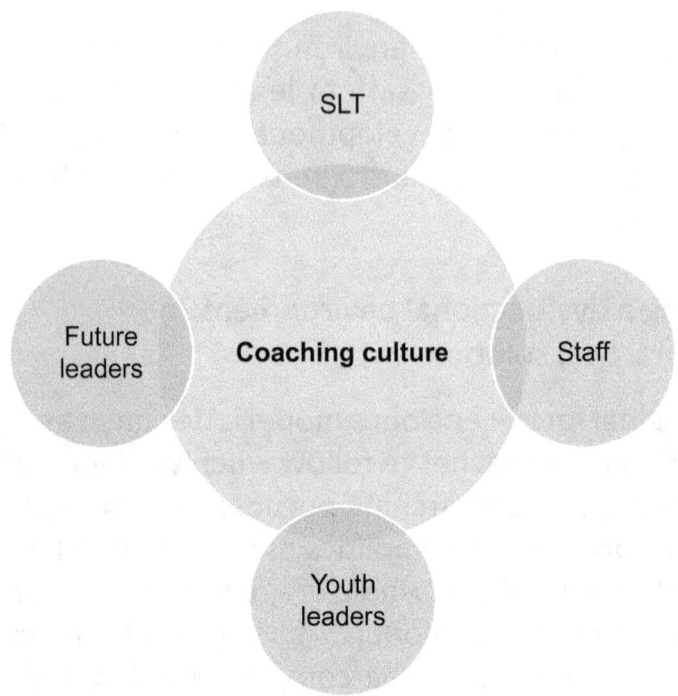

Working with the system

Rather than collide with the environment, we adopted a Trojan horse approach with schools, whereby we aligned leadership coaching with the accepted language, theories and outcomes of conventional education as a companion to teaching and learning. Therefore, we did not attempt to embed leadership coaching in the environment but infiltrate the school curriculum by connecting it to relevant academic targets. In Chapters 4 and 6, we present detailed case studies of Trojan horse projects where we have connected coaching, active and self-regulated learning to relatable educational outcomes.

The Education Endowment Foundation (2021) defines self-regulated learning as a breakdown of three components: cognition, metacognition and motivation. In Figure 9.3, we present a framework used at the proposal stage of a leadership coaching project with a school. In this instance, we have used the recognisable components of self-regulated learning to connect coaching and leadership to a given school task. The framework should be treated as a template where different learning methodologies and specific school targets including intangibles can be dropped in.

Figure 9.3 Template for leadership coaching proposal

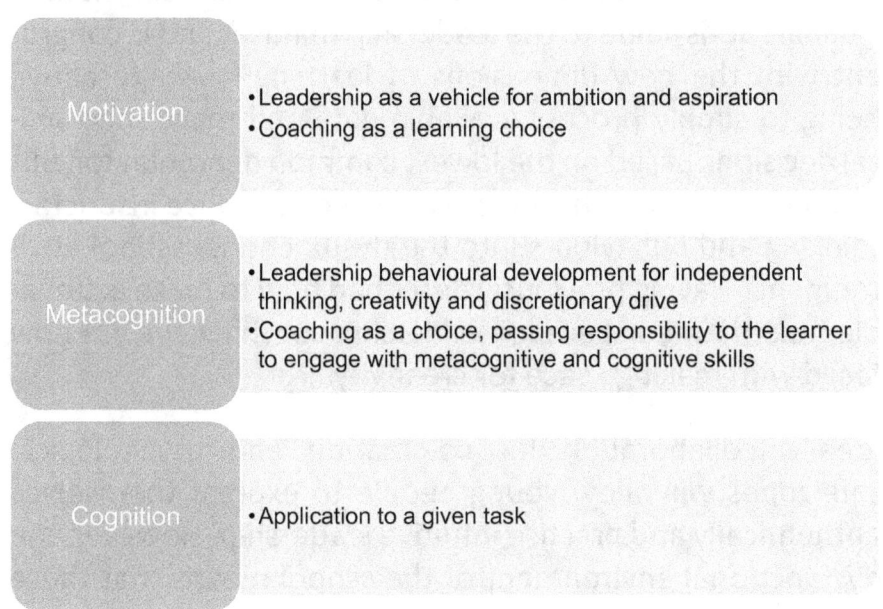

- Motivation
  - Leadership as a vehicle for ambition and aspiration
  - Coaching as a learning choice

- Metacognition
  - Leadership behavioural development for independent thinking, creativity and discretionary drive
  - Coaching as a choice, passing responsibility to the learner to engage with metacognitive and cognitive skills

- Cognition
  - Application to a given task

Making space for intangibles

Let us remember that school outcomes are not one-dimensionally focused on academic results but include intangible goals such as inclusion, mental health and well-being.

In our experience, any leadership coaching programme can be pivoted using the framework in Figure 9.3 to include subjective intangible outcomes. For instance, the case study in Chapter 4 (Ambassadors of Difference) is a leadership coaching programme designed as part of a wider strategy for inclusion. What is more challenging for the coach is to get the school to make space for intangible instincts, such as intuition and imagination, that contribute to the development of the young leader's mindset and a new way of thinking about learning.

Why should we care about instinctive thought processes such as intuition or imagination? Generally, exercising human instincts adds value to the leadership mindset and is congruent with the new dimensions of learning, the alternative being to simply process available data and make mechanical decisions based on the lowest common denominator. But how do we explain the inexplicable and introduce instinctive thinking and behaviours into the dysfunctional school environment? Having previously described how to make actionable task-oriented space for leadership coaching, we are now faced with making space for creativity.

Ideally, collaboration for co-creation and psychological safe zones will allow young people to express themselves authentically and practise intuitive leadership. However, the dysfunctional environment of the school means that these ideas are a fiction, along with other notions such as curiosity, enquiry and judgement. For instance, the intransigence of the curriculum means that curiosity is neither expected nor required, but optional. Enquiry emphasises answers rather than great questions and calls on judgement are limited to personal behaviours and attitudes rather than an expression of free thinking. So, how does the school make space for intangibles as part of a leadership coaching programme? By connecting soft skills to hard targets.

In the framework (Figure 9.4) selected intangibles are connected to actions that teachers can take and then aligned with school targets. This particular school is focused on academic results, the reputation of the school in the local community and its growing status in wider (schools) society. By purposefully engaging with recognisable leadership behaviours, teachers can create the space for leadership coaching and the development of intangibles with one eye on the curriculum or desired school outcomes.

Figure 9.4 Template framework – connecting soft skills to hard targets to make space for intangibles

Autonomy for judgement to contribute to school community	• Leadership: an expectation for independent thinking • Coaching to take personal responsibility for decisions and choices, making space for instinctive thought processes
Delegation for curiosity to achieve academic goals	• Empowerment through positive and supported delegation • Expectation for active learning through developed curiosity
Intention for enquiry to engage with wider society	• Clear goals and task setting • Ownership of goals and engagement through active enquiry

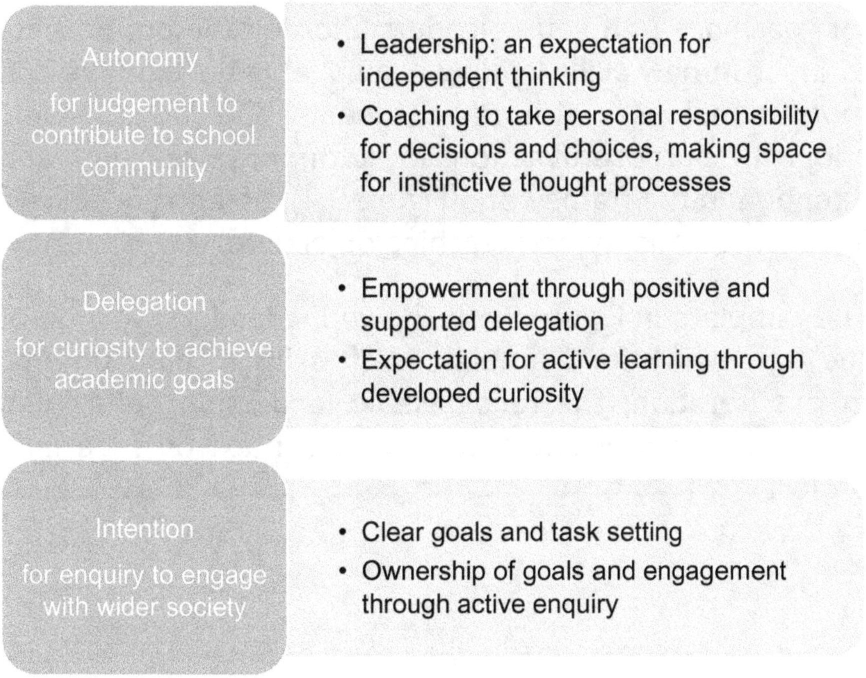

CRITICAL QUESTION

- How would you introduce instinctive intangible learning skills such as intuition into your lessons?

Working with the curriculum

Many of our leadership coaching programmes have been delivered as part of intense projects or workshops aligned to the curriculum but in addition to the school's provision. Therefore, one way to look at introducing leadership coaching is to identify leadership opportunities in the curriculum. For instance, most schools now follow a spiral curriculum model where learners revisit the same topics, each time deepening their understanding. Here, there is a legitimate entry point for coaching, with young leaders afforded the opportunity to practise new skills leading cognitive, metacognitive and motivational tasks with other students. The young leaders adopt the purposeful actions of autonomy, delegation and intention in the framework (Figure 9.4), essentially delivering peer-led quality-first teaching objectives.

The template in Figure 9.5 is the young leaders' version of the framework for connecting soft skills to hard targets. In this iteration, the recognisable leadership behaviours are shown as real outcomes in the context of a learning project.

Figure 9.5 Young leaders' version of template framework for connecting leadership behaviours to real outcomes in the context of an academic task

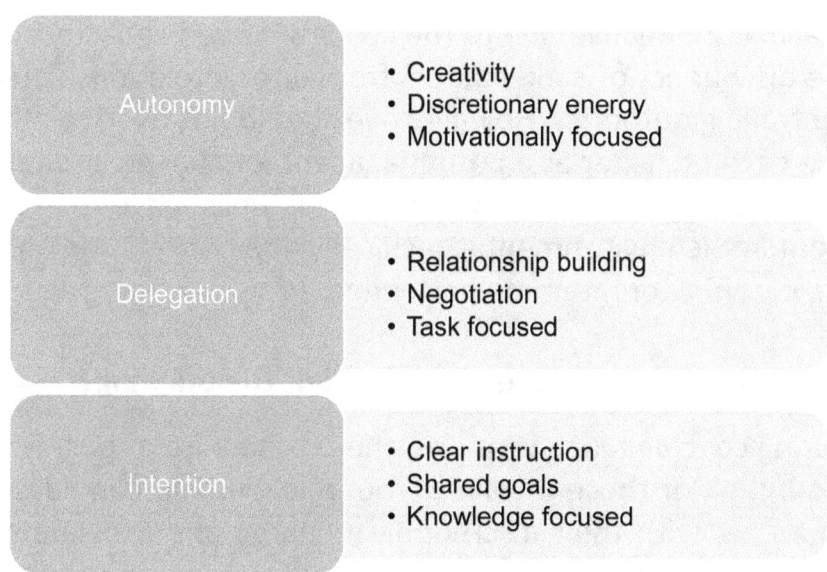

In this example, the young person is actively engaged as a leader of a group of students, focused on autonomy, delegation and intention. Almost inadvertently, the young leader is immersed in learning as part of a spiral curriculum model, revisiting the topic over and over again in their capacity as an expert, guiding and instructing younger pupils towards an end goal.

Making space for teachers

In this chapter we have concentrated on the dysfunctional environment as a mitigation for the seemingly immiscible relationship between leadership coaching and the current education system. Accordingly, we have designed frameworks to accommodate, rather than challenge, the system and employed Trojan horse strategies to gain entry. We have so far prioritised these strategies over individual coaching targets to change the system, which we describe as impractical and ineffective due to the coach's limited capacity and the disconnect of stakeholders from a remote and isolated controlling authority. However, we should not overlook the role of the teacher as a potential agent for change and take the time to explore opportunities for their active engagement in the environment, specifically at a critical time once the coaching programme has ended.

What happens once the coach has left the building?

During coaching interventions, there is an aura of positivity around all of those involved. Young leadership candidates amaze us with their discretionary energy and accelerated learning, and teachers become creative hubs contributing new ideas and perspectives to the project. In terms of visible impact, reorientation candidates show a huge spike in short-term progress, specifically in attitude and engagement in school activities, while developmental candidates now have licence through coaching to plot pathways towards long-term ambitions. However, this chapter is not focused on assessing the impact of coaching but on its long-term sustainability as part of the learning and development fabric of the school. Therefore, the critical question is, what next? How do we prevent teachers from returning to that inhibitive space that characterises the dysfunctional environment? Because, regardless of short-term success, coaching young people for leadership is destined to fail without self-sufficient (from the school) continuity.

> **CRITICAL QUESTIONS**
>
> - How would you maintain momentum once a coaching programme has finished?
> - What are the particular environmental challenges you face?

At this critical moment in the coaching process, we believe that teachers can have an active say in the success (or not) of the programme and the future direction of youth leadership coaching in the school. If we are to make space for a coaching culture, then teachers need to play an active part and schools must make the space for them to so do. To secure this space we must first understand the practical implications of navigating a dysfunctional environment and the operational space needed. If the coaching partnership is to work with, not against, the system, teachers need to:

- plan, co-ordinate, implement and review the impact of the leadership coaching intervention;
- exploit links and opportunities for leadership and creative learning within the curriculum;
- develop their own coaching behaviours.

To deliver these operational essentials, schools must somehow design a safe space outside of the wider dysfunctional environment. In other words, schools need to be prepared to act independently within the system. From our research and experience of working with teachers and senior leadership teams, four mechanisms emerged: real time, value, continuing professional development (CPD) and will (Figure 9.6).

Figure 9.6 The four mechanisms to create a safe space for teachers

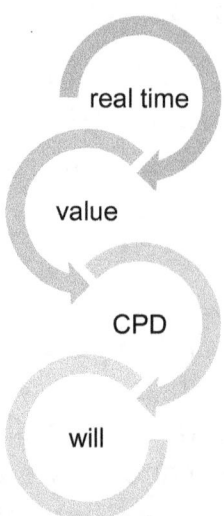

Real time

We have previously discussed the fact that the environment within which teachers operate means that they are time poor. Furthermore, the transience of the workplace means that time management is a reactive function rather than a deliberate action. In our experience, teachers are constantly called from programmes to cover for absentees or respond to unexpected contingencies. However, teachers are not only time poor; they are real-time poor. By real time, we mean purposeful blocks of uninterrupted time as opposed to 45-minute snatches here and there. If teachers are to make space for reflection and personal creativity, they need to be afforded dedicated quality time. This can be achieved by reallocating non-contact time (intended for administrative and operational management) to create meaningful stretches of real time that allow the teacher space for reflection and intellectual creativity as well as day-to-day chores.

Value

Placing value on coaching is a major problem for schools. The fact that schools prioritise urgent routine tasks for teachers over their involvement in important innovative learning programmes and place emphasis on mundane (but categorised as essential) operational tasks is indicative of coaching as an undervalued resource. There are two reasons schools undervalue coaching: firstly, they do not currently pay for it (in general, most of our programmes are funded by an external sponsor) and, secondly, it sits outside of the curriculum. To achieve buy-in, individual schools must look to their leadership. Attitudes to coaching and the value attributed to it are generated from the top. SLTs must provide collective endorsement for not only coaching programmes but a wider coaching culture capable of incorporating the operational essentials (plan, exploit, develop) and the real time teachers need.

Development

We have previously discussed teachers as a misdirected focus for coaching. However, in the context of integrating a leadership coaching culture, coaching becomes a significant intervention for advocacy, practice and continuity. Accepting that limited investment in coaching is likely to be a choice between different groups of coachees, we would obviously promote young people as primary candidates. But if schools have created real time for teachers and bought in to reflective practice, continuing professional development including coaching behaviours is positively insinuated, endorsed and encouraged.

As part of the cascade effect from SLT buy-in, CPD is reoriented away from conventional professional practice towards soft skills, creativity and innovation. In this way it becomes an intellectual stimulant and a space to explore pioneering ideas. In our various conversations with teachers, there is a real appetite for intellectual development as a way of remaining connected to purpose. If teaching talent is to be retained, teachers need to be kept interested in their work.

Will

Coaching is a choice. In the same way that learners are invited to choose their approach and application to academic targets, teachers have a choice about how they interact with the coaching culture. The first three mechanisms in our model make way for the teacher to facilitate a coaching culture, but where there is a way there must also be a will. This is the psychological space teachers need to find.

The will to act is not straightforward. Failure to make choices despite having the skills and a genuine commitment to cultural change cannot always be blamed on individual recalcitrance. Organisational psychologists suggest that a psychological dynamic called *competing commitment* (Kegan and Lahey, 2001) is at play here, where a subconscious bias undermines our efforts towards a shared goal. In the wider organisational context, this theory explains an individual's difficulty in committing to an agreed strategy as part of a personality flaw, which, once diagnosed, can be coached out. In schools, we found that *competing commitments* were more likely as a result of the teacher becoming institutionalised by the system, where long-held assumptions have become reality. Therefore, radical departures from familiar operating systems are treated with suspicion or half-heartedly because of the number of short-lived initiatives that have come and gone and the underlying belief that nothing ever changes. Accordingly, a psychological dimension needs to be added to the three operational mechanisms to support and encourage teachers to commit.

Progress towards these four mechanisms is likely to be phased over the longer term, which means that internal funding and investment for programmes and operational roles like coaching co-ordinator will have to wait. On a positive note, a gradual evolution means that leadership coaching is likely to emerge as an established part of the curriculum rather than a short-term fad.

> **CRITICAL QUESTION**
>
> - Given a regular tranche of real time, how would you make space for reflective practice?

A final irony

You might perhaps appreciate the irony of an environment specifically designed for functionality being described as dysfunctional. As this chapter unfolded, despite being written as a practical guide, we were constantly being drawn back into the wider debate around education, covered in the earlier conceptual chapters in the book. Therefore, choosing to work within the system rather than trying to change it does not reflect a lack of ambition but a practical realisation that the real politics of education are currently outside of our reach. We accept that making space for leadership coaching is a complex multi-dimensional conundrum to which we don't have all the answers, but early inroads made suggest that, in time, the environment will evolve to naturally accommodate coaching as an accepted mainstream way of learning.

References

Department for Education (DfE) (2022) Research at DfE. [online] Available at: www.gov.uk/government/organisations/department-for-education/about/research (accessed 26 January 2024).

Education Endowment Foundation (2021) *Metacognition and Self-regulated Learning:* Guidance Report. [online] Available at: https://d2tic4wvo1iusb.cloudfront.net/production/eef-guidance-reports/metacognition/EEF_Metacognition_and_self-regulated_learning.pdf?v=1706320906 (accessed 26 January 2024).

Kegan, R and Lahey, L (2001) The Real Reason People Won't Change. *Harvard Business Review*, November 2001.

Lencioni, P (2002) *The Five Dysfunctions of a Team*. San Francisco, CA: Jossey-Bass.

Chapter 10
PSYCHOLOGICAL DIMENSIONS

CHAPTER OVERVIEW

This chapter sets out to explore the psychological dimensions of coaching in the classroom. We examine how educational psychology currently serves young people and how a relationship with coaching might work. Drawing on our experience of working with educational psychologists, we investigate the shared challenges of the dysfunctional environment, characterised by idealised goals and mundane solutions. Based on the premise that coaching reimagines extraordinary behaviours, to be developed rather than fixed, we suggest a new model for the triumvirate relationship – coaching, psychology and education – that directly interacts with the learner via clearly defined but complementary roles.

Introduction: four questions

Coaches need not be psychologists but they do need to have a relationship with psychology. The current emphasis in schools on mental health and well-being amplifies the call to coaches to become familiar with the psychological dimensions of learning currently embedded in the school system. Accordingly, this section focuses on four fundamental questions: how does educational psychology currently serve young people? Does educational psychology crowd out coaching or make space for it? What is the relationship between educational psychology and coaching? What are the psychological dimensions of coaching learners? This chapter sets out to investigate these questions as a basis for a collaborative model, guiding schools and coaches working together to enhance learning in a psychological context.

How does educational psychology serve young people?

To assess the effectiveness of educational psychology in serving the needs of learners, we observed how educational psychologists (EPs) interacted with the dysfunctional environment in schools. We found that despite high ambitions to respond to the psychologically problematic areas in education, the current system underserved learners by providing reactive mundane solutions to highly complex issues. Here, the dysfunctional environment within which EPs operate is characterised by budgetary restrictions, local politics and a lack of investment (intellectual and financial) in external research to deliver durable and radical solutions. We arrived at four underlying reasons to back up our assertion that learners are underserved: non-collaboration, default attitudes, subjective judgements and lack of expert knowledge. To address these areas, we began by looking at the role of the EP and their place in the system.

The role of the educational psychologist

As part of the relationship-building process with schools, we have gone out of our way to understand the different perspectives of our colleagues. We found EPs to be highly receptive to the work we were doing in the classroom and professionally curious about coaching as an accompaniment to learning. Young people with special educational needs and/or disabilities (SEND) emerged as the primary focus for EPs, where pupils are deemed to be in need of *above and beyond* quality first teaching (QFT) at a high-quality level to reach age-appropriate expectations for a given academic year. This is perhaps unsurprising and symptomatic of the reactionary approach taken by schools (according to available data, the number of young people reported to have special educational needs (SEN) is on an upward trajectory, with 13 per cent of learners in schools classified as SEN support, while 4.3 per cent of pupils have an education, health and care plan (Gov.UK, 2023)).

Initially, we set out to understand the relationship between EPs and schools. Our starting point was to accept that EPs, unlike coaches, are already embedded in the system and therefore operate within a homogeneous job description as part of a standardised strategy to deliver agreed institutional targets. Accordingly, Figures 10.1 and 10.2 provide a thumbnail description of the role of the EP. In Figure 10.1, the formal job description of the EP is defined, describing the cycle of functions employed to make assessments and intervene with those who have difficulty in learning and social behaviours. Figure 10.2 represents a graduated response strategy generally used by schools as a framework for interventions.

Figure 10.1 The functions of the educational psychologist

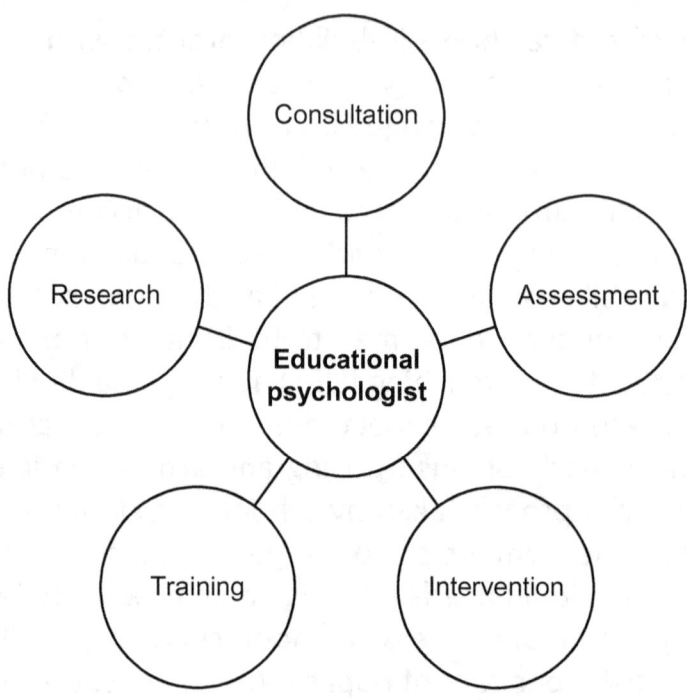

Figure 10.2 A graduated response framework for interventions

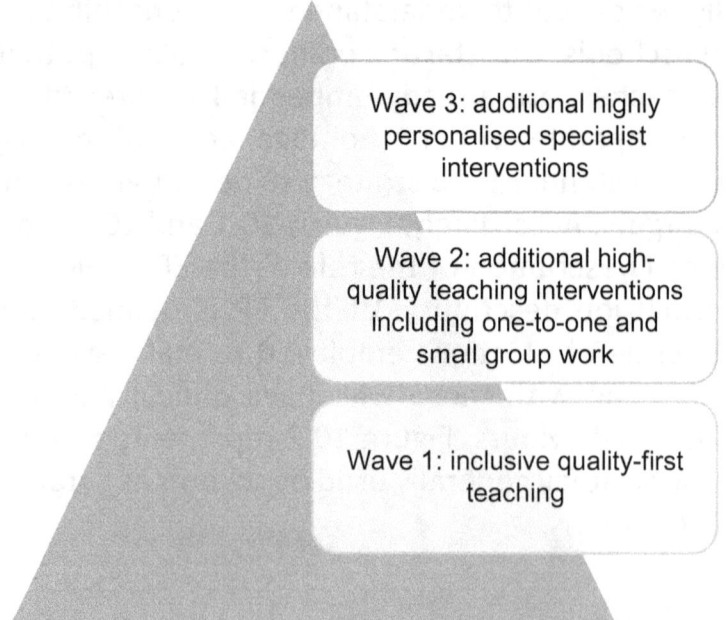

In practice, we found this operating system produced a very one-sided relationship, characterised by convenient delegation, where schools were using EPs as conduits for additional support, as a way to abdicate responsibility for learners with special needs or complex behaviours. In turn, being straitjacketed by the system meant that, as with many teachers, EPs are liable to become detached from their vocation as they are called upon to deliver tasks aligned to dominant non-vocational targets, specifically for assessment and intervention, rather than explore and research new ideas and their application.

> *I am overrun with statutory assessments for EHCPs (education, health and care plans). It seems to me that schools are only really interested in getting SEN into the system. I am basically seen as a tick-box for referrals to alternative provision. Often, I've had no input into the acceptance process.*
>
> A, educational psychologist, Manchester

And, whereas a graduated response strategy is undoubtedly an intelligent way of controlling focused interventions for SEN, ensuring that the young person is not overwhelmed, the dominance of school targets means that interventions are always remedial and reactionary rather than developmental and preventionist.

> *Basically, we get called in when the school doesn't know what to do with the young person because they don't fit in. When what's needed is above and beyond what they can offer – not in terms of the actual offering but the best way to offer it. By then, it feels too late...*
>
> K, educational psychologist, Bradford

Perhaps the most damning indictment we found of EPs' relationship with schools was the reported lack of emphasis on training and research and the space afforded to experiment and explore new ideas, applying non-cognitive solutions to cognitive or behavioural problems.

> *Yes, I'm worried about this tick-box mentality that governs schools. Take absenteeism – ghost children – that's a big issue and, if I'm honest, I think EPs are complicit by just being part of the system and accepting it. The DfE (Department for Education) say that we all share responsibility for improving attendance by creating spaces where young people want to be and are motivated to learn. That's all well and good, but the key to keeping kids in school is to focus on their individual psychological needs – make them feel included and then work on their self-esteem. That's why standards are declining; young people simply don't have the psychological space to succeed academically.*
>
> S, educational psychologist, Surrey

From an understanding of the educational context – the unique psychological dysfunctional environment – for EPs, and the subordinate relationship with schools, four reasons emerged as to why learners are underserved: non-collaboration, default attitudes, subjective judgements and lack of expert knowledge.

Four reasons why educational psychology underserves learners

Non-collaborative relationship

EPs appear to accept the role of subordinate partner in the relationship they have with schools and this means that they do not have to fit into the system because they are already part of it. The school's relationship is generally with the Child and Adolescent Mental Health Services (CAMHS) or the local authority educational psychology services; therefore, it could be argued, EPs lack the autonomy of coaches (as external consultants). However, despite being generally compliant, the peripheral role of EPs becomes a point of high tension when professional integrity is called into question: specifically, the lack of opportunities to collaborate, using teacher's insights into the personalities of learners to positively affect outcomes. Many of the EPs we talked to were frustrated by this, adding to the overhanging sense of tick-box functionality seemingly applied to their role and a missed opportunity to contribute to early intervention prevention strategies.

Default attitudes

Throughout our work, we found many similarities between the challenges faced by EPs and those faced by coaches to integrate effectively into schools. Generally speaking, these arise when the dysfunctional environment rejects intangible dimensions of youth development and support, in favour of the tangible targets that constitute the rigid education mindset. In terms of educational psychology, the intractability of schools to look beyond entrenched mainstream academic outcomes means that two overarching themes emerge: firstly, schools are generally focused on the deficit of the child and, secondly, the special educational needs of learners are pathologised. Along with a preoccupation with averages, these two themes say a lot about the relationship that schools have with psychology, specifically where extraordinary behaviours (non-mainstream) are treated as psychologically abnormal. This is a specific iteration of the dysfunctional environment for EPs.

> *Their attitude is — what is wrong with the child, why can't they access what schools teach? This means that targets get skewed and assessment criteria can be at odds with our work. It's not a great place to start from.*
>
> M, educational psychologist, London

Subjective judgements

The main focus for the EP is SEN; however, many of the practitioners we worked with agreed that outside of those categorised as SEN, there remains a large number of pupils who are not achieving age-appropriate expectations but are unclassified and left to drift in the mainstream. As coaches we were interested in the criteria for classification and, due to the systematic nature of the EPs' work, we expected a rigorous framework for assessment. What we found was the opposite:

> *It's crazy, it's down to the perception of the school — or even the individual teacher. It is purely a subjective opinion which means there is a lot of inconsistency and kids get overlooked.*
>
> R, educational psychologist, London

The implications of subjective judgements were asserted to be a major concern to the EPs we talked to and exposed systematic and systemic failings in meeting young people's needs:

> *Again, when we're talking about the behavioural, social and emotional needs of young people, the default position of pastoral teams with responsibility to manage presenting behaviours or emotional dysregulation is more stick than carrot. This*

means that the go-to response for disruptive behaviours is often detention or exclusion – depending on the approach of the individual teacher. In turn, this exposes the conflicting personalities of teachers making judgements: how are we inclusive? or how do we mete out hard-line discipline? If you're a young person struggling, it's down to the luck of the draw.

R, educational psychologist, London

Lack of expert knowledge

As part of the subjective and non-scientific approach to what is a highly scientific area, too many teachers are uneducated about the psychological dimensions of the special educational needs of young people. SEND does not really feature in teacher training despite the expectation that teachers will be competent to deal with it as part of inclusive QFT. Therefore, at best, there exists a well-intentioned but casual acquaintance with learning difficulties arising from conditions such as dyslexia, autism and ADHD. An awareness of these areas is enough to tick a box but not sufficient to inform an effective working relationship with EPs. This also means that teachers cannot always see the potential impact of a more psychological approach where a focus on non-cognitive solutions can deliver learning outcomes.

Is psychology a potential advocate for coaching in schools?

The question we then asked EPs was, does educational psychology crowd out coaching in schools or make space for it? Evidence, albeit anecdotal, suggests that EPs would welcome coaching as both a companion and ally in supporting young people to simultaneously survive in the system and thrive outside of it. There will always be conversations around boundaries when two professions negotiate an alliance, but more generally there was recognition that coaching is compatible with the work of psychologists on the basis that it is 'similar but different'.

> *I would welcome a working relationship with coaching. The idea of coaching in schools gets consumed by mentoring and pastoral care schemes. There is no structure, just a group of well-meaning teachers giving it a go and showing that they care [to varying degrees]. Unfortunately, schools tend to default to correction strategies even when supposedly focused on well-being.*
>
> C, educational psychologist, Surrey

There was no evidence that schools eschewed the services of coaches because they deemed the presence of a psychologist sufficient to cover the non-cognitive skills and emotional needs of learners. But as we played the coaching/EP relationship forward, we could see a time when the coming together of EPs and coaches in a classroom setting might spawn a new hybrid role, such was their compatibility, and this would give the school an easy option in an either–or debate.

CRITICAL DISCUSSION POINT

Coaching psychology

Coaching psychology in education (Adams, 2015) is already a recognised concept for EPs to expand their offering, combining coaching methodologies and psychology theory in a school setting. Here, the EP is using psychological insights in a non-directive collaboration with the young person to achieve a mainstream academic goal. It could be argued that, in this way, the EP is providing a more than adequate two-for-the-price-of-one alternative that precludes coaching. However, the limited access to EPs that schools currently have, restrictive budgets and the lack of professional autonomy to work outside the curriculum and mainstream academic targets suggest a false economy. As an option, coaching psychology also underestimates the unique skill-set, training and experience of the coach. The assumption that EPs might simply develop a coaching dimension is perhaps typical of the underlying bias in education towards recognised professional qualifications over the perceived unstructured arcane procedures of coaching.

The relationship between educational psychology and coaching

Coaching and psychology in the classroom are highly compatible; however, the current idea of coaching psychology in schools reorients coaching away from the learner towards the professional to enhance practitioner performance. As with the general misconception about coaching in schools, coaching psychology, albeit helpful, relies on an incidental relationship with the learner resulting in serendipitous outcomes. The relationship between educational psychology and coaching is positive because both disciplines are naturally aligned. It is the context for that relationship (the classroom) that challenges the natural harmony by potentially heightening conflict between an intractable system and a disruptive force. In the work we have done with EPs there has been a tendency to form alliances to counter the dysfunctional environment; however, these are usually flirtations rather than definitive actions due to the EP's place in the system.

This relationship reimagined sees the coach collaborating with the EP and teacher as part of a triumvirate, directly interacting with the learner with clearly defined but complementary roles. At the end of the chapter, we produce a model that shows how this can work, but in order to achieve a collaborative state the barriers that inhibit the current relationship need to be negated and the following characteristics adopted: non-reactive, autonomous and adaptive.

Non-reactive

In schools, it takes a crisis to create change; therefore, since the Covid-19 pandemic, we have seen a groundswell in concern about mental health and well-being. Because schools are generally reactive, investment in research (for the EP) and radical new ideas (for coaching) is missing, meaning that they are always playing catch-up rather than anticipating future long-term issues. Becoming non-reactive allows schools to prioritise longer-term solutions over short-term fixes and is a basis for the relationship with psychology and coaching to thrive.

Autonomous

Mental health is a moving target and can change for all of us depending on a unique set of circumstances. The current absence of autonomy to make judgements and take decisions in schools facilitates a one-size-fits-all approach. In terms of mental health, this approach is especially flawed as many of the symptoms do not meet the threshold of clinical diagnosis, implying that a number of young people are slipping through the net. Whereas EPs are currently hamstrung by the system that employs them, a truly collaborative working relationship would provide them with a more authoritative voice to inform future strategies and individual interventions. On the other hand, coaches sit outside of the system and levels of autonomy are a matter of negotiation with the school. If the system prohibits sufficient levels of autonomy for the coach to carry out their work effectively, any relationship will falter.

> **CRITICAL DISCUSSION POINT**
>
> **Adaptive**
>
> To play their part in a triumvirate relationship, schools need to be adaptive to learners' needs, coming into line with the EP and coach, by responding to learners as unique individuals rather than applying the law of averages. There are encouraging signs that schools are beginning to take responsibility for the learning environment in a psychological context. For instance, emotionally based school avoidance (EBSA) is a term that is coming into regular usage as a reference to reduced or non-attendance at school, replacing the term *school refusal*. EBSA recognises that avoidance has its roots in emotional, mental health or well-being issues and
>
> →

should not be classified as an act of defiance. EBSA is a complex issue and is usually caused by a combination of factors; however, the common theme that underpins it is that the school is not able to adapt to meet the young person's psychological needs. Whereas being sensitive to the nuance of language is a start, it is not sufficient to make a real difference. Acknowledging the psychological dimensions of learning and collaborating with professionals outside of teaching lays the foundations for significant impact.

The psychological dimensions of coaching learners

Finally, we wanted to investigate the psychological dimensions of coaching young people in the classroom. We felt that this would help us to locate a logical entry point for coaching and start to form a truly hybrid learning offering as an alternative version of the coach psychologist.

The psychological needs of learners: an entry point for coaching

To examine the psychological impact of coaching, we began by looking for a natural entry point for coaching interventions. Using Maslow's theory of human motivation as a reference point (Figure 10.4) provided us with a convenient way of illustrating the distinct approaches of schools, psychologists and coaches. To design a working relationship between all three, we were looking for pinch-points in the psychological needs of learners: where one discipline logically takes over from another or where one approach's limitations become exposed or superseded by an alternative.

From this process, we would confidently argue that schools do not see beyond the two low-level needs: basic physiological and safety. Yes, it is entirely true that a young person cannot function in school if physiological needs (nutrition, warmth and rest) are not met. Similarly, young people need to experience safety through having order, control and predictability in their lives. Schools are highly focused on these two areas but seemingly abdicate responsibility for the social and higher-level needs posited by Maslow.

Figure 10.3 Hierarchy of learners' needs and the entry point for coaching

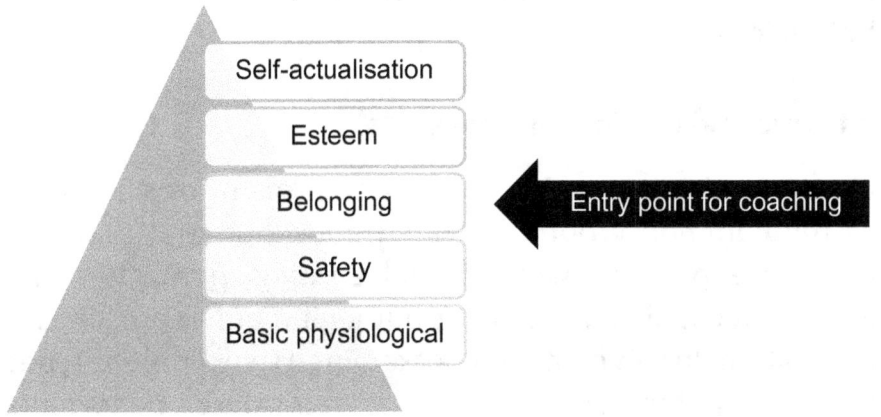

Maslow's seminal book was entitled *Motivation and Personality* (1954) and his theory was concerned with the process of human decision making. The sidebars on Figure 10.3 confirm the psychological nature of the framework and insinuate an access point for coaching. Unlike the original linear theory, where one level needs to be achieved before progressing to the next, in the context of the psychological impact of coaching, the process is binary, split between deficiency needs (school and psychology) and growth needs (coaching and psychology). Here, psychology has a foot in both camps and is required to flex between operational short-term outcomes (for the school) and long-term development outcomes (for the learner delivered by the coach). The graphic (Figure 10.3) suggests that the natural entry level for coaching is at the pivotal *belonging* level: the social and emotional need for interpersonal relationships and being accepted as part of a group. We see *belonging* as a connector of low-level and high-level needs, where emotional and physical affiliations combined can help young people thrive, with the school creating a sense of community (physical belonging) and the coach eliciting a sense of purpose (emotional belonging).

Intrinsic and extrinsic motivations

An alternative way of interpreting the role of psychology is as the common ground between education and coaching giving rise to a framework of valid learning approaches. The linking mechanism for distinct but legitimate approaches is motivation. In this context, we examined two different types of basic motivations: extrinsic and intrinsic. Behaviours and actions that are extrinsically motivated are those in which the controlling trigger – rules, recognition, financial compensation – is clear and visible. Intrinsically motivated efforts, in contrast, are internally motivated, often with no obvious reward except the action itself and the accompanying sense of self-satisfaction.

In a recent coaching programme carried out in a school in Bradford, we recorded examples of extrinsic and intrinsic motivations reported by learners (Table 10.1).

Table 10.1 Extrinsic and intrinsic motivations in learners

Extrinsic motivation in learners	Intrinsic motivation in learners
Achievement points	Team performance over individual performance
Praise	Respect
Disciplined work	Leadership behaviours
Acknowledgement	Sense of achievement and self-worth
What now?	What next?

In this exercise, we were not setting out to make the case for one set of motivations over another but to draw a clear distinction between the two. In doing so, we can see the diverse approaches of teachers and coaches in action, while EPs might favour a balanced approach despite being firmly entrenched in the mainstream education system. The obvious question arising is, what is the dominant motivation to achieve mainstream education targets? A more nuanced version of this question might be, does a focus on intrinsically motivated learning effectively satisfy educational targets by emphasising learners' needs?

This is a complex conundrum because both extrinsic and intrinsic motivations make important contributions to learning. Rewarding performance can increase the learner's enjoyment while pursuing mainstream academic goals, whereas intrinsically motivated learning unlocks discretionary energy, widens the purview of knowledge and introduces the young person to valuable adult behaviours such as independent thought, decision making and originality. At the same time, seen as mutually exclusive, each can undermine the other. For instance, emphasising external rewards (achievement points, grades, etc) discourages learners from exploring intrinsic drivers. Furthermore, research has shown that, where external rewards are assumed to be the main incentive, existing intrinsically motivated behaviours towards an internally rewarding goal can be compromised.

From a coach's perspective, intrinsic motivation is instinctively a superior (if yet unproven) driver; however, the school environment is not set up to accommodate or incentivise intrinsically motivated efforts. Besides, some learners might simply not have the desire to engage. Therefore, as coaches we should not underestimate that development of the learner is at an early stage. Drawing on programmes we have delivered in schools, there is still a clear sense of wanting to win when we introduce a competitive element to the work. This may be in response to a return to more familiar carrot and stick classroom etiquette or the individual learner's need for affirmation.

Bearing in mind the environment and the problematic nature of evaluating the impact of intangible unknown coaching outcomes, the coach should strive for a balanced approach. This means using extrinsic motivation to influence intrinsic drivers, in order to simultaneously achieve academic targets and enrich the learning experience. Such an approach should consider three factors: firstly, the negative impact of external rewards, decreasing intrinsic motivation and limiting the scope of achievement to a given target; secondly, the positive influence of praise and encouragement, affording learners the space to explore intrinsically motivated internal behaviours and thought patterns; and finally, the sweet-spot of unexpected external rewards for intrinsically motivated achievement.

CRITICAL DISCUSSION POINT

Maslow revisited

Maslow is a useful guide but, used in the context of coaching, needs to be adapted because it emphasises deficiency needs (decisions are motivated by depravation) and only includes growth needs at the self-actualisation level. In contrast, coaching uses growth needs (decisions are motivated by a desire to develop) to motivate intellectual and creative capacity to achieve personal goals.

Maslow continued to revisit his model, specifically the idea that it was not necessary to follow a strict linear progression but that individuals were unique multi-motivated personalities and could access different levels as they required. For instance, the need for creativity may supersede some basic physiological needs or self-esteem might be deemed more important than love. These refinements align with the leadership coaching approach – growth goals over remedial targets and the unique nature of the individual coachee – as well as reflecting the psychological health of young people as a moving target.

One of the undoubted attractions to Maslow's theory is its accessibility and transferability; however, its convenience encourages professionals outside the domain of expertise to practise cod psychology, which, in the context of working with young people, can have damaging or dangerous consequences.

CRITICAL QUESTIONS

- As a teacher, what can you do to motivate learners to make good decisions?
- What does your school do to create a learning community?
- How will you negotiate a development strategy for learners that emphasises growth over deficiency needs?
- Explain your approach to balancing intrinsic and extrinsic motivations.

Esteem and self-actualisation

The coach's focus on esteem and self-actualisation effectively accesses the learner's intrinsic motivation and develops a non-cognitive and psychological support system to accelerate learning.

- Esteem, in simple terms, is a sense of self-worth, respect and achievement. It has two classifications: esteem for oneself (accomplishment, adherence to personal values, mastery, originality and integrity) and to be held in high esteem by others (respect, status and prestige). Coaching young people to develop self-esteem allows them to understand the value they have and the contribution they make. In turn, this enables them to be confident in their learning. A consistent theme arising from our work with EPs is the assertion that academic underachievement (below age-appropriate expectations) is directly connected to an inferiority complex or low self-esteem.

Coaching at this level centres on Levels 1 and 2 of the LCH (Leadership Coaching Hierarchy – self-awareness and awareness of others), developing the learner's authentic and authoritative voice. A strong sense of self-esteem must be achieved before the coachee can be held in high esteem by others.

- Self-actualisation in learners is more difficult to explain. By definition, self-actualisation is a destination: the realisation of potential and a state of self-fulfilment; whereas, in coaching, the emphasis is placed upon ambition and aspiration as a vehicle for potential. No final destination is envisaged but achievement is accumulative, realising success at a series of milestones along a pathway under the guidance of the coach.

To achieve self-actualisation, coaches support learners to define long-term ambitions while teachers are encouraged to provide feedback and insights with reference to these ambitions. Self-actualisation should be seen as a fluid concept, where learners attain objectives and gain confidence from their achievements before moving on to new goals.

Table 10.2 is a selection of coaching questions we use when working at esteem and self-actualisation levels with learners. Essentially, these are focused on self-perception and purpose, encouraging the coachee to explore psychological dimensions of learning and attitudes to intrinsic and extrinsic motivation.

Table 10.2 Example coaching questions for esteem and self-actualisation

Esteem questions for learners	Self-actualisation questions for learners
How much do you worry about what others think about you?	How closely are your ambitions connected to your aspirations?
How do you think others might describe you?	How closely is your school work connected to your ambitions?
How would you describe the contribution you make to school?	How do you feel about the contribution you make to school?
Do you consider yourself a leader and, if so, why would anyone want to be led by you?	How do you feel when you achieve a personal goal?
How would you describe the way you communicate with teachers?	Think of the goals you set yourself last year; how much have these changed today?

Sharing the load: coaches and schools working together

Figure 10.4 is our model for coaches and schools to work together to deliver the psychological needs of learners. The graphic identifies the complementary roles played by the school and the coach. The order of *school* and *coach* as they appear in the model denotes the dominant natural partner (above) at each level. It is envisaged that the non-dominant partner (below) will adapt and adopt new ideas and methodologies as a way to contribute.

Figure 10.4 Coaches and schools working together in a psychological context

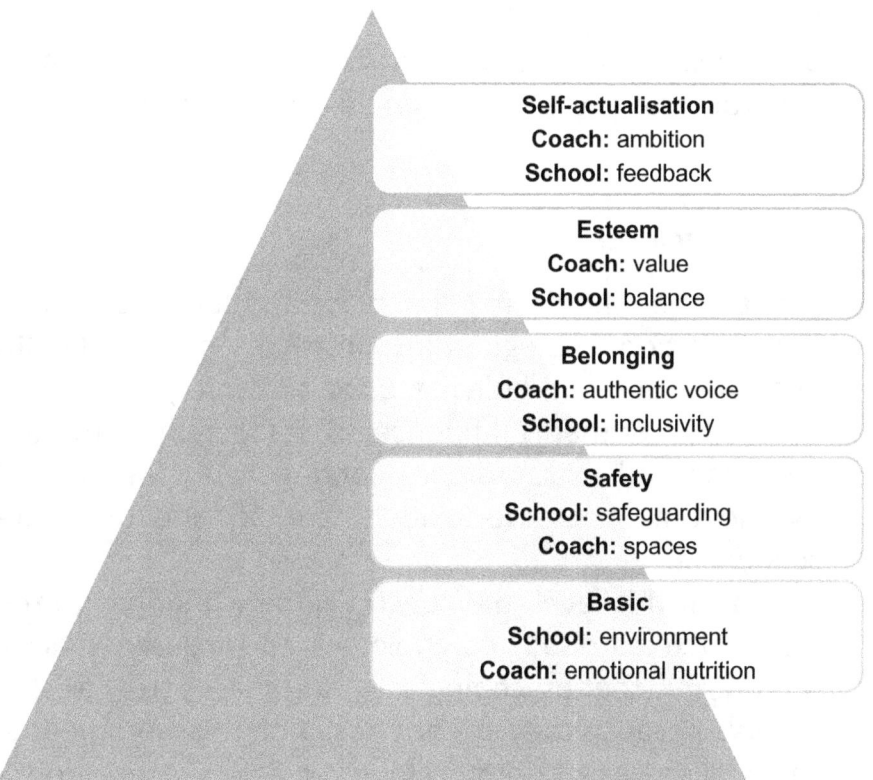

At the basic level

- **School:** The basic learning environment is the responsibility of the school. Outside of the school, this is difficult to influence; however, teachers can play their part by being aware that young people have their dietary needs met and are well rested to enhance learning. Schools are also responsible for signposting to external agencies for issues at this level.
- **Coach:** The coach has no say in the learning environment but they can provide emotional nutrition at this level.

Emotional nutrition is defined as a positive mindset that counter-acts negativity or physical discomfort, creating the emotional space to be able to focus on learning. At a basic level, it can also act as an introduction to the coaching process and the more complex developing leadership mindset.

At the safety level

- **School:** The school will put in place and supervise essential operational safeguarding processes such as health and safety and anti-bullying. *Basic* and *safety*-level operational foci primarily influence school responses to both everyday and extraordinary contingencies (as evinced by the Covid-19/post-Covid-19 period) and dominate school life.
- **Coach:** At this level, the coach will be working with the learner to create safe, psychological and inclusive spaces. It is unlikely that psychologically safe spaces truly exist in schools because they are not designed to accommodate the challenging of norms. However, safe spaces – to try and fail – and inclusive spaces – to be heard and listened to – are essential for intrinsic motivation and highly valued by learners.

At the belonging level

*This is the pivotal point where the emphasis switches from the school to the coach.

- **Coach:** Focusing on self-awareness (the authentic voice) and awareness of others encourages the learner to develop, value and express their natural personality traits. An acute awareness of others creates empathetic behaviours and inclusion. This mental state enables a sense of

connection and a culture of sharing. Emphasising leadership behaviours and values adds a sense of responsibility as a member of a team or a friendship group. Belonging is the ultimate inclusive space.
- **School:** At this level, the school is focused on inclusivity. Leadership groups, clubs and societies are natural outlets; however, emotional support and adopting coaching behaviours are the basis for a sense of connection and belonging in learners.

At the esteem level

- **Coach:** Building esteem is the coach's stock in trade. Creating a sense of value and self-worth reinforces confidence and enables the young person to find their authoritative voice and use it as an independent and original thinking learner.
- **School:** At this level, the school is supporting the work of the coach, providing consistent back-up and a balanced view of curriculum-based academic targets and wider learning goals.

At the self-actualisation level

- **Coach:** Focusing on leadership, the coach has a natural opening to work with the learner to explore the idea of ambition. At the self-actualisation level, ambition need not necessarily take the form of a formal life plan but emphasise emotional, sensory and instinctive dynamics to allow the learner to connect potential to meaningful (to them) goals, within and without the curriculum.
- **School:** Schools can play their part at this level by making the time and space to become interested and involved in the learner's intrinsic motivations. Engaging with

learners at this level makes sense of extrinsic motivators used to encourage learners, such as insightful feedback, respect and hard-earned praise.

References

Adams, M (2015) *Coaching Psychology in Schools: Enhancing Performance, Development and Wellbeing.* Abingdon: Routledge.

Gov.UK (2023) *Education, Health and Care Plans.* [online] Available at: https://explore-education-statistics.service.gov.uk/find-statistics/education-health-and-care-plans/2023 (accessed 26 January 2024).

Maslow, A H (1954) *Motivation and Personality.* New York: Harper & Row.

Chapter 11

WHAT THE FUTURE HOLDS: SIX CRITICAL QUESTIONS

CHAPTER OVERVIEW

This chapter imagines the future of coaching in schools through six critical questions, applied to three key areas: knowledge, value and collaboration. These questions guide our discussions and provide an understanding of the terrain for education as we journey into the future. We conclude that leadership is essential for an education renaissance and show how leaders can create a positive cognitive contagion (where the pressure of peer influence changes the way we think) to underpin the work of coaching and other active learning collaborations.

Introduction

Coaching in schools is at a pivotal moment. In this book, we have recorded our working observations to provide a reliable treatise evidencing the potential benefits of coaching as an accompaniment to conventional learning. Out of necessity (to enter the education mainstream), we have emphasised the transferability of coaching to adapt to schools, specifically the national curriculum, and the environment for learning – described here as dysfunctional. But now, as the influence of coaching continues to grow, schools face an existential dilemma: capture progress to maintain the education stasis or harness it to bridge the ideological gap between the curriculum and the new dimensions of learning.

Reflecting our experiences, this final chapter sets out to identify and eliminate some of the current contradictions and assumptions in education, helping schools and coaches to unravel their hitherto complex relationship and make mutually beneficial decisions about future direction. Using a series of critical questions, it interrogates three key areas for discussion that have emerged from our work to date – knowledge, value and collaboration – which we believe will determine the future of coaching in schools.

Knowledge

Knowledge in this context refers to what is learnt and how it is learnt. In Chapter 3, we set out the new dimensions of learning. It would be difficult to argue against the ideological relevance of these; however, what is in doubt is their legitimacy. While the required artfulness currently needed to inveigle schools into looking beyond the curriculum should not be a focus for future professional development, teachers should anticipate the advent of a learning reset and prepare themselves to develop a new set of active learning techniques.

First critical question

- How can the new dimensions of learning (or an iteration thereof) be accepted and subsequently integrated into the education mainstream?

What is learnt

For any version of the new dimensions of learning to be integrated into the education mainstream, achieving legitimacy is critical. Currently, coaching works hard, with little formal credit, as a kind of teaching assistant to support the academic endeavours of learners. At this time, coaching, and a learning focus outside of the national curriculum, are surreptitiously insinuated into schools through an alliance of like-minded pioneers as part of an intellectual experiment. The informal status of coaching means that the relationship between engaged professionals is almost conspiratorial. The necessity to employ disguised tactics to enter the academic mainstream adds to the sense of subversive activity:

> *Coaching doesn't always get a fair hearing at staff meetings and that means it doesn't get the credit it deserves. I could say more to fight its corner and about the focus on different aspects of knowledge, but I'm not sure anybody's really listening. At the moment it feels like I'm part of a secret enlightenment while being a card-carrying member of the Flat Earth Society.*
>
> S-A, teacher, Surrey

The six new dimensions of learning suggested in Chapter 3 are not steeped in academic theory but have come about as a result of aligning the interests of stakeholders. The practical characteristics of these dimensions mean that they are readily transferable to what is currently being learnt in schools and, despite going generally unnoticed, they make a telling contribution to learning outcomes. In this way, new learning dimensions are already effectively being applied and, because they are aligned to conventional targets, accommodated by schools. In the future it is envisioned that, buoyed by the groundswell of intellect and popular opinion, this process will be reversed and the spotlight will fall on schools to try harder to adapt to a version of new learning dimensions. This implies that integration will only be a matter of time; what is uncertain is when and what to do in the meantime.

In short, we must accept that moving to the new dimensions of learning is a gradual process and progress will be incremental. Timing is an unknown contingency; therefore, patience and perseverance are required. As the balance of interest continuously shifts, there will no doubt be a tipping point when the onus is on schools to adapt, but for now, pioneers of new learning must be resilient and schools must show thought-leadership in the way they respond to positive outcomes.

> **Second critical question**
>
> - In a dysfunctional environment, what do teachers need in order to adopt active learning techniques?

How it is learnt

Adapting to a new curriculum requires a deliberate shift from passive to active learning for both teachers and pupils. We see coaching as an informal iteration of active learning – not yet recognised as a legitimate pedagogy but with a proven and growing track record to positively impact academic achievement and enrich the learning experience. In general terms, active learning requires the teacher to challenge the learner to interrogate knowledge rather than passively receive it – transitioning from a student to researcher mindset (Figure 11.1).

Figure 11.1 The transition process from a learner to a researcher mindset

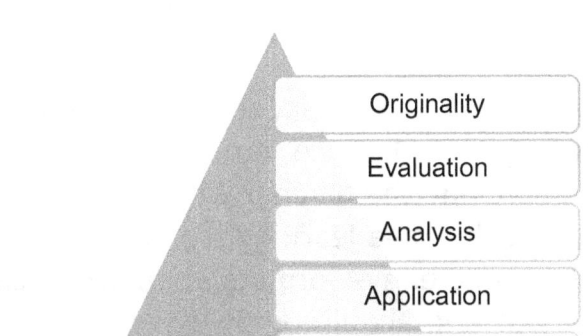

Adopting active learning techniques is not the focus of this chapter and their application should be a straightforward process for the professional educator; however, practically applying them in a dysfunctional environment is another matter altogether. We found three prerequisites for teachers to adopt active learning in such an environment: intellect, co-operation and management.

Intellect

Intellectual investment is essential to active learning. At one level, intellect is seen as a source of curiosity, enabling teachers to develop a mastery over creative outlets for new knowledge. At another level, it provides emotional support for teachers, reinforcing their purpose and encouraging personal development as a coping mechanism for routine mundane activities. In our experience, *being interested* underpins the relationship with both coaching and the new dimensions of learning, allowing teachers to become co-creators of any future design for education and equipping them with the resolve necessary to navigate the current environment.

Co-operation

Co-operation refers to the support system that the teacher may, or may not, have in place. A reassuring senior leadership team can provide the teacher with the space and time to experiment with active learning techniques and encourage pupils through creative formats to unlock discretionary learning energies and acquire knowledge beyond the curriculum. Alternatively, cynical leadership completely devitalises and undermines the teacher's efforts.

Management

Developing a new set of vital management skills is essential for the teacher to deliver an active learning agenda in a dysfunctional environment. This refers to political intelligence: the ability to manage up and down the organisational hierarchy. The current environment discourages teacher autonomy and is a psychologically unsafe space to challenge rigid norms and structures. Managing the politics of the organisation requires the teacher to be proficient in switching between charm offensive and authoritative voice.

Value

This section treats value as two-dimensional – esteem and assessment of impact – and discusses the broad concept of what is valued and what gets valued. Esteem refers to the value that the school places on the contribution of the coach and the respect it has for coaching as a viable learning methodology. The second dimension, assessment of impact, asks the questions: are we valuing the things we care about and how are we putting data to use?

> **Third critical question**
> - Why don't schools take coaching seriously?

Value dimension: esteem

In short, schools do not take coaching seriously. For coaching to have a future, this needs to change. Despite the enthusiasm of many of the teachers we have worked with, we find a significant number of schools generally disinterested in our work, undervaluing it and treating it with a collective sigh as yet another initiative to be accommodated within an already impossible workload. As with the dimensions of learning, we must accept that radical institutional change will take time; however, we posit two reasons why schools undervalue the services of coaches in the current climate: a paradoxical relationship and reactive strategies.

Final thoughts on a paradoxical relationship

Our working relationship with schools has been both marvellously invigorating and dishearteningly fractious. We have been welcomed with open arms by some and ignored by others – often in the same school. In some cases, our partnership with teachers has been casually delegated to an uninformed junior member of the team, while in others, senior teachers have, driven by intellectual curiosity, fully invested their personalities. In side discussions, we have reignited idealists' interest in education, exploring realities and reframing them for creative excursions into learning. On other occasions, those same realities have weighed too heavily, leaving no space for new ideas, nurturing cynicism rather than intelligent inquiry. Due to the current dominance of the negative side of the paradox, institutional indifference, coaching is held in low esteem, casting a shadow over its future role in schools.

Today the power of least interest defines the relationship between schools and coaching (the party with the least interest in a partnership holds the most power). Early successes against curriculum targets are a cause for optimism, but it is the thematic engagement of young people with coaching that shines a light on the future, suggesting an inevitable tipping point in the relationship in favour of the coach. In the meantime, schools will persist in underestimating coaching, treating it as an intellectual curiosity of little relevance in the context of imperative academic targets.

Reactive strategies: a word on fads
The second reason schools do not take coaching seriously is the culture of reactive strategies, specifically faddism. In trying to adapt to the presumed needs of learners, it can be argued that schools end up being guilty of reactive correction, where there is a continuous movement to put right issues that have already come and gone. This means that education is playing catch-up and constantly responding to new, moving targets. Knee-jerk policies lacking meta-analysis, made in live pressurised environments, can reduce serious issues to fads, meaning impact is limited and short term. Reactive responses have consequences for the way each school operates on a day-to-day basis; where, as one new problem-solving initiative gets implemented, other strategies are disrupted, in a cycle of reaction, action and counteraction.

Significant areas of concern like mental health, emotional well-being, trauma, attainment gaps, special educational needs and disabilities (SEND), north–south divide (levelling up) and socio-economic disparity are currently all in danger of being reduced to fad status. This also means teachers are burdened with implementation of initiatives they are wholly underqualified to deliver. For instance, *trauma-informed schools* commit to tackling a specific mental health crisis from inside the school. Teachers are required to develop an acute awareness of how their professional practice affects a young person with adverse childhood experience (ACE). With minimum support, they are expected to develop the social and emotional intelligence to anticipate possible pressure points that might induce negative responses from pupils who have experienced trauma. This assumes that teachers can conjure up the time and space for intense self-assessment and a possible practice reset, navigate an entrenched curriculum and act autonomously within an inflexible structure that discourages personal judgements.

By adopting short-term reactive tactics, schools are creating the illusion of dealing with a crisis but in reality simply bury it under a newer shinier one. The problem for coaching is that schools see it as a fad they can probably do without. Whereas other institutions, particularly in the private sector, might be attracted to experimental development strategies, especially those accompanied by slick marketing campaigns, coaching in schools is a financial and intellectual non-starter – a fad they cannot afford and with no relevant outcome. Accordingly, coaching must adopt various subversive strategies by attaching itself to current issues as a way of getting accepted.

Fourth critical question

- How does education move from rigid structures for known targets to flexible approaches for unknown goals?

Value dimension: assessment of impact

We present the following case study as typical of the way we currently set out to assess impact, illustrating the disconnect between what we claim to be valuable and what we actually measure.

CASE STUDY

The (hidden) relationship between leadership coaching and Ofsted

A secondary state school, where we had recently delivered a history project, was visited by Ofsted soon after completion of our programme. The head of history at the school reported back to us that the inspection was extremely positive and that the combination of leadership coaching and Team-Based Learning we employed was highly praised:

> *... there is comprehensive coverage of the national curriculum alongside opportunities to explore wider concepts. The Key Stage 3 curriculum has been enhanced ...*
>
> Ofsted inspector in 2023

The head of history reinforced this point and directly linked the success of the project to our interpretation of the curriculum and the alternative learning methodology used. In assessing the longer-term impact of the coaching, the headline findings from the school included:

- all of the Year 9 leaders who were on the programme requested to continue with the leadership coaching;
- all of the Year 9 leaders attended a leadership forum with the sponsor to plan a further history workshop following the same format as the original programme (leading individual groups of Year 7 historians);
- four of the leaders piloted a heritage trail of the local area on behalf of the sponsor;
- seven of the Year 9 leaders participated in a panel discussion and sat alongside professors and professionals for a Corporate Finance Development Centre presentation task.

On the one hand, we considered this assessment data evidenced the impact of our work, successfully putting theory into practice. It proved the transferability of coaching as an active learning methodology to mainstream education, facilitated an alternative hidden curriculum (implicitly learnt behaviours and ways of thinking) and enriched the young person's experience of being at school. On the other hand, we were painfully aware that these findings would be considered in isolation and were not sufficient to balance the current inequitable relationship between coaching and education. As there are no qualifications or league tables for the intangible outcomes produced by coaching and evaluation is currently limited to the individual schools with which we work (see Chapter 8), we sought guidance from Ofsted as the only recognised statutory measurement available.

→

We found Ofsted recognises that children are influenced by factors outside of the school's control and while schools can teach young people how to build confidence and resilience, they cannot always determine how well they will draw on this learning. Accordingly, they judge a school on their offer of provision rather than the impact the provision has on students. These provisions include:

- ways of developing responsible, respectful and active citizens;
- promoting equality of opportunity;
- promoting an inclusive environment;
- developing pupils' character and giving them the qualities that they need to flourish in society;
- developing pupils' confidence and resilience so that they can keep themselves mentally healthy;
- preparing pupils for the next phase of education.

The type of evidence they stated they were looking for included:

- the range, quality and take-up of extracurricular activities;
- how the education provided develops pupils' character;
- how curriculum subjects contribute to pupils' personal development;
- the quality of careers information and guidance.

As part of our own evaluation process, we placed our findings into the Ofsted framework (Table 11.1).

Table 11.1 Overlaying findings from coaching programme assessment of impact onto Ofsted framework

Examples of Ofsted provision targets	Examples of Ofsted evidence of provision	Outcomes of learners attributed to leadership coaching programme
Future citizenship	Extracurricular activities	Membership of school leadership forum Renewed participation in clubs and groups outside of school Participation in clubs and societies inside of school
Equality of opportunity	Unbiased careers advice	Development and reorientation candidates considered for leadership coaching Focus on the transferable skills rather than the 'job' goal

→

Table 11.1 (Continued)

Examples of Ofsted provision targets	Examples of Ofsted evidence of provision	Outcomes of learners attributed to leadership coaching programme
Inclusivity	Demonstrate all learners are accessing all provisions	Development and reorientation candidates considered for leadership coaching
		Social influence through leadership behaviours
		A sense of 'belonging' to new groups
Social and workplace skills	Work experience	Participation in Corporate Finance Development Centre
		Real-life leadership experience leading Year 7 historians in heritage project
		Complex problem-solving
		Social interactions with peers, teachers and external bodies
		Project management

Mental health and well-being	Aspirational career plans for personal development	Anecdotal evidence of positive impact on mental health and well-being as a result of coaching for ambition encouraging aspiration Improved confidence, engagement and academic performance resulting from focus on leadership
Future education	Guidance for options	Coaching new learning skills for original thinking, critical analysis and creativity to undertake curriculum task

We are confident that the evaluation frameworks introduced in Chapter 8 provide a workable and strategically useful way of connecting intangible outcomes to tangible (conventionally measurable) targets. However, these are innovative ideas not yet accepted into the mainstream and, therefore, being able to interpret evaluation data in a way that complies with Ofsted is critical to the future progress of coaching in schools – another example of fitting in to the system.

Goodhart's Law and the trouble with Ofsted

The previous case study proves the adaptability of alternative learning methodologies to comply with statutory assessment criteria – assuming that criteria is fit for purpose. Current criticisms of Ofsted, led by the former Chief Inspector of Schools, Sir Michael Wilshaw (UK Parliament, 2023), include assertions that simplistic judgements are misleading and unhelpful, and dismiss claims that nine out of ten state schools in England are classified as *good*. In particular, one-word inspection grades are now argued to underserve parents by providing them with a skewed perspective about what is happening in a school, lulling them into a false sense of security. Subjective judgements mean inconsistent unreliable classifications.

From our point of view, as external consultants, the tension between Ofsted and schools is representative of the current combative state of education, where argument and counter-argument rage over maintaining the stasis. Those arguing for change claim that simplistic subjective judgements, eliciting one-word outcome measures, are no longer relevant in a more complex post-Covid-19 world for learners. They challenge as specious Ofsted's assertion that the education inspection framework was designed in consultation with the wider stakeholder group and call for new measures that create a more meaningful impression of how a school is performing.

Under Ofsted's watch, targets have become overbearing, focused on the immeasurable and the meaningless, corrupting stressed teachers to find ways to navigate the system, too exhausted and demotivated to challenge their relevance. Therefore, schools are in danger of following Goodhart's Law, where as soon as a measurement becomes a target, it ceases to be a measurement of any value. We see this moment as a fork in the road. If education is to stop obsessing about short-term known targets and focus on long-term unknown goals, it must dismantle the tick-box culture and punitive legislative management structures that limit its scope and vision. To achieve this, there must be an acceptance that one size does not fit all, a meaningful partnership with stakeholders to align needs and a focus on what happens next to learners. But, most importantly, whatever inevitably replaces Ofsted must take a breath to reset and identify what is really valuable and then measure it.

Collaboration

Collaboration is referenced here in terms of a reimagining of the professional development relationship between coaching and education practitioners, as well as the logic that, in the future, coaching will not be the only active learning methodology working in schools.

> **Fifth critical question**
> - Not everyone wants to be a coach – how do coaching outliers fit into the future relationship with learning?

Coming full circle: the coach-teacher

The original premise for this book is that coaching in schools is misplaced by being focused on teachers and senior leadership teams rather than young people. We now appear to have come full circle, arriving at the final destination question: how might coaching re-form its offering to teachers in the context of the new dimensions of learning?

Context: supporting a teacher reset

We are in the midst of the *technological revolution*. According to research (McKinsey Global Institute, 2017), over half of recognised jobs today are at risk of becoming automated in the future. Logically, job descriptions will evolve and be redefined, but how are schools preparing future generations to contribute and thrive? Due to the rapid pace of change, we can only guess what the future might look like (as non-scientists, we cannot even begin to fathom out the advance of AI set within its own moral maze), but what we do know is that teaching the new dimensions of learning as part of an after-school club culture is wholly inadequate. Therefore, we must accept that teaching methodologies will need to undergo a radical rethink.

The advent of a technical revolution is heralded as a positive for teachers, doing much of the heavy lifting of the day-to-day workload and enabling new methods of digital delivery to engage and enthral learners. Teachers need reprogramming to exploit the space created by technology and the new learning opportunities it affords, moving learners away from replication towards originality. This means adopting a new set of teaching foci and a reimagining of the coaching offer for teachers (Table 11.2).

Table 11.2 How coaching can reprogramme teachers to deliver the six new dimensions of learning

The six new dimensions of learning	New teaching outcomes	Coaching outcomes for teachers
Creativity	Original thinking	Time management – making space for learners.
	Curiosity	Insightful enquiry.
Society	Inspiring purpose	How do I tap into purpose?
	Entrepreneurship	Developing connections between people and ideas.
Leadership	Professionalism	How do I help learners find their authoritative voice?
	Ambition	How do I help learners find their authentic voice?
Industry	Work ethic	Purpose for performance.
	Social and political intelligence	Coaching behaviours to develop intelligent learners.
Technology	Problem-solving	How to teach non-cognitive skills such as judgement.
	Differentiation (soft skills)	Understanding value propositions.

→

Table 11.2 (Continued)

The six new dimensions of learning	New teaching outcomes	Coaching outcomes for teachers
Well-being	Active learning skills	How do I help learners to think independently?
	Leadership	How do I support learners to become leaders?

The advent of the coach-teacher hybrid

In Table 11.2, the new foci of teaching are placed in the context of the six dimensions of learning, while the final column resets the coach offering for teachers. This table suggests that the notion of a coach-teacher hybrid is now more than just an interesting idea but a necessity for the future of learning – reinventing teaching today to fit the learning requirement we anticipate for tomorrow. This is a very different proposition to the current professional development of teachers, specifically because it is directly connected to the learner.

This model debunks the arcane aura around coaching that might discourage teachers from developing their own professional offering. Rather, it represents a gradual move towards coaching reflecting the evolution of education rather than an either–or proposition necessitating a move towards formal coaching. In other words, the two professions begin to morph as part of a learning renaissance and the teacher is coach by proxy, equipped to deliver intangible and non-cognitive skills for learners.

What the Future Holds: Six Critical Questions

> **Sixth critical question**
> - Can alternative active learning methodologies realistically act in concert?

Other methodologies working in concert

The short answer to our final critical question is yes. We have shown that Team-Based Learning (TBL) complements and enhances the leadership coaching model, offering instant and relevant leadership opportunities, inextricably linked to the curriculum and students' everyday lives. Furthermore, the LCTBL (Leadership Coaching Team-Based Learning) model described in Chapter 6 coincides with an assessment made by the Education Endowment Foundation (EEF), asserting that active collaborative learning (ACL – learners working together in small groups, ensuring everyone participates and contributes to a given task) is a cost-effective method for raising attainment.

A structured approach that thrives on a high level of interaction between learners means there is an obvious ideological congruency between coaching and ACL, making them natural collaborators. In practice, we were interested in the dynamic between the two and how shared ideologies played out in the classroom. Was the relationship equitable? Did it matter? Were there distinct roles to play for each methodology? Our work in collaboration with TBL proved to be seamless. The two approaches were highly complementary, and preparation for the overall programme and individual sessions required a minimum of choreography. Most importantly, the two methodologies learnt from each other during the process, adapting and developing organically while remaining true to the core principles of their philosophies. There are numerous active learning approaches under the umbrella of ACL and enquiry-based learning, which we have yet to work with and have been filed under *Future Research.* However, none of these are referred to in the Education Inspection Framework (2019) and there is no guidance or evidence about how ACL can be effectively facilitated in the classroom.

Due to the similarities between coaching and other ACL approaches, we do not envisage any ideological friction to hinder a positive collaboration in the future. What is not so certain is the silo instincts of distinct professions to willingly co-operate and the influence of the dysfunctional environment. For instance, we have noticed a professional qualification hierarchy emerging from our work with educational psychologists, suggesting a bias towards science and a continued distrust of unfamiliar less-formal approaches. We would also suggest that state schools and teachers are wary of collaborative learning, partly due to the skill and professional management that is involved in these types of methodologies. At the same time, in the secondary independent sector (more often inspected by the Independent Schools Council (ISC)) there is more confidence in engaging with leadership coaching as part of a parallel curriculum, with ACL considered as the subordinate partner working alongside leadership development strategies. We can only guess about the future for collaborative learning but we must be inspired by our experiences to date and the mutual development of hybrid approaches, in order to persevere as part of a long-term creative process.

And finally ... leadership contagion

We have argued in this book how a tick-box culture, where schools are compelled to follow meaningless guidelines to achieve irrelevant standards and classify learners into discrete units, sits at the heart of a failing education system. Such a culture, where a rigidly defined set of rules precludes independent thought and individual autonomy, means that professionals are restricted to thinking inside the box (Boyle, 2020). Furthermore, as the technical revolution takes hold, more and more decisions are likely to be dehumanised. This suggests a move to the ultimate tick-box culture where those who have ticked the boxes to create the algorithms that make the decisions insinuate their own particular brand of bias, ironically in the name of objectivity and unambiguous judgements.

The answer to such a culture is in leadership and we believe that the diverse range of leaders in education – from learners to government – will ultimately shape the future for education. As coaches, we treat leadership as a state of mind. In the first book in this series, *Coaching Young People for Leadership*, it is posited that leadership, regardless of external interventions, can only ever achieve real change as part of a positive cognitive contagion (Jamieson, 2023). The theory of positive cognitive contagion asserts that, in a significant social context, lasting change is only ever possible when the pressure of peer influence is sufficient to change thinking – when socially destructive behaviours or attitudes have desisted as a result of becoming unequivocally reviled as unacceptable. We must begin by placing the failings of education in the category of unacceptability and social destruction, and those with an interest must lead the charge to change the way we think about learning. By so doing, we can be certain that coaching and other ACL methodologies have a future in our schools.

How to create leadership contagion

To create a leadership contagion, the leader is aiming to turn a cause into a movement. In the context of education, this means gathering advocacy to enable the design of a system that serves the learner, not, as it currently does, the system itself. The framework suggested in *Coaching Young People for Leadership* is for a general overview of youth leadership. Table 11.3 is a refined version of that model, specifically designed for an education context.

Table 11.3 How to build leadership contagion in the context of education

Tools	User guide
Fight the impulse to conform.	Navigate the dysfunctional environment.
Value targets.	Identify value and measure it.
Evidence success.	Success is marketable.
Respond to feedback.	Accept that the coaching relationship is evolving.
Collaborate with like-minded partners.	Seek out alternative active learning methodologies to work with.
Gather advocacy.	Network outside the domain of education to gather advocacy.

Concluding thoughts

This book is not intended to be a polemic but is written as a guide and provocation; hence the structure of this final chapter is deliberately laid out as a series of questions. In other words, it does not claim to have all the answers but believes that continuous enquiry and practical experimentation will contribute to durable long-term change. It borrows data from the numerous reports and research commissioned around the future of education but prefers to rely on first-hand intelligence of working across the country with diverse schools, faithfully reporting real-life experiences. Nevertheless, we are encouraged by the approach of current formal investigations in stepping outside the domain of conventional education expertise and eliciting the opinions of entrepreneurs, cultural headliners and celebrity academics. But, at the same time, we are disappointed that the informal status of coaching means that it is not yet invited to contribute to these discussions. This seems like a missed opportunity because, throughout the writing of this book, we have been constantly surprised by the alignment of ideas, framing of challenges and common interests of those involved in the wider debate, suggesting that change is a matter of time and a co-ordinated effort.

As a professional guidebook, we have avoided a self-help format, leaving space for practitioners to find their own interpretations and develop surprising networks of like-minded people with whom they choose to collaborate. Being open to individual interpretation means that our ideas are designed to flex between different methodologies, contexts and goals. We acknowledge that the six new dimensions of learning are unauthorised, but we are confident that a version of these will shape a future curriculum. Similarly, the dysfunctional environment has no formal recognition but is presented as an accurate depiction of the operational landscape for education as we experienced it. Furthermore, we accept that, despite workable models, evaluation remains a nebulous concept, not least because of the chasm between what is said to be valued and what actually gets valued. But what is not a matter for conjecture is the awe-inspiring engagement of learners, consistent throughout our work. This book gives voice to those young people. Their endorsement means that we are constantly striving, using reciprocal energy, to develop evermore creative and effective programmes. Their advocacy means that coaching in schools is now a compelling proposition.

Further reading

Boyle, D (2020) *Tickbox*. London: Little, Brown.

References

Boyle, D (2020) *Tickbox*. London: Little, Brown.

Gov.UK (2019) Guidance: Education Inspection Framework (EIF). [online] Available at: www.gov.uk/government/publications/education-inspection-framework (accessed 26 January 2024).

Jamieson, M (2023) *Coaching Young People for Leadership*. St Albans: Critical Publishing.

McKinsey Global Institute (2017) *Jobs Lost, Jobs Gained: What the Future of Work Will Mean for Jobs, Skills, and Wages*. [online] Available at: www.mckinsey.com/featured-insights/future-of-work/jobs-lost-jobs-gained-what-the-future-of-work-will-mean-for-jobs-skills-and-wages (accessed 26 January 2024).

UK Parliament (2023) *Ofsted's Work with Schools: Inquiry*. [online] Available at: https://committees.parliament.uk/work/7761/ofsteds-work-with-schools (accessed 26 January 2024).

INDEX

Page numbers in *italics* and **bold** denote figures and tables, respectively.

accountability, 197, 230
active citizenship project (case study), 152–61
active collaborative learning, 147, 151
active collaborative learning (ACL), 291
active environment, 191
active learning techniques, 274–6
    alternative, 291–2
    cooperation, 276
    intellectual investment, 275–6
    value, 276
activism, 39–40
activist candidates, 131, 137–40
activist teachers, 41–3
adaptation to learners' needs, 257–8
advocacy, 30–2
    and alignment, 33
    and alliances, 34
    awareness, 30
    and clarity, 32–3
    and evaluation, 34
    and navigation, 34
    and originality, 33
    and perspective, 33–4
    prompts, 32
affordability, for coaching, 9–10
ambassadors of difference (case study), 111–14
ambidexterity, 189–90
ambition, 19, 28, 56, 90, *91*, **91**, 136, 170, 173
aspiration, 28, 56
authentic self, 107
authentication, 19, 95, 124–6, 170
authoritative voice, 41
autonomous characteristic, in psychological context, 256–8

blind obedience, 61
Bradford, legacy leaders for (case study), 96–9

Centrepoint, 15
change, pace of, 47
Child and Adolescent Mental Health Services (CAMHS), 251
clarity, and advocacy, 32–3
coach teachers, 287
    coach-teacher hybrid, 290
    teacher reset, 288
coaches–schools collaboration, 267, *267*
    at basic level, 267–8
    at belonging level, 268–9
    at esteem level, 269
    at safety level, 268
    at self-actualisation level, 269–70
coaching and education, relationship between, 9
    affordability, 9–10
    aiming for average, 13–14
    complexity versus creativity, 20–1
    connectedness, 18–20
    developmental and reorientation coaching, 16–18
    imagined, 11–12
    inundation, 10
    misconception, 10–11
    potentiality, 13–18
    self, connection to, 18–19
    work, connection to, 20
    youth leadership, 15–16
coaching bubble, 48–53
coaching hubris, 170–1

coaching psychology, 254–5
Cobden, Richard, 38
co-creation, 234
cognitive bias, 171–2
    ambition projection, 173–4
    countertransference, 172–3
    illusory bias, 174–5
    saviour complex, 174
    vicarious living, 175
collaboration, 287
commitment, 229–30
communication targets, 45–6
    colleagues, 45
    learners, 44
    senior leadership team, 44–5
competing commitment, 242
conflicts, 229
connection, 49–50
cooperation, 276
countertransference, 172–3
CREATES brainsets model, 84–9, 134
creativity, 20–1, 83–4
    absorb level, 86
    coaching in classroom, 84–9
    connection level, 86–7
    envision level, 86
    evaluate level, 87
    reason level, 87
    self-development, 71
    stream level, 88
    transactional, 70–1
    transform level, 88
curriculum
    intransigence, 226–7
    working with, 236–7

data reliability, 168–9
development agenda, 186–7
developmental candidates, 123
    different reactions to, 131–7
    integrating into leadership group, 126–30
    at the introduction and authentication stage, 124–6

developmental coaching, 16–18, **17**, 19
developmental leadership candidate, 199–211
drive, 49
dysfunctional environment, 48, 227–8, 234, 251–2, 274–6, 296
    and accountability, 230
    changing, 231–2
    and commitment, 229–30
    and conflict, 229
    and objectives, 230
    and trust, 228–9

education
    coach's definition of the role of, 29
    functions of, 28
    vision for, 27
Education Endowment Foundation (EEF), 291
educational hybrid model, 67
educational psychologists (EPs), 246–50
educational psychology
    advocacy, 253–5
    and coaching, relationship between, 255–8
    dysfunctional environment, 251–2
    non-collaborative relationship, 250–1
    subjective judgements, 252–3
    for young people, 246–53
emergent outcomes, **68**
    aligning across stakeholders, 69–70, **69**
    summary of, 65–8
    young people's need, 59–64
emotional intelligence, 67, 74, 107
emotional resilience, 89
emotionally-based school avoidance (EBSA), 257
end goals, of leadership, 191
entrepreneur, teacher as, 43

environment, 35
- active, 191
- balance, 189–90
- current, 224–30
- development agenda, 186–7
- dysfunctional. *See* dysfunctional environment
- inclusivity, 188
- positive relationships, 178–85
- relevant, 188–9
- safe space, 185–6
- workable hybrid environment, 177–8

esteem, 151, 264–6, 276–9
evaluation, 50–1
- and accountability, 197
- and connection, 196
- dimensions of, 196–7
- dual functions of, *195*
- impact, framework for, 198
- and leading in the future, 198–218
- and learning in the future, 197
- overlooking, reasons for, 192–4
- schools' interest in, significance of, 196–7
- unexpected data, 218–19

exam pressures, 7
experimentation, 51
expert knowledge, lack of, 253
extrinsic motivations, 260–3

failing intelligently, 51
feedback, 51, 168
Five Dysfunctions of a Team model (Lencioni), 227
flexible approaches for unknown goals, 279–87
'4-S' model, 149
future leadership, environment for, 170
- coaching hubris, 170–1
- cognitive bias, 171–5
- leadership gestures, 176–7

future workplace, preparing young people for aiming for known targets, 56
- originality over replication, 56–7
- reality check, 57–9

future, learning in, 197

generation sameness, 227
gesture leadership, 168, 176–7
Goodhart's Law, 286–7

hero coach, 171
hierarchy of human needs (Maslow), 62, 258–60, 263
Hirsch, E D, 143
hybrid leadership environment, guiding principles, *178*

illusory bias, 174–5
illustrative narrative, and advocacy awareness, 31
inclusion, 16, 233
inclusivity, 188
incrementalism, 50
industry, as a learning dimension, 103
- coaching in classroom, 103–5
- self-development, 74
- transactional, 74

institutional transience, 225–6
intangibles, making space for, 233–6
intellectual investment, 275–6
intrinsic motivations, 260–3
inundation of coaches, 10

knowledge, 272
known targets, aiming for, 56

leadership, 91–2
- coaching in classroom, 93–103
- disempowerment and empowerment capacity, 35
- inclusion, 36–7
- interaction with education, 36

leadership (*continued*)
    as part of a hybrid learning, *94*
    potential, 36–7
    preparedness, 37–8
    relevance, 38–9
    self-development, 73
    significance of, 119–22
    three stage model, 94–5
    transactional, 72–3
Leadership Coaching Hierarchy, 19, *19*
Leadership Coaching Team-Based Learning (LCTBL) model, 161–2, 291, 161–2, 291
leadership contagion
    creating, 294
    overview, 293–4
leadership reimagined, and inclusion, 16
learners, as communication targets, 44
learners' needs, schools' adaptation to, 257–8
learning dimensions, 70
    creativity, 70–1
    different reactions to, 131–7
    industry, 74
    integration into mainstream education, 272–4
    leadership, 72–3
    society, 71–2
    technology, 75
    well-being, 76
life skills, 67
Local Authority Educational Psychology Services, 251

mainstream learning, integrating coaching into, 29–30
    activism, 39–40
    advocacy, 30–4
    environment, 35–9
management, 276
mental health, 7, 233
#MeToo movement, 39
modern slavery, 39
motivations, 260–3

navigation, 34
negative behaviours of authorities, 61
negative peer pressure, 180
negotiating to normal, 48–9
    connection, 49–50
    drive, 49
    evaluation, 50–1
    experimentation, 51
    incrementalism, 50–3
non-collaborative relationship, 250–1
non-reactive characteristic, in psychological context, 256
normalisation of coaching, 48

objective, 230
Ofsted, 280–7
optimal learning
    characteristics of, 142, *142*
    impact of leadership coaching on, 147–8
    versus knowledge-rich curriculum, 143–4
organisational reluctance, 193
originality
    and advocacy, 33
    and replication, 56–7
outcomes for education
    balancing needs, 64–5
    emergent outcomes, 65–8

personality, 119–22
personality traits, 121
perspectives, 33–4, 60
pivotal moments, 117
positive peer detachment, 180
positive relationships, 178–85
    pupils with peers, 180–1
    pupils with teachers, 178–9
    teachers with the curriculum, 182–91

positivity, 238
prevention strategy, 16, 213–18
professional mindset, 74
professionalisation, 51–3
psychological dimensions of coaching, 258
    coaches and schools working together, 266–70
    esteem and self-actualisation, 264–6
    intrinsic and extrinsic motivations, 260–3
    psychological needs, 258–60
psychological safe spaces, 52–3
psychological safe zones, 234
purpose, identification of, 49

questions for young leaders, 165–8

reactive strategies, 278–9
refugees, moral dilemmas around, 39
relevancy, 188–9
reorientation candidates, 123, 169
    different reactions to, 131–7
    integrating into leadership group, 126–30
    at the introduction and authentication stage, 124–6
reorientation coaching, 16–18, **17**
replication and originality, 56–7

safe space, 185–6
saviour complex, 174
schools
    seriousness towards coaching, value dimension, 277–9
    working relationship with, 277–8
self-actualisation, 151, 264–6
self-exploration, and leadership, 73
self-help-book coach, 10
self-motivation, 106
self-regulated learning, 233

senior leadership team (SLT), 43–5
skills gap, 57–9
social intelligence, 67
society, 89–90
    coaching in classroom, 90–1
    self-development, 72
    transactional, 71–2
soft skills, 69, 74, 89, 107
special educational needs and/or disabilities (SEND), 247
strategic narrative, and advocacy awareness, 31
subconscious bias, 242
subjective judgements, 252–3
system, working with, 232–3
systematic inflexibility, 61

teachers
    as arbiters, 46–8
    and coaching, relationship between, 21–4
    as communicators, 43–6
    as counsellors, 46
    as entrepreneurs, 43
teachers, making space for, 237–43
    development, 241–2
    real-time mechanism, 240
    value mechanism, 241
    will, 242–3
Team-Based Learning (TBL), 291, *see also* Leadership Coaching Team-Based Learning (LCTBL) model
    mechanism of, 149
    overview, 147–8
technology, as a learning dimension, 105
    coaching in classroom, 105–8
    self-development, 75
    transactional, 75
time management, 224–5
timing, 117–18

transformative characteristics of coaching, **12**
trauma informed schools, 279
trust, 228–9

underperformance, 47

valuable insights, mining for, 211–18
value, 241, 276
values table, 108
vicarious living, 175
vision for education, 27
vocational context, coaching in, 170

well-being agenda, 67
well-being, as a learning dimension, 108–9, 233
    coaching in classroom, 109–14
    self-development, 76
    transactional, 76
willingness
    to coach, 287–90
    to lead, 164–5

youth leadership, 15–16
Youth Leadership Coaching model, 19, *19*, 95, 144

For Product Safety Concerns and Information please contact our EU
representative GPSR@taylorandfrancis.com
Taylor & Francis Verlag GmbH, Kaufingerstraße 24, 80331 München, Germany

www.ingramcontent.com/pod-product-compliance
Lightning Source LLC
Chambersburg PA
CBHW061430300426
44114CB00014B/1626